YESTERDAY AND TODAY

BOOKS BY LOUIS UNTERMEYER

Poetry

FOOD AND DRINK
BURNING BUSH
ROAST LEVIATHAN
CHALLENGE
THE NEW ADAM
THESE TIMES

Parodies

INCLUDING HORACE
— AND OTHER POETS
HEAVENS
COLLECTED PARODIES

Tales

CHIP: MY LIFE AND TIMES
THE DONKEY OF GOD
THE FAT OF THE CAT
  AND OTHER STORIES
MOSES

Travel

BLUE RHINE—BLACK FOREST

Essays

AMERICAN POETRY SINCE 1900
THE FORMS OF POETRY

Critical Collections

THE BOOK OF LIVING VERSE
AMERICAN POETRY FROM THE
  BEGINNING TO WHITMAN
MODERN AMERICAN POETRY
MODERN BRITISH POETRY
THIS SINGING WORLD
YESTERDAY AND TODAY
POEMS OF HEINRICH HEINE

YESTERDAY AND TODAY: *A Comparative Anthology of Poetry by* LOUIS UNTERMEYER

New York

HARCOURT, BRACE AND COMPANY

1940

COPYRIGHT, 1926, BY

HARCOURT, BRACE AND COMPANY, INC.

PRINTED IN THE U.S.A.

PREFACE

THE PLAN OF THE BOOK

Considering the great interest in modern poetry, and the various anthologies covering the period, one is struck by two outstanding facts — first, the similarity of most compilations of contemporary verse and second, the neglect (and, in many cases, the disparagement) of the poetry of the immediate past. For some time the editor has thought of a volume which would answer both of these objections. The result is this *comparative* collection, which hopes to bring to light first, a number of the fully representative poems of the period, and second, to provide not merely a background to contemporary verse but an equally satisfying record of the poetry which preceded it.

To accomplish this object it has seemed wise to divide the book sharply in two, and, though all boundaries between historical epochs are usually vague in outline, a certain definiteness of date has been achieved. *Yesterday and Today: A Comparative Anthology* represents the poetic achievements of the last one hundred and twenty-five years. The Nineteenth Century marks the dividing line — literature produced before that time does not come within the scope of this volume. The First Part (*Yesterday*) includes the work of authors born between 1800 and 1850; any poet born before that date has been ruthlessly though often regretfully excluded. (An exception has been made in the single case of William Cullen Bryant, born 1794, who is identified so closely with the famous New England group that it would be impossible to omit him.) The Second Part (*Today*) includes the work of authors born *after* 1850 and is, as the subtitle suggests, devoted to the poets of our own times, represented, for the greater part, by living authors. Thus the volume separates itself almost equally into the two divisions. These divisions, incidentally, are self-contrasting. A reader will be interested to note certain differences between the two periods: differences in point of view as well as in form and structure, differences in the actual subjects as well as in the manner of treating them, differences in the underlying spirit as well as in poetic diction. And even the most casual reader will be sure to find many similarities relating both parts, giving a unity to the work as a whole.

It has already been implied that an effort has been made to select, for the most part, poems not duplicated in the usual anthologies for high schools. However, it should be added, there are certain authors for whom the choice is inevitable, certain poems without which no collection of the kind would be complete. It is no longer necessary to enter a defense of modern poetry. Every educator aims to establish the relation between life and literature. And that, it has been proved, can be accomplished most easily by letting the reader begin with the work of the present. The introduction to a remote past with which the reader has no contact should be gradual, not immediate, and this introduction can be made far more satisfactorily *after* the student has been introduced to the thought and spirit of his own age. Chaucer's and Shakespeare's world will mean more to him if he approaches it with a knowledge of the one in which he lives.

REASON FOR THE CONTENTS

In a desire to prepare this book for a particular audience, the editor gladly acknowledges the assistance of many teachers to whom he turned for advice. When work on this book was first started, a number of questionnaires were sent to teachers and heads of English Departments (as recorded under the *Acknowledgments*) and the contents of this volume are, to a great extent, the result of their invaluable coöperation.

The answers to most of the questionnaires, it must be confessed, were extremely varied and often actually contradictory. Taste and experience were, obviously, the determining factors in these replies — but in a country as geographically and temperamentally diverse as America, it is not surprising that there should be two opposed views on practically every subject. Thus, referring to the definite matter of *choice* of poems, a number of teachers insisted, " select poems by only the best known poets " — whereas others agreed with Charles L. Sanders, of the High School in Greenwich, Connecticut, who wrote: " To me a sufficiency of poems — especially modern poems —seems to appear in print only because a particular author produced them. The measure of poetry is not the name of an author but the nobility inherent in the work. No poem should be chosen simply because a certain well known writer is responsible for it."

As to the *kind* of poetry, many (though less than half) of the responses indicated that young people were interested only in stories and refused to listen to anything the smallest degree beyond their mental grasp — " Young people care for no other kind but narrative poetry; lyrical poems do not appeal to them at all. . . . Do not allow any poem beyond the unformed mind to creep into your book."

On the other hand, William B. Elwell, of the Crosby High School, in Waterbury, Connecticut, expressed the contrary point of view of many when he wrote, " I hope that you will give a good deal of your space to lyric poetry. I feel strongly that lyric poetry is the best medium through which one can give a real introduction to poetry and to the abiding love of it. Here is the very essence of that intangible thing which all good teachers hope to impart to their students. . . . One can only expose oneself to a fine poem; one can never ' teach ' it. The teacher can only hope that, if the pupils are saturated in real poetry, some of it may filter into the very marrow of their beings and they too may know it — to love it. . . . For this reason, I hope you will also include some poems that are just a bit *above* the heads of the average students — not too many, of course, but a number to which they can grow; with meat enough for a second helping."

SUBJECTS — AND OBJECTS

Under the heading of *subject,* the advisors were less specific, the answers more scattered. There were, however, two distinct standpoints regarding anything sombre in tone. Several suggested that " young people do not like depressing subjects; poems about death should be omitted." The contrary opinion was presented by Mary S. Kline of the High School at Easton, Pennsylvania, who said, " My Juniors tell me that they ' love poems about death,' and the Sophomores seem to select poems with ' sadness ' in them."

The division of opinion was strongest along these lines. The two questions continually presented to the editor were: How really representative of the period could he make the book without sacrificing the interest of those to whom poetry makes little or no appeal? How simple could it be without insulting the intelligence of the more sensitive and appreciative groups? The editor was informed that " the book should contain nothing but the most simple verses which a young student could grasp at the very first reading." But he was reassured by many like Bertha Evans Ward, of the Hughes High School, Cincinnati, Ohio, who felt strongly that " A collection containing only the obvious would fail in the very purpose for which it was made. . . . Most important of all, there should be scattered here and there carefully selected poems which seem to the editor to represent the very best in poetry, so beautiful in form and so fine in music that the young reader would appreciate them even though he did not always understand them fully. These best poems would be grasped first by the unusual ones in each class, but would doubtless charm many besides."

The question of didactic poetry was another hotly disputed point. A great part of the reading as well as the
teaching public seems to have revolted against a poetry that
laid down morals of any sort. Yet many replies coincided
with that of Edith Adams of the Senior High School, New
Britain, Connecticut, who concluded that, " Though the
'teens generally like action, rhythm, humor and studies of
simple characters, they have a curious liking for morals
and, guided by nothing more disciplinary than their own
free will, often seek ' moral lessons ' in their reading."

Even the details concerning supplementary matter were
far from unanimous. " Why not," said one, " give the
instructor some hints as to the construction of the different
kinds of poetry and an analysis of the various forms? "
" Whatever you do," urged another, " do not be technical.
Young people care only for the *matter*; they have absolutely no interest in pattern-making or construction."
" Ask as few questions as possible," maintained one faction.
" Let the poems suggest their own questions. Fully half
of the class will be able to find the answers either in the
poems themselves or in their own experiences." Yet A.
Francis Trams, of the Joliet Township High School, Joliet,
Illinois, voicing the other sentiment, declared, " The setting
of good questions is almost the most important part of the
editing."

The result, it may be stated at once, is a compromise —
but a compromise which, while satisfying the majority, will,
it is hoped, disappoint but few. It is, frankly, a combination of the suggestions given the editor *and* his own preferences. The difficulties were great. The problem has been
pithily summed up by Ellen E. Garrigues of the De Witt
Clinton High School of New York City, in two sentences:
" Our boys come to us as children and leave us as young
men. Transformation in taste ought to be as apparent as
that in body."

This volume frankly endeavors to appeal to all classes
and tastes. There are sufficiently simple, popular verses

almost to touch bottom, but there is plenty of slightly
" advanced " poems for those who desire something a bit
above the general level.   There are poems that teach a
" moral lesson," and there are many delightful ones which
do not teach anything at all.   The two groups of narrative
poems show that this age is not lacking in action.   There
are dozens of lyrics revealing the fact that even our complex civilization has not destroyed the impulse to sing.
For those interested in structures, the ballades and rondeaus, breathing an old world grace, are mingled with the
most modern poems.   Death as a theme (though in a
buoyant rather than in a depressing key) has its place
here as well as the quaint turns of dialect and boisterous
humor.   In short, instead of catering to one type of taste,
the scope of this volume is broad and inclusive.   The
chief object, thus, is catholicity.   The collection is pur-
posely varied that each teacher and every pupil may discover just what is suited to his individual requirements.

THE TWO PERIODS

Although the book has been divided into two contrasting
sections, it should be stated that the editor does not intend
to point to either section as superior to the other.   The
course of poetry may be temporarily changed, new influ-
ences may bring certain differences in direction, yet poetry
itself is not a series of separate movements but one con-
tinuous stream.   It is this sense of *unity* as well as surface
differences which this collection hopes to show.   Each age
is prone to believe its own product the most significant and
we who respond to the spirit of our times are all too likely
to glorify the present at the expense of the past.

On the other hand, the ultra-conservative who, in his
fidelity to the past, belittles the present, is equally at fault.
With a few exceptions, the living poets are carrying on the
great traditions of English verse in a manner which the
future will be quick to acclaim.   In Robert Frost, Thomas
Hardy, E. A. Robinson, John Masefield, Walter de la Mare,

William Butler Yeats, Edna St. Vincent Millay, and many other contemporaries, there is the same beauty of language which we can find in Tennyson, Longfellow, Swinburne, Emerson, Henley and Christina Rossetti. One might say that the chief feature distinguishing the poetry of today from yesterday seems to be not so much a departure from the traditions, but a certain straight-forwardness. Yet even here the distinction is uncertain. The great writers have always used the speech of their own times, have always avoided the *clichés*, have never employed the stereotyped rhetoric affected by the lesser writers. One finds traces of the classics in even the most original of living poets: John Masefield's narratives are obviously indebted to Chaucer's; E. A. Robinson's monologues owe something to Browning's; Sara Teasdale's lyrics are related to Christina Rossetti's; Amy Lowell, though the average reader might not suspect it, owed as much to Keats as she did to the modern French poets.

The principal difference between the two periods is the difference between the *spirit* of today and yesterday. Never in the history of art, music and literature has there been such variety of expression, so many different forms, so wide a choice of subject. Modern inventions have brought people's thoughts closer together; more rapid means of communication are responsible for the greater diversity of interest. Just as English poetry was definitely influenced by the French singers, so contemporary American poetry responds to its own mixture of races and temperaments — one can even see traces of old Chinese and Japanese forms in the free verse of today. Much current writing may be experimental. But even here it faithfully reflects its backgrounds — and if we allow the scientist to experiment as freely as he wishes, why should we deny the poet that right?

Certain objectors have claimed that, in spite of the apparently familiar subjects, modern poetry is too complicated. On the other hand a great proportion of present day writing is actually *simpler* than poetry has ever been; most of the contemporaries speak with remarkable directness to their audience, using a speech and a background of experience which the reader can comprehend immediately. It might be observed that if any difficulty exists, it is a natural reflection of the age. In an essay on " The Metaphysical Poets," T. S. Eliot, writing on this theme, remarks, " It appears likely that poets in our civilization, as it exists at present, must be difficult. Our civilization comprehends great variety and complexity, and this variety and complexity, playing upon refined sensibilities, must produce various and complex results." However, much of what, at first glance, may seem involved and obscure becomes clear on closer inspection; the obstacles to a complete enjoyment are not alone superficial but pass away if the reader is at all sympathetic.

To appreciate the variety of any art, an open mind is all that one needs to begin with. And if beauty is in the eye of the beholder, poetry is surely in the ear of the listener — which is one reason why poetry demands to be read aloud. A line of verse on the printed page is like a bar of music; it does not actually live until it is heard. The fewer a reader's prejudices, the greater will be his reward. If his mind is as open as his ears, he will share something of the splendor and the mystery which is the very heart of the poet's vision.

L. U.

New York City.

CONTENTS

Contents

TODAY

DAILY LIFE

THE GOOD GROUND

Contents

HOOF, CLAW, AND WING

PORTRAITS OF PEOPLE

Contents

YESTERDAY

Being selections from poets born in the first half of the nineteenth century

THE POETS[1]

We are the music-makers,
  And we are the dreamers of dreams,
Wandering by lone sea-breakers,
  And sitting by desolate streams;
World-losers and world-forsakers,
  On whom the pale moon gleams:
Yet we are the movers and shakers
  Of the world for ever, it seems.

With wonderful deathless ditties
We build up the world's great cities,
  And out of a fabulous story
  We fashion an empire's glory:
One man with a dream, at pleasure,
  Shall go forth and conquer a crown;
And three with a new song's measure
  Can trample an empire down.

We, in the ages lying
  In the buried past of the earth,
Built Nineveh with our sighing,
  And Babel itself with our mirth;
And o'erthrew them with prophesying
  To the old of the new world's worth;
For each age is a dream that is dying,
  Or one that is coming to birth.

— ARTHUR O'SHAUGHNESSY

[1] This is the first and most famous part of the "Ode" celebrating the power of poetry.

My heart leaps up when I behold
  A rainbow in the sky:
So was it when my life began;
So is it now I am a man;
So be it when I shall grow old,
  Or let me die!

— WILLIAM WORDSWORTH

A MEMORY

Four ducks on a pond,
A grass-bank beyond,
A blue sky of spring,
White clouds on the wing;
What a little thing
To remember for years —
To remember with tears!

William Allingham

SUNRISE AND SUNSET [1]

I'll tell you how the sun rose, —
A ribbon at a time.
The steeples swam in amethyst,
The news like squirrels ran.

The hills untied their bonnets,
The bobolinks begun.
Then I said softly to myself,
" That must have been the sun! "

.   .   .   .

1 Copyright by Little, Brown and Company.

3

But how he set, I know not.
There seemed a purple stile
Which little yellow boys and girls
Were climbing all the while

Till when they reached the other side,
A dominie in gray
Put gently up the evening bars,
And led the flock away.

Emily Dickinson

THE LONELY HOUSE [2]

I know some lonely houses off the road
A robber'd like the look of, —
Wooden barred,
And windows hanging low,
Inviting to
A portico,
Where two could creep:
One hand the tools,
The other peep
To make sure all's asleep.
Old-fashioned eyes,
Not easy to surprise!

How orderly the kitchen'd look by night,
With just a clock, —
But they could gag the tick,
And mice won't bark.
And so the walls don't tell,
None will.

A pair of spectacles ajar just stir —
An almanac's aware.
Was it the mat winked,
Or a nervous star?

[2] Copyright by Little, Brown and Company.

The moon slides down the stair
To see who's there.

There's plunder, — where?
Tankard, or spoon,
Earring, or stone,
A watch, some ancient brooch
To match the grandmamma,
Staid sleeping there.

Day rattles, too,
Stealth's slow;
The sun has got as far
As the third sycamore.
Screams chanticleer,
" Who's there? "
And echoes, trains away,
Sneer — " Where? "
While the old couple, just astir,
Fancy the sunrise left the door ajar!

Emily Dickinson

THE SNOW–STORM

Announced by all the trumpets of the sky,
Arrives the snow, and, driving o'er the fields,
Seems nowhere to alight; the whited air
Hides hills and woods, the river, and the heaven,
And veils the farm-house at the garden's end.
The sled and traveller stopped, the courier's feet
Delayed, all friends shut out, the housemates sit
Around the radiant fireplace, enclosed
In a tumultuous privacy of storm.

Come see the north wind's masonry.
Out of an unseen quarry evermore
Furnished with tile, the fierce artificer
Curves his white bastions with projected roof
Round every windward stake, or tree, or door.

Speeding, the myriad-handed, his wild work
So fanciful, so savage, nought cares he
For number or proportion.   Mockingly,
On coop or kennel he hangs Parian wreaths; [3]
A swan-like form invests the hidden thorn;
Fills up the farmer's lane from wall to wall,
Maugre [4] the farmer's sighs; and, at the gate,
A tapering turret overtops the work.
And when his hours are numbered, and the world
Is all his own, retiring, as he were not,
Leaves, when the sun appears, astonished Art
To mimic in slow structures, stone by stone,
Built in an age, the mad wind's night-work,
The frolic architecture of the snow.

Ralph Waldo Emerson

FROM " SNOW–BOUND "

As night drew on, and, from the crest
Of wooded knolls that ridged the west,
The sun, a snow-blown traveller, sank
From sight beneath the smothering bank,
We piled with care, our nightly stack
Of wood against the chimney-back, —
The oaken log, green, huge, and thick,
And on its top the stout back-stick;
The knotty forestick laid apart,
And filled between with curious art
The ragged brush; then, hovering near,
We watched the first red blaze appear,
Heard the sharp crackle, caught the gleam
On whitewashed wall and sagging beam,
Until the old, rude-furnished room
Burst, flower-like, into rosy bloom;

---

[3] Parian wreaths = wreaths of snow which look as though they were carved
out of Parian marble, a particularly white and almost translucent marble used
by the ancient Greek sculptors.

[4] maugre = originally a French word meaning " in spite of."

While radiant with a mimic flame
Outside the sparkling drift became,
And through the bare-boughed lilac-tree
Our own warm hearth seemed blazing free.
The crane and pendent trammels showed,
The Turks' heads on the andirons glowed;
While childish fancy, prompt to tell
The meaning of the miracle,
Whispered the old rhyme: *" Under the tree*
When fire outdoors burns merrily,
There the witches are making tea."
The moon above the eastern wood
Shone at its full; the hill-range stood
Transfigured in the silver flood,
Its blown snows flashing cold and keen,
Dead white, save where some sharp ravine
Took shadow, or the sombre green
Of hemlocks turned to pitchy black
Against the whiteness at their back.
For such a world and such a night
Most fitting that unwarming light,
Which only seemed where'er it fell
To make the coldness visible.

John Greenleaf Whittier

" DE GUSTIBUS —— " [5]

Your ghost will walk, you lover of trees,
   (If our loves remain)
   In an English lane,
By a cornfield-side a-flutter with poppies.
Hark, those two in the hazel coppice —
A boy and a girl, if the good fates please,
   Making love, say, —
   The happier they!

---

[5] The complete quotation is *De gustibus non est disputandum*, which, freely translated, means "There is no accounting for tastes."

Draw yourself up from the light of the moon,
And let them pass, as they will too soon,
　With the bean-flowers' boon,
　And the blackbird's tune,
　And May and June!

Robert Browning

NOVEMBER BLUE

(The golden tint of the electric lights seems to give a complementary color to the air in the early evening. — *Essay on London*)

O heavenly color, London town
　Has blurred it from her skies;
And, hooded in an earthly brown,
　Unheaven'd the city lies.
No longer standard-like this hue
　Above the broad road flies;
Nor does the narrow street the blue
　Wear, slender pennon-wise.

But when the gold and silver lamps
　Color the London dew,
And, misted by the winter damps,
　The shops shine bright anew —
Blue comes to earth, it walks the street,
　It dyes the wide air through;
A mimic sky about their feet,
　The throng go crowned with blue!

Alice Meynell

SPRING

(*From " In Memoriam "*)

Now fades the last long streak of snow,
　Now burgeons every maze of quick [6]
　About the flowering squares, and thick
By ashen roots the violets blow.

[6] quick, used as a noun = a living thing. Here it refers to plants like the hawthorn.

Now rings the woodland loud and long,
   The distance takes a lovelier hue,
   And drowned in yonder living blue
The lark becomes a sightless song.

Now dance the lights on lawn and lea,
   The flocks are whiter down the vale,
   And milkier every milky sail,
On winding stream or distant sea;

Where now the seamew pipes, or dives
   In yonder greening gleam, and fly
   The happy birds, that change their sky
To build and brood, that live their lives

From land to land; and in my breast
   Spring wakens too, and my regret
   Becomes an April violet,
And buds and blossoms like the rest.

                       Alfred Lord Tennyson

THE HOUNDS OF SPRING

(From " Atalanta in Calydon ")

When the hounds of spring are on winter's traces,
   The mother of months in meadow or plain
Fills the shadows and windy places
   With lisp of leaves and ripple of rain;
And the brown bright nightingale amorous
Is half assuaged for Ityius,
For the Thracian ships and the foreign faces,
   The tongueless vigil, and all the pain.

Come with bows bent and with emptying of quivers,
   Maiden most perfect, lady of light,
With a noise of winds and many rivers,
   With a clamor of waters, and with might;

Bind on thy sandals, O thou most fleet,
Over the splendor and speed of thy feet;
For the faint east quickens, the wan west shivers,
  Round the feet of the day and the feet of the night.

Where shall we find her, how shall we sing to her,
  Fold our hands round her knees, and cling?
O that man's heart were as fire and could spring to her,
  Fire, or the strength of the streams that spring!
For the stars and the winds are unto her
As raiment, as songs of the harp-player;
For the risen stars and the fallen cling to her,
  And the southwest-wind and the west-wind sing.

For winter's rains and ruins are over,
  And all the season of snows and sins;
The days dividing lover and lover,
  The light that loses, the night that wins;
And time remembered is grief forgotten,
And frosts are slain and flowers begotten,
And in green underwood and cover
  Blossom by blossom the spring begins.

The full streams feed on flower of rushes,
  Ripe grasses trammel a travelling foot,
The faint fresh flame of the young year flushes
  From leaf to flower and flower to fruit;
And fruit and leaf are as gold and fire,
And the oat is heard above the lyre,
And the hoofèd heel of a satyr crushes
  The chestnut-husk at the chestnut-root.

Algernon Charles Swinburne

MIRACLES

Why, who makes much of a miracle?
As to me I know of nothing else but miracles,
Whether I walk the streets of Manhattan,

Or dart my sight over the roofs of houses toward the sky,
Or wade with naked feet along the beach just in the edge
    of the water,
Or stand under trees in the woods,
Or talk by day with any one I love,
Or sit at table at dinner with the rest,
Or look at strangers opposite me riding in the car.
Or watch honey-bees busy around the hive of a summer
    forenoon,
Or animals feeding in the fields,
Or birds, or the wonderfulness of insects in the air,
Or the wonderfulness of the sundown, or of stars shining so
    quiet and bright,
Or the exquisite delicate thin curve of the new moon in
    spring;
These with the rest, one and all, are to me miracles,
The whole referring, yet each distinct and in its place.

To me every hour of the light and dark is a miracle,
Every cubic inch of space is a miracle,
Every square yard of the surface of the earth is spread with
    the same,
Every foot of the interior swarms with the same.

To me the sea is a continual miracle,
The fishes that swim — the rocks — the motion of the
    waves — the ships with men in them,
What stranger miracles are there?

Walt Whitman

WHEN I HEARD THE LEARN'D ASTRONOMER

When I heard the learn'd astronomer,
When the proofs, the figures, were ranged in columns before
    me,
When I was shown the charts and diagrams, to add, divide,
    and measure them,

When I, sitting, heard the astronomer where he lectured
    with much applause in the lecture-room,
How soon unaccountable I became tired and sick,
Till rising and gliding out I wander'd off by myself,
In the mystical moist night-air, and from time to time,
Look'd up in perfect silence at the stars.

Walt Whitman

"THIS SPACIOUS EARTH"

Here at the fountain's sliding foot,
Or at some fruit-tree's mossy root,
Casting the body's vest aside,
My soul into the boughs does glide;
There, like a bird, it sits and sings,
Then whets and combs its silver wings,
And, till prepared for longer flight,
Waves in its plumes the various light.

— ANDREW MARVELL

TO MAKE A PRAIRIE [1]

To make a prairie it takes a clover and one bee, —
One clover, and a bee,
And revery.
The revery alone will do
If bees are few.

Emily Dickinson

THE MOUNTAIN [1]

The mountain sat upon the plain
In his eternal chair,
His observation omnifold,
His inquest everywhere.

The seasons played around his knees,
Like children round a sire:
Grandfather of the days is he,
Of dawn the ancestor.

Emily Dickinson

[1] Copyright by Little, Brown and Company.

THE GRASS [2]

The grass so little has to do, —
A sphere of simple green,
With only butterflies to brood,
And bees to entertain,

And stir all day to pretty tunes
The breezes fetch along,
And hold the sunshine in its lap
And bow to everything;

And thread the dews all night, like pearls,
And make itself so fine, —
A duchess were too common
For such a noticing.

And even when it dies, to pass
In odors so divine,
As lowly spices gone to sleep,
Or amulets of pine.

And then to dwell in sovereign barns,
And dream the days away, —
The grass so little has to do,
I wish I were the hay!

Emily Dickinson

MY GARDEN

A garden is a lovesome thing, God wot!
Rose plot,
Fringed pool,
Fern'd grot —
    The veriest school
    Of peace; and yet the fool
Contends that God is not —
Not God! in gardens! when the eve is cool?

[2] Copyright by Little, Brown and Company.

Nay, but I have a sign;
'Tis very sure God walks in mine.

Thomas Edward Brown

WEATHERS

This is the weather the cuckoo likes,
   And so do I;
When showers benumble the chestnut spikes,
   And nestlings fly;
And the little brown nightingale bills his best,
And they sit outside the " Traveller's Rest,"
And maids come forth sprig-muslin drest,
And citizens dream of the South and West,
   And so do I.

This is the weather the shepherd shuns,
   And so do I:
When beeches drip in browns and duns,
   And thresh, and ply;
And hill-hid tides throb, throe on throe,
And meadow rivulets overflow,
And drops on gate-bars hang in a row,
And rooks in families homeward go,
   And so do I.

Thomas Hardy

QUIET WORK

One lesson, Nature, let me learn of thee,
One lesson which in every wind is blown,
One lesson of two duties kept at one
Though the loud world proclaim their enmity —
Of toil unsevered from tranquillity;
Of labor, that in lasting fruit outgrows
Far noisier schemes, accomplished in repose,
Too great for haste, too high for rivalry.

Yes, while on earth a thousand discords ring,
Man's fitful uproar mingling with his toil,
Still do thy sleepless ministers move on,
Their glorious tasks in silence perfecting;
Still working, blaming still our vain turmoil;
Laborers that shall not fail, when man is gone.

Matthew Arnold

HOME–THOUGHTS FROM ABROAD

I

Oh, to be in England
Now that April's there,
And whoever wakes in England
Sees, some morning, unaware,
That the lowest boughs and the brush-wood sheaf
Round the elm-tree bole are in tiny leaf,
While the chaffinch sings on the orchard bough
In England — now!

II

And after April, when May follows,
And the whitethroat builds, and all the swallows —
Hark! where my blossomed pear-tree in the hedge
Leans to the field and scatters on the clover
Blossoms and dewdrops — at the bent spray's edge —
That's the wise thrush; he sings each song twice over,
Lest you should think he never could recapture
The first fine careless rapture!
And though the fields look rough with hoary dew,
All will be gay when noontide wakes anew
The buttercups, the little children's dower,
— Far brighter than this gaudy melon-flower!

Robert Browning

A SONG OF THE ROAD

The gauger [3] walked with willing foot,
And aye the gauger played the flute;
And what should Master Gauger play
But *Over the hills and far away?*

Whene'er I buckle on my pack
And foot it gaily in the track,
O pleasant gauger, long since dead,
I hear you fluting on ahead.

You go with me the self-same way —
The self-same air for me you play;
For I do think and so do you
It is the tune to travel to.

For who would gravely set his face
To go to this or t'other place?
There's nothing under Heaven so blue
That's fairly worth the travelling to.

On every hand the roads begin,
And people walk with zeal therein;
But wheresoe'er the highways tend,
Be sure there's nothing at the end.

Then follow you, wherever hie
The travelling mountains of the sky.
Or let the streams in civil mode
Direct your choice upon a road;

For one and all, or high or low,
Will lead you where you wish to go;
And one and all go night and day
Over the hills and far away!

Robert Louis Stevenson

[1] gauger = an exciseman, an officer in the King's service.

SONG OF THE OPEN ROAD

(*A Fragment*)

Afoot and light-hearted I take to the open road,
Healthy, free, the world before me,
The long brown path before me leading wherever I choose.

Henceforth I ask not good-fortune, I myself am good-for-
tune,
Henceforth I whimper no more, postpone no more, need
nothing;
Done with indoor complaints, libraries, querulous criticisms,
Strong and content I travel the open road.

Walt Whitman

WHEN THE GREEN GITS BACK IN THE TREES [4]

In Spring, when the green gits back in the trees,
    And the sun comes out and *stays*,
And yer boots pulls on with a good tight squeeze,
    And you think of your bare-foot days;
When you *ort* to work and you want to *not*,
    And you and yer wife agrees
It's time to spade up the garden-lot,
    When the green gits back in the trees —
        Well! work is the least o' *my* idees
        When the green, you know, gits back in the trees!

When the green gits back in the trees, and bees
    Is a-buzzin' aroun' ag'in
In that kind of a lazy go-as-you-please
    Old gait they bum roun' in;
When the groun's all bald where the hay-rick stood,
    And the crick's riz, and the breeze

[4] From *Neighborly Poems*, copyright 1891-1925. Used by special permission of the publishers, The Bobbs-Merrill Company.

Coaxes the bloom in the old dogwood,
  And the green gits back in the trees, —
    I live, as I say, in sich scenes as these,
    The time when the green gits back in the trees!

When the whole tail-fethers o' Wintertime
  Is all pulled out and gone!
And the sap it thaws and begins to climb,
  And the swet it starts out on
A feller's forrid, a-gittin' down
  At the old spring on his knees —
I kindo' like jest a-loaferin' roun'
  When the green gits back in the trees —
    Jest a-potterin' roun' as I — durn — please —
    When the green, you know, gits back in the trees!

James Whitcomb Riley

THE WIND

I saw you toss the kites on high
And blow the birds about the sky;
And all around I heard you pass,
Like ladies' skirts across the grass —
  O wind, a-blowing all day long!
  O wind, that sings so loud a song!

I saw the different things you did,
But always you yourself you hid.
I felt you push, I heard you call,
I could not see yourself at all —
  O wind, a-blowing all day long,
  O wind, that sings so loud a song!

O you that are so strong and cold,
O blower, are you young or old?
Are you a beast of field and tree,
Or just a stronger child than me?
  O wind, a-blowing all day long,
  O wind, that sings so loud a song!

Robert Louis Stevenson

A VISIT FROM THE SEA

Far from the loud sea beaches
    Where he goes fishing and crying,
Here in the inland garden
    Why is the sea-gull flying?

Here are no fish to dive for;
    Here is the corn and lea;
Here are the green trees rustling.
    Hie away home to sea!

Fresh is the river water
    And quiet among the rushes;
This is no home for the sea-gull
    But for the rooks and thrushes.

Pity the bird that has wandered!
    Pity the sailor ashore!
Hurry him home to the ocean,
    Let him come here no more!

High on the sea-cliff ledges
    The white gulls are trooping and crying;
Here among rooks and roses,
    Why is the sea-gull flying?

Robert Louis Stevenson

MARINERS' SONG

To sea, to sea! The calm is o'er;
    The wanton water leaps in sport,
And rattles down the pebbly shore;
    The dolphin wheels, the sea-cows snort,
And unseen Mermaids' pearly song
Comes bubbling up, the weeds among,
    Fling broad the sail, dip deep the oar:
    To sea, to sea! The calm is o'er.

To sea, to sea!   Our wide-winged bark
   Shall billowy cleave its sunny way,
And with its shadow, fleet and dark,
   Break the caved Tritons' azure day,
Like mighty eagle soaring light
O'er antelopes on Alpine height,
   The anchor heaves, the ship swings free,
   The sails swell full.   To sea, to sea!

                        Thomas Lovell Beddoes

He prayeth best, who loveth best
All things both great and small;
For the dear God who loveth us,
He made and loveth all.

— SAMUEL TAYLOR COLERIDGE

VESPERS

O blackbird, what a boy you are!
How you do go it!
Blowing your bugle to that one sweet star —
How you do blow it!
And does she hear you, blackbird boy, so far?
Or is it wasted breath?
" Good Lord!   She is so bright
To-night! "
The blackbird saith.

Thomas Edward Brown

TO A WATERFOWL

Whither, 'midst falling dew,
While glow the heavens with the last steps of day,
Far, through their rosy depths, dost thou pursue
Thy solitary way?

Vainly the fowler's eye
Might mark thy distant flight to do thee wrong,
As, darkly painted on the crimson sky,
Thy figure floats along.

22

Seek'st thou the plashy brink
Of weedy lake, or marge of river wide,
Or where the rocking billows rise and sink
   On the chafed ocean side?

There is a Power whose care
Teaches thy way along that pathless coast,
The desert and illimitable air —
   Lone wandering, but not lost.

All day thy wings have fanned,
At that far height, the cold, thin atmosphere,
Yet stoop not, weary, to the welcome land,
   Though the dark night is near.

And soon that toil shall end;
Soon shalt thou find a summer home, and rest,
And scream among thy fellows; reeds shall bend,
   Soon, o'er thy sheltered nest.

Thou'rt gone, the abyss of heaven
Hath swallowed up thy form; yet, on my heart
Deeply hath sunk the lesson thou hast given,
   And shall not soon depart.

He who, from zone to zone,
Guides through the boundless sky thy certain flight,
In the long way that I must tread alone
   Will lead my steps aright.

William Cullen Bryant

BIRDS IN APRIL

In the red April dawn,
  In the wild April weather,
From brake and thicket and lawn
  The birds sing all together.

The look of the hoyden [1] Spring
　　Is pinched and shrewish and cold;
But all together they sing
　　Of a world that can never be old:

Of a world still young — still young!
　　Whose last word won't be said,
Nor her last song dreamed and sung,
　　Till her last true lover's dead!

William Ernest Henley

A THRUSH SINGS

Deep in my gathering garden
　　A gallant thrush has built;
And his quaverings on the stillness
　　Like light made song are spilt.

They gleam, they glint, they sparkle,
　　They glitter along the air,
Like the song of a sunbeam netted
　　In a tangle of red-gold hair.

And I long, as I laugh and listen,
　　For the angel-hour that shall bring
My part, pre-ordained and appointed
　　In the miracle of Spring.

William Ernest Henley

THE EAGLE

He clasps the crag with crooked hands;
Close to the sun in lonely lands,
Ringed with the azure world, he stands.

[1] hoyden = a bold, rustic girl.

The wrinkled sea beneath him crawls;
He watches from his mountain walls,
And like a thunderbolt he falls.

Alfred Lord Tennyson

UNSATISFIED YEARNING

Down in the silent hallway
   Scampers the dog about,
And whines, and barks, and scratches,
   In order to get out.

Once in the glittering starlight,
   He straightway doth begin
To set up a doleful howling
   In order to get in!

R. K. Munkittrick

THE SNAKE [2]

A narrow fellow in the grass
Occasionally rides;
You may have met him, — did you not,
His notice sudden is.

The grass divides as with a comb,
A spotted shaft is seen;
And then it closes at your feet
And opens further on.

He likes a boggy acre,
A floor too cool for corn,
Yet when a child, and barefoot,
I more than once, at morn,

[2] Copyright by Little, Brown and Company.

Have passed, I thought, a whip-lash
Unbraiding in the sun, —
When, stooping to secure it,
It wrinkled, and was gone.

Several of nature's people
I know, and they know me;
I feel for them a transport
Of cordiality;

But never met this fellow,
Attended or alone,
Without a tighter breathing,
And zero at the bone.

Emily Dickinson

THE CHAMBERED NAUTILUS

This is the ship of pearl, which, poets feign,
   Sails the unshadowed main, —
   The venturous bark that flings
On the sweet summer wind its purpled wings
In gulfs enchanted, where the Siren sings,
   And coral reefs lie bare,
Where the cold sea-maids rise to sun their streaming hair.

Its webs of living gauze no more unfurl;
   Wrecked is the ship of pearl!
   And every chambered cell,
Where its dim dreaming life was wont to dwell,
As the frail tenant shaped his growing shell,
   Before thee lies revealed, —
Its irised ceiling rent, its sunless crypt unsealed!

Year after year beheld the silent toil
   That spread his lustrous coil;
   Still, as the spiral grew,

He left the past year's dwelling for the new,
Stole with soft step its shining archway through,
   Built up its idle door,
Stretched in his last-found home, and knew the old no more.

Thanks for the heavenly message brought by thee,
   Child of the wandering sea,
   Cast from her lap, forlorn!
From thy dead lips a clearer note is born
Than ever Triton blew from wreathèd horn!
   While on mine ear it rings,
Through the deep caves of thought I hear a voice that
   sings: —

Build thee more stately mansions, O my soul,
   As the swift seasons roll!
   Leave thy low-vaulted past!
Let each new temple, nobler than the last,
Shut thee from heaven with a dome more vast,
   Till thou at length art free,
Leaving thine outgrown shell by life's unresting sea!

                  Oliver Wendell Holmes

THE OAK

   Live thy Life,
      Young and old,
   Like yon oak,
   Bright in spring,
      Living gold;

   Summer-rich
      Then; and then
   Autumn-changed,
   Soberer-hued
      Gold again.

All his leaves
 Fallen at length,
Look, he stands,
Trunk and bough,
 Naked strength.

     Alfred Lord Tennyson

FROM " LEAVES OF GRASS "

I believe a leaf of grass is no less than the journey work of
 the stars,
And the pismire [3] is equally perfect, and a grain of sand,
 and the egg of the wren,
And the tree-toad is a *chef-d'œuvre* [4] for the highest,
And the running blackberry would adorn the parlors of
 heaven,
And the narrowest hinge in my hand puts to scorn all machinery,
And the cow crunching with depressed head surpasses any
 statue,
And a mouse is a miracle enough to stagger sextillions of
 infidels.

     Walt Whitman

TO THE FRINGED GENTIAN

Thou blossom bright with autumn dew,
And colored with the heaven's own blue,
That openest, when the quiet light
Succeeds the keen and frosty night,

Thou comest not when violets lean
O'er wandering brooks and springs unseen,
Or columbines, in purple dressed,
Nod o'er the ground-bird's hidden nest.

[3] pismire=an ant.
[4] *chef d'œuvre*=French for "a masterpiece."

Thou waitest late, and com'st alone,
When woods are bare and birds are flown,
And frosts and shortening days portend
The aged year is near his end.

Then doth thy sweet and quiet eye
Look through its fringes to the sky,
Blue — blue — as if that sky let fall
A flower from its cerulean wall.

I would that thus, when I shall see
The hour of death draw near to me,
Hope, blossoming within my heart,
May look to heaven as I depart.

William Cullen Bryant

FROM "TO THE DANDELION"

Dear common flower, that grow'st beside the way,
Fringing the dusty road with harmless gold,
   First pledge of blithesome May,
Which children pluck, and, full of pride, uphold,
   High-hearted buccaneers, o'erjoyed that they
An Eldorado in the grass have found,
Which not the rich earth's ample round
   May match in wealth, thou art more dear to me
   Than all the prouder summer-blooms may be.

Gold such as thine ne'er drew the Spanish prow
Through the primeval hush of Indian seas,
   Nor wrinkled the lean brow
Of age, to rob the lover's heart of ease;
   'Tis the Spring's largess,[5] which she scatters now
To rich and poor alike, with lavish hand,

     [5] largess=a generous gift.

Though most hearts never understand
To take it at God's value, but pass by
The offered wealth with unrewarded eye.

James Russell Lowell

THE RHODORA:
(*On being asked, whence is the flower?*)

In May, when sea-winds pierced our solitudes,
I found the fresh Rhodora in the woods,
Spreading its leafless blooms in a damp nook,
To please the desert and the sluggish brook.
The purple petals, fallen in the pool,
Made the black water with their beauty gay;
Here might the red-bird come his plumes to cool,
And court the flower that cheapens his array.
Rhodora! if the sages ask thee why
This charm is wasted on the earth and sky,
Tell them, dear, that if eyes were made for seeing,
Then Beauty is its own excuse for being:
Why thou wert there, O rival of the rose!
I never thought to ask, I never knew;
But, in my simple ignorance, suppose
The self-same Power that brought me there brought you.

Ralph Waldo Emerson

GHOSTS

Out in the misty moonlight, the first snow flakes I see,
  As they frolic among the leafless boughs of the apple-
  tree.
Faintly they seem to whisper, as round the boughs they
  wing,
    "We are the ghosts of the flowers who died in the early
    spring."

R. K. Munkittrick

FLOWER IN THE CRANNIED WALL

Flower in the crannied wall,
I pluck you out of the crannies,
I hold you here, root and all, in my hand,
Little flower — but if I could understand
What you are, root and all, and all in all,
I should know what God and man is.

Alfred Lord Tennyson

All the world's a stage,
And all the men and women merely players.
They have their exits and their entrances;
And one man in his time plays many parts.

— WILLIAM SHAKESPEARE

A DUTCH PICTURE

Simon Danz has come home again,
  From cruising about with his buccaneers;
He has singed the beard of the King of Spain
And carried away the Dean of Jaen
  And sold him in Algiers.

In his house by the Maese, with its roof of tiles,
  And weathercocks flying aloft in air,
There are silver tankards of antique styles,
Plunder of convent and castle, and piles
  Of carpets rich and rare.

In his tulip-garden there by the town,
  Overlooking the sluggish stream,
With his Moorish cap and dressing-gown,
The old sea-captain, hale and brown,
  Walks in a waking dream.

A smile in his gray mustachio lurks
  Whenever he thinks of the King of Spain,
And the listed tulips look like Turks,
And the silent gardener as he works
  Is changed to the Dean of Jaen.

32

The windmills on the outermost
  Verge of the landscape in the haze,
To him are towers on the Spanish coast,
With whiskered sentinels at their post,
  Though this is the river Maese.

But when the winter rains begin,
  He sits and smokes by the blazing brands,
And old seafaring men come in,
Goat-bearded, gray, and with double chin,
  And rings upon their hands.

They sit there in the shadow and shine
  Of the flickering fire of the winter night;
Figures in color and design
Like those by Rembrandt of the Rhine,
  Half darkness and half light.

And they talk of ventures lost or won,
  And their talk is ever and ever the same,
While they drink the red wine of Tarragon,
From the cellars of some Spanish Don,
  Or convent set on flame.

Restless at times with heavy strides
  He paces his parlor to and fro;
He is like a ship that at anchor rides,
And swings with the rising and falling tides,
  And tugs at her anchor-tow.

Voices mysterious far and near,
  Sound of the wind and sound of the sea,
Are calling and whispering in his ear,
" Simon Danz! Why stayest thou here?
  Come forth and follow me! "

So he thinks he shall take to the sea again
   For one more cruise with his buccaneers,
To singe the beard of the King of Spain,
And capture another Dean of Jaen
   And sell him in Algiers.

Henry Wadsworth Longfellow

KING ROBERT OF SICILY

Robert of Sicily, brother of Pope Urbane
And Valmond, Emperor of Allemaine,
Apparelled in magnificent attire,
With retinue of many a knight and squire,
On St. John's eve, at vespers, proudly sat
And heard the priests chant the Magnificat.
And as he listened, o'er and o'er again
Repeated, like a burden or refrain,
He caught the words, " *Deposuit potentes
De sede, et exaltavit humiles* ";
And slowly lifting up his kingly head
He to a learnèd clerk beside him said,
" What mean these words? " The clerk made answer meet.
" He has put down the mighty from their seat,
And has exalted them of low degree."
Thereat King Robert muttered scornfully,
" 'Tis well that such seditious words are sung
Only by priests and in the Latin tongue;
For unto priests and people be it known,
There is no power can push me from my throne!"
And leaning back, he yawned and fell asleep,
Lulled by the chant monotonous and deep.

When he awoke, it was already night;
The church was empty, and there was no light,
Save where the lamps, that glimmered few and faint,
Lighted a little space before some saint.

He started from his seat and gazed around,
But saw no living thing and heard no sound.
He groped towards the door, but it was locked;
He cried aloud, and listened, and then knocked,
And uttered awful threatenings and complaints,
And imprecations upon men and saints.
The sounds re-echoed from the roof and walls
As if dead priests were laughing in their stalls!
At length the sexton, hearing from without
The tumult of the knocking and the shout,
And thinking thieves were in the house of prayer,
Came with his lantern, asking, " Who is there? "
Half choked with rage, King Robert fiercely said,
" Open: 'tis I, the King!   Art thou afraid? "
The frightened sexton, muttering, with a curse,
" This is some drunken vagabond, or worse! "
Turned the great key and flung the portal wide;
A man rushed by him at a single stride,
Haggard, half naked, without hat or cloak,
Who neither turned, nor looked at him, nor spoke,
But leaped into the blackness of the night,
And vanished like a spectre from his sight.

Robert of Sicily, brother of Pope Urbane
And Valmond, Emperor of Allemaine,
Despoiled of his magnificent attire,
Bare-headed, breathless, and besprent ¹ with mire,
With sense of wrong and outrage desperate,
Strode on and thundered at the palace gate;
Rushed through the court-yard, thrusting in his rage
To right and left each seneschal ² and page,
And hurried up the broad and sounding stair,
His white face ghastly in the torches' glare,
From hall to hall he passed with breathless speed;
Voices and cries he heard, but did not heed,
Until at last he reached the banquet room,

1 besprent=the old form of the word "sprinkled."
2 seneschal=a steward.

Blazing with light, and breathing with perfume.
There on the dais sat another king,
Wearing his robes, his crown, his signet-ring,
King Robert's self in features, form and height,
But all transfigured with angelic light!
It was an Angel; and his presence there
With a divine effulgence filled the air,
An exaltation, piercing the disguise,
Though none the hidden Angel recognize.

A moment speechless, motionless, amazed,
The throneless monarch on the Angel gazed,
Who met his looks of anger and surprise
With the divine compassion of his eyes;
Then said, " Who art thou? and why com'st thou here? "
To which King Robert answered, with a sneer,
" I am the King, and come to claim my own
From an impostor, who usurps my throne! "
And suddenly, at these audacious words,
Up sprang the angry guests, and drew their swords;
The Angel answered, with unruffled brow,
" Nay, not the King, but the King's Jester, thou
Henceforth shalt wear the bells and scalloped cape,
And for thy counsellor shalt lead an ape;
Thou shalt obey my servants when they call,
And wait upon my henchmen in the hall!"

Deaf to King Robert's threats and cries and prayers,
They thrust him from the hall and down the stairs;
A group of tittering pages ran before;
And as they opened wide the folding-door,
His heart failed, for he heard, with strange alarms,
The boisterous laughter of the men-at-arms,
And all the vaulted chamber roar and ring
With the mock plaudits of " Long live the King! "
Next morning, waking with the day's first beam,
He said within himself, " It was a dream! "

But the straw rustled as he turned his head,
There were the cap and bells beside his bed,
Around him rose the bare, discolored walls,
Close by, the steeds were champing in their stalls,
And in the corner, a revolting shape,
Shivering and chattering sat the wretched ape.
It was no dream; the world he loved so much
Had turned to dust and ashes at his touch!

Days came and went; and now returned again
To Sicily the old Saturnian reign;
Under the Angel's governance benign
The happy island danced with corn and wine,
And deep within the mountain's burning breast
Enceladus, the giant, was at rest.
Meanwhile King Robert yielded to his fate,
Sullen and silent and disconsolate.
Dressed in the motley garb that Jesters wear,
With looks bewildered and a vacant stare,
Close shaven above the ears, as monks are shorn,
By courtiers mocked, by pages laughed to scorn,
His only friend the ape, his only food
What others left, — he still was unsubdued.
And when the Angel met him on his way,
And half in earnest, half in jest, would say,
Sternly, though tenderly, that he might feel
The velvet scabbard held a sword of steel,
" Art thou the King? " the passion of his woe
Burst from him in resistless overflow,
And, lifting high his forehead, he would fling
The haughty answer back, " I am, I am the King! "

Almost three years were ended; when there came
Ambassadors of great repute and name
From Valmond, Emperor of Allemaine,
Unto King Robert, saying that Pope Urbane
By letter summoned them forthwith to come

On Holy Thursday to his city of Rome.
The Angel with great joy received his guests,
And gave them presents of embroidered vests,
And velvet mantles with rich ermine lined,
And rings and jewels of the rarest kind.
Then he departed with them o'er the sea
Into the lovely land of Italy,
Whose loveliness was more resplendent made
By the mere passing of that cavalcade,
With plumes, and cloaks, and housings, and the stir
Of jewelled bridle and of golden spur.

And lo! among the menials, in mock state,
Upon a piebald steed, with shambling gait,
His cloak of fox-tails flapping in the wind,
The solemn ape demurely perched behind,
King Robert rode, making huge merriment
In all the country towns through which they went.

The Pope received them with great pomp, and blare
Of bannered trumpets, on Saint Peter's square,
Giving his benediction and embrace,
Fervent, and full of apostolic grace.
While with congratulations and with prayers
He entertained the Angel unawares,
Robert, the Jester, bursting through the crowd,
Into their presence rushed, and cried aloud,
" I am the King! Look, and behold in me
Robert, your brother, King of Sicily!
This man, who wears my semblance to your eyes,
Is an impostor in a king's disguise.
Do you not know me? does no voice within
Answer my cry, and say we are akin? "
The Pope in silence, but with troubled mien,
Gazed at the Angel's countenance serene;
The Emperor, laughing, said, " It is strange sport
To keep a madman for thy Fool at court! "

And the poor, baffled Jester in disgrace
Was hustled back among the populace.

In solemn state the Holy Week went by,
And Easter Sunday gleamed upon the sky;
The presence of the Angel, with its light,
Before the sun rose, made the city bright,
And with new fervor filled the hearts of men,
Who felt that Christ indeed had risen again.
Even the Jester, on his bed of straw,
With haggard eyes the unwonted splendor saw,
He felt within a power unfelt before,
And, kneeling humbly on his chamber floor,
He heard the rushing garments of the Lord
Sweep through the silent air, ascending heavenward.

And now the visit ending, and once more
Valmond returning to the Danube's shore,
Homeward the Angel journeyed, and again
The land was made resplendent with his train,
Flashing along the towns of Italy
Unto Salerno, and from there by sea.
And when once more within Palermo's wall,
And, seated on the throne in his great hall,
He heard the Angelus from convent towers,
As if the better world conversed with ours,
He beckoned to King Robert to draw nigher,
And with a gesture bade the rest retire;
And when they were alone, the Angel said,
" Art thou the King? " Then bowing down his head,
King Robert crossed both hands upon his breast,
And meekly answered him: " Thou knowest best!
My sins as scarlet are; let me go hence,
And in some cloister's school of penitence,
Across those stones, that pave the way to heaven,
Walk barefoot, till my guilty soul is shriven! "
The Angel smiled, and from his radiant face

A holy light illumined all the place,
And through the open window, loud and clear,
They heard the monks chant in the chapel near,
Above the stir and tumult of the street,
" He has put down the mighty from their seat,
And has exalted them of low degree! "
And through the chant a second melody
Rose like the throbbing of a single string:
" I am an Angel, and thou art the King! "

King Robert, who was standing near the throne,
Lifted his eyes, and lo! he was alone!
But all apparelled as in days of old,
With ermined mantle and with cloth of gold;
And when his courtiers came, they found him there
Kneeling upon the floor, absorbed in silent prayer.

Henry Wadsworth Longfellow

HER LETTER

I'm sitting alone by the fire,
    Dressed just as I came from the dance,
In a robe even *you* would admire, —
    It cost a cool thousand in France;
I'm be-diamonded out of all reason,
    My hair is done up in a cue:
In short, sir, " the belle of the season "
    Is wasting an hour upon you.

A dozen engagements I've broken;
    I left in the midst of a set;
Likewise a proposal, half spoken,
    That waits — on the stairs — for me yet.
They say he'll be rich, — when he grows up, —
    And then he adores me indeed;
And you, sir, are turning your nose up,
    Three thousand miles off, as you read.

" And how do I like my position? "
   " And what do I think of New York? "
" And now, in my higher ambition,
   With whom do I waltz, flirt, or talk? "
" And isn't it nice to have riches,
   And diamonds and silks, and all that? "
" And aren't they a change to the ditches
   And tunnels of Poverty Flat? "

Well, yes, — if you saw us out driving
   Each day in the Park, four-in-hand,
If you saw poor dear mamma contriving
   To look supernaturally grand, —
If you saw papa's picture, as taken
   By Brady, and tinted at that, —
You'd never suspect he sold bacon
   And flour at Poverty Flat.

And yet, just this moment, when sitting
   In the glare of the grand chandelier, —
In the bustle and glitter befitting
   The " finest *soirée* of the year," —
In the midst of a *gaze de Chambéry,*
   And the hum of the smallest of talk, —
Somehow, Joe, I thought of the " Ferry,"
   And the dance that we had on " The Fork ";

Of Harrison's barn, with its muster
   Of flags festooned over the wall;
Of candles that shed their soft lustre
   And tallow on head-dress and shawl;
Of the steps that we took to one fiddle,
   Of the dress of my queer *vis-à-vis;* [3]
And how I once went down the middle
   With the man that shot Sandy McGee;

---

[3] *vis-à-vis* (pronounced *veez-ah-vee*) = the one opposite; in this sense, her partner.

Of the moon that was quietly sleeping
  On the hill, when the time came to go;
Of the few baby peaks that were peeping
  From under their bedclothes of snow;
Of that ride, — that to me was the rarest;
  Of — the something you said at the gate.
Ah! Joe, then I wasn't an heiress
  To " the best-paying lead in the State."

Well, well, it's all past; yet it's funny
  To think, as I stood in the glare
Of fashion and beauty and money,
  That I should be thinking, right there,
Of some one who breasted high water,
  And swam the North Fork, and all that,
Just to dance with old Folinsbee's daughter,
  The Lily of Poverty Flat.

But goodness! what nonsense I'm writing!
  (Mamma says my taste still is low),
Instead of my triumphs reciting,
  I'm spooning on Joseph, — heigh-ho!
And I'm to be " finished " by travel, —
  Whatever's the meaning of that.
Oh, why did papa strike pay gravel
  In drifting on Poverty Flat?

Good-night! — here's the end of my paper;
  Good-night! — if the longitude please, —
For maybe, while wasting my taper,
  Your sun's climbing over the trees.
But know, if you haven't got riches,
  And are poor, dearest Joe, and all that,
That my heart's somewhere there in the ditches,
  And you've struck it, — on Poverty Flat.

Bret Harte

THE COURTIN'

God makes sech nights, all white an' still
    Fur'z you can look or listen,
Moonshine an' snow on field an' hill,
    All silence an' all glisten.

Zekle crep' up quite unbeknown
    An' peeked in thru' the winder,
An' there sot Huldy all alone,
    'Ith no one nigh to hender.

A fireplace filled the room's one side
    With half a cord o' wood in —
There war n't no stoves (tell comfort died)
    To bake ye to a puddin'.

The wa'nut logs shot sparkles out
    Towards the pootiest, bless her,
An' leetle flames danced all about
    The chiny on the dresser.

Agin the chimbley crook-necks hung,
    An' in amongst 'em rusted
The ole queen's arm thet gran'ther Young
    Fetched back from Concord busted.

The very room, coz she was in,
    Seemed warm from floor to ceilin',
An' she looked full ez rosy agin
    Ez the apples she was peelin'.

'T was kin' o' kingdom-come to look
    On sech a blessed cretur,
A dogrose blushin' to a brook
    Ain't modester nor sweeter.

He was six foot o' man, A 1,
  Clear grit an' human natur';
None could n't quicker pitch a ton
  Nor dror a furrer straighter.

He'd sparked it with full twenty gals,
  He'd squired 'em, danced 'em, druv 'em,
Fust this one, an' then thet, by spells —
  All is, he could n't love 'em.

But long o' her his veins 'ould run
  All crinkly like curled maple,
The side she breshed felt full o' sun
  Ez a south slope in Ap'il.

She thought no v'ice hed sech a swing
  Ez hisn in the choir;
My! when he made Ole Hunderd ring,
  She *knowed* the Lord was nigher.

An' she'd blush scarlit, right in prayer,
  When her new meetin'-bunnet
Felt somehow thru' its crown a pair
  O blue eyes sot upun it.

Thet night, I tell ye, she looked *some!*
  She seemed to 've gut a new soul,
For she felt sartin-sure he'd come,
  Down to her very shoe-sole.

She heered a foot, an' knowed it tu,
  A-raspin' on the scraper, —
All ways to once her feelin's flew
  Like sparks in burnt-up paper.

He kin' o' l'itered on the mat
  Some doubtfle o' the sekle,[4]
His heart kep' goin' pity-pat,
  But hern went pity Zekle.

---

[4] *sekle* is, as most of you have guessed, this New Englander's way of pronouncing "sequel."

An' yit she gin her cheer a jerk
    Ez though she wished him furder,
An' on her apples kep' to work,
    Parin' away like murder.

" You want to see my Pa, I s'pose! "
    " Wal . . . no . . . I come designin' " —
" To see my Ma?   She's sprinklin' clo'es
    Agin to-morrer's i'nin'."

To say why gals act so or so,
    Or don't, 'ould be presumin';
Mebby to mean *yes* an' say *no*
    Comes nateral to women.

He stood a spell on one foot fust,
    Then stood a spell on t'other,
An' on which one he felt the wust
    He could n't ha' told ye nuther.

Says he, " I'd better call agin ";
    Says she, " Think likely, Mister ":
Thet last word pricked him like a pin,
    An' . . . Wal, he up an' kist her.

When Ma bimeby upon 'em slips,
    Huldy sot pale ez ashes,
All kin' o' smily roun' the lips
    An' teary roun' the lashes.

For she was jes' the quiet kind
    Whose naturs never vary,
Like streams that keep a summer mind
    Snowhid in Jenooary.

The blood clost roun' her heart felt glued
    Too tight for all expressin',
Tell mother see how metters stood,
    An' gin 'em both her blessin'.

Then her red come back like the tide
    Down to the Bay o' Fundy,
An' all I know is they was cried
    In meetin' come nex' Sunday.

James Russell Lowell

A SONNET IN DIALOGUE

Frank (on the Lawn)
Come to the Terrace, May, — the sun is low.

May (in the House)
Thanks, I prefer my Browning here instead.

Frank
There are two peaches by the strawberry bed.

May
They will be riper if we let them grow.

Frank
Then the Park-aloe is in bloom, you know.

May
Also, her Majesty Queen Anne is dead.

Frank
But surely, May, your pony must be fed.

May
And was, and is. I fed him hours ago.
It's useless, Frank, you see I shall not stir.

Frank
Still, I had something you would like to hear.

May
No doubt some new frivolity of men.

Frank

Nay, — 'tis a thing the gentler sex deplores
Chiefly, I think . . .

    May (*coming to the window*)
                What is this secret, then?

    Frank (*mysteriously*)

There are no eyes more beautiful than yours!
                         Austin Dobson

THE FORSAKEN MERMAN

Come, dear children, let us away;
Down and away below.
Now my brothers call from the bay;
Now the great winds shoreward blow;
Now the salt tides seaward flow;
Now the wild white horses play,
Champ and chafe and toss in the spray.
   Children dear, let us away.
     This way, this way!

Call her once before you go.
   Call once yet.
In a voice that she will know:
   'Margaret! Margaret!'
Children's voices should be dear
(Call once more) to a mother's ear;
Children's voices, wild with pain.
Surely she will come again.
Call her once and come away.
   This way, this way!
'Mother dear, we cannot stay,'
The wild white horses foam and fret.
   Margaret! Margaret!

Come, dear children, come away down.
 Call no more.
One last look at the white-wall'd town,
And the little grey church on the windy shore.
 Then come down.
She will not come though you call all day.
 Come away, come away.

Children dear, was it yesterday
We heard the sweet bells over the bay?
In the caverns where we lay,
Through the surf and through the swell,
The far-off sound of a silver bell?
Sand-strewn caverns, cold and deep,
Where the winds are all asleep;
Where the spent lights quiver and gleam;
Where the salt weed sways in the stream;
Where the sea-beasts, ranged all round,
Feed in the ooze of their pasture-ground;
Where the sea-snakes coil and twine,
Dry their mail, and bask in the brine;
Where great whales come sailing by,
Sail and sail, with unshut eye,
Round the world for ever and aye?
When did music come this way?
Children dear, was it yesterday?

 Children dear, was it yesterday
 (Call yet once) that she went away?
 Once she sat with you and me,
On a red gold throne in the heart of the sea,
 And the youngest sat on her knee.
She combed its bright hair, and she tended it well,
When down swung the sound of the far-off bell.
She sigh'd, she look'd up through the clear green sea.
She said, 'I must go, for my kinsfolk pray
In the little grey church on the shore to-day.

'Twill be Easter-time in the world — ah me!
And I lose my poor soul, Merman, here with thee.'
I said, ' Go up, dear heart, through the waves,
Say thy prayer, and come back to the kind sea-caves.'
She smiled, she went up through the surf in the bay.
      Children dear, was it yesterday?

    Down, down, down;
   Down to the depths of the sea.
She sits at her wheel in the humming town,
   Singing most joyfully.
Hark what she sings: ' O joy, O joy,
For the humming street, and the child with its toy,
For the priest, and the bell, and the holy well.
   For the wheel where I spun,
   And the blessèd light of the sun.'
   And so she sings her fill,
   Singing most joyfully,
   Till the shuttle falls from her hand,
   And the whizzing wheel stands still.
She steals to the window, and looks at the sand;
   And over the sand at the sea;
   And her eyes are set in a stare;
   And anon there breaks a sigh,
   And anon there drops a tear,
   From a sorrow-clouded eye,
   And a heart sorrow-laden,
    A long, long sigh
For the cold, strange eyes of a little Mermaiden,
   And the gleam of her golden hair.

   Come away, away, children.
   Come children, come down.
   The hoarse wind blows colder;
   Lights shine in the town,
   She will start from her slumber
   When gusts shake the door;

She will hear the winds howling,
Will hear the waves roar.
We shall see, while above us
The waves roar and whirl,
A ceiling of amber,
A pavement of pearl.
Singing, ' Here came a mortal,
But faithless was she:
And alone dwell for ever
The kings of the sea.'

But, children, at midnight,
When soft the winds blow;
When clear falls the moonlight;
When spring-tides are low:
When sweet airs come seaward
From heaths starr'd with broom;
And high rocks throw mildly
On the blanch'd sands a gloom:
Up the still, glistening beaches,
Up the creeks we will hie;
Over banks of bright seaweed
The ebb-tide leaves dry.
We will gaze, from the sand-hills,
At the white, sleeping town;
At the church on the hill-side —
And then come back down.
Singing, ' There dwells a loved one,
But cruel is she.
She left lonely for ever
The kings of the sea.'

Matthew Arnold

THE TOYS

My little Son, who look'd from thoughtful eyes
And moved and spoke in quiet grown-up wise,
Having my law the seventh time disobey'd,
I struck him, and dismiss'd

With hard words and unkiss'd,
— His Mother, who was patient, being dead.
Then, fearing lest his grief should hinder sleep,
I visited his bed,
But found him slumbering deep,
With darken'd eyelids, and their lashes yet
From his late sobbing wet.
And I, with moan,
Kissing away his tears, left others of my own.
For, on a table drawn beside his head,
He had put, within his reach,
A box of counters, and a red-vein'd stone,
A piece of glass abraded by the beach,
And six or seven shells,
A bottle with bluebells,
And two French copper coins, ranged there with careful art,
To comfort his sad heart.
So when that night I pray'd
To God, I wept, and said:
Ah, when at last we lie with trancèd breath,
Not vexing Thee in death,
And Thou rememberest of what toys
We made our joys,
How weakly understood
Thy great commanded good,
Then, fatherly not less
Than I whom Thou hast moulded from the clay,
Thou'lt leave Thy wrath, and say,
' I will be sorry for their childishness.'

Coventry Patmore

" WHEN I SAW YOU LAST, ROSE "

When I saw you last, Rose,
You were only so high; —
How fast the time goes!

Like a bud ere it blows,
You just peeped at the sky,
When I saw you last, Rose!

Now your petals unclose,
Now your May-time is nigh; —
How fast the time goes!

And a life, — how it grows!
You were scarcely so shy,
When I saw you last, Rose!

In your bosom it shows
There's a guest on the sly;
(How fast the time goes!)

Is it Cupid?   Who knows!
Yet you used not to sigh,
When I saw you last, Rose.
How fast the time goes!

Austin Dobson

ROSE

Rose, round whose bed
Dawn's cloudlets close
Earth's brightest-bred
    Rose!

No song, love knows,
May praise the head
Your curtain shows.

Ere sleep has fled,
The whole child glows:
One sweet, live, red
    Rose.

Algernon Charles Swinburne

LADY CLARA VERE DE VERE

Lady Clara Vere de Vere,
   Of me you shall not win renown:
You thought to break a country heart
   For pastime ere you went to town,
At me you smiled, but unbeguiled
   I saw the snare, and I retired;
The daughter of a hundred earls,
   You are not one to be desired.

Lady Clara Vere de Vere,
   I know you proud to bear your name,
Your pride is yet no mate for mine,
   Too proud to care from whence I came.
Nor would I break for your sweet sake
   A heart that dotes on truer charms.
A simple maiden in her flower
   Is worth a hundred coats-of-arms.

Lady Clara Vere de Vere,
   Some meeker pupil you must find,
For, were you queen of all that is,
   I could not stoop to such a mind,
You sought to prove how I could love,
   And my disdain is my reply.
The lion on your old stone gates
   Is not more cold to you than I.

Lady Clara Vere de Vere,
   You put strange memories in my head,
Not thrice your branching limes have blown
   Since I beheld young Laurence dead.
O, your sweet eyes, your low replies!
   A great enchantress you may be;
But there was that across his throat
   Which you had hardly cared to see.

Lady Clara Vere de Vere,
  There stands a spectre in your hall;
The guilt of blood is at your door;
  You changed a wholesome heart to gall.
You held your course without remorse,
  To make him trust his modest worth,
And, last, you fix'd a vacant stare,
  And slew him with your noble birth.

Trust me, Clara Vere de Vere,
  From yon blue heavens above us bent
The gardener Adam and his wife
  Smile at the claims of long descent.
Howe'er it be, it seems to me,
  'T is only noble to be good.
Kind hearts are more than coronets,
  And simple faith than Norman blood.

Clara, Clara Vere de Vere,
  If time be heavy on your hands,
Are there no beggars at your gate,
  Nor any poor about your lands?
O, teach the orphan-boy to read,
  Or teach the orphan-girl to sew;
Pray Heaven for a human heart,
  And let the foolish yeoman go.

                              Alfred Lord Tennyson

AN ANSWER [5]

The Lady Clara V. de V.
  Presents her very best regards
To that misguided Alfred T.
  (With one of her enamelled cards).

[5] This is a rather cruel but witty parody on Tennyson's famous poem (beginning on page 53), which should be read first.

Though uninclined to give offence,
  The Lady Clara begs to hint
That Master Alfred's common sense
  Deserts him utterly in print.

The Lady Clara can but say,
  That always from the very first,
She snubbed in her decisive way
  The hopes that silly Alfred nursed.
The fondest words that ever fell
  From Lady Clara, when they met,
Were " How d'ye do? I hope you're well,"
  Or else " The weather's very wet! "

To show a disregard for truth
  By penning scurrilous attacks,
Appears to Lady C. in sooth
  Like stabbing folks behind their backs.
The age of chivalry, she fears,
  Is gone for good, since noble dames
Who irritate low sonneteers
  Get pelted with improper names.

The Lady Clara cannot think
  What kind of pleasure can accrue
From wasting paper, pen, and ink,
  On statements the reverse of true.
If Master Launcelot, one fine day,
  (Urged on by madness or by malt,)
Destroyed himself — can Alfred say
  That Lady Clara was at fault?

Her ladyship needs no advice
  How time and money should be spent,
And can't pursue at any price
  The plan that Alfred T. has sent.

She does not in the least object
  To let the " foolish yeoman " go,
But wishes — let him recollect —
  That he should move to Jericho.

H. S. Leigh

> " *Piper, sit thee down and write*
> *In a book that all may read.*"
> *So he vanish'd from my sight;*
> *And I pluck'd a hollow reed,*
>
> *And I made a rural pen,*
> *And I stained the water clear,*
> *And I wrote my happy songs*
> *Every child may joy to hear.*

— WILLIAM BLAKE

SONG OF THE CHATTAHOOCHEE

Out of the hills of Habersham,
  Down the valleys of Hall,
I hurry amain to reach the plain,
Run the rapid and leap the fall,
Split at the rock and together again,
Accept my bed, or narrow or wide,
And flee from folly on every side
With a lover's pain to attain the plain
  Far from the hills of Habersham,
  Far from the valleys of Hall.

All down the hills of Habersham,
  All through the valleys of Hall,
The rushes cried *Abide, abide*,
The wilful waterweeds held me thrall,
The laving laurel turned my tide,
The ferns and the fondling grass said *Stay*,

The dewberry dipped for to work delay,
And the little reeds sighed *Abide, abide,*
 Here in the hills of Habersham,
 Here in the valleys of Hall.

 High o'er the hills of Habersham,
 Veiling the valleys of Hall,
The hickory told me manifold
Fair tales of shade; the poplar tall
Wrought me her shadowy self to hold;
The chestnut, the oak, the walnut, the pine,
Overleaning, with flickering meaning and sign,
Said, *Pass not, so cold, these manifold*
 Deep shades of the hills of Habersham,
 These glades in the valleys of Hall.

 And oft in the hills of Habersham,
 And oft in the valleys of Hall,
The white quartz shone, and the smooth brook-stone
Did bar me of passage with friendly brawl,
And many a luminous jewel lone
— Crystals clear or a-cloud with mist,
Ruby, garnet, and amethyst —
Made lures with the lights of streaming stone
 In the clefts of the hills of Habersham,
 In the beds of the valleys of Hall.

 But oh, not the hills of Habersham,
 And oh, not the valleys of Hall
Avail; I am fain for to water the plain.
Downward the voices of Duty call —
Downward, to toil and be mixed with the main,
The dry fields burn, and the mills are to turn,
And a myriad flowers mortally yearn,
And the lordly main from beyond the plain
 Calls o'er the hills of Habersham,
 Calls through the valleys of Hall.

Sidney Lanier

"TO ONE IN PARADISE"

Thou wast that all to me, love,
  For which my soul did pine —
A green isle in the sea, love,
  A fountain and a shrine,
All wreathed with fairy fruits and flowers,
  And all the flowers were mine.

And all my days are trances,
  And all my nightly dreams,
Are where thy dark eye glances,
  And where thy footstep gleams —
In what ethereal dances,
  By what eternal streams!

Edgar Allan Poe

TO HELEN

Helen, thy beauty is to me
  Like those Nicean barks of yore,
That gently, o'er a perfumed sea,
  The weary, wayworn wanderer bore
To his own native shore.

On desperate seas long wont to roam,
  Thy hyacinth hair, thy classic face,
Thy Naiad airs have brought me home
  To the glory that was Greece,
To the grandeur that was Rome.

Lo! in yon brilliant window niche,
  How statue-like I see thee stand,
  The agate lamp within thy hand!
Ah, Psyche, from the regions which
  Are Holy Land!

Edgar Allan Poe

A MUSICAL INSTRUMENT

What was he doing, the great god Pan,
   Down in the reeds by the river?
Spreading ruin and scattering ban,
Splashing and paddling with hoofs of a goat,
And breaking the golden lilies afloat
   With the dragon-fly on the river.

He tore out a reed, the great god Pan,
   From the deep cool bed of the river;
The limpid water turbidly ran,
And the broken lilies a-dying lay,
And the dragon-fly had fled away,
   Ere he brought it out of the river.

High on the shore sat the great god Pan,
   While turbidly flowed the river;
And hacked and hewed as a great god can,
With his hard bleak steel at the patient reed,
Till there was not a sign of a leaf indeed
   To prove it fresh from the river.

He cut it short, did the great god Pan,
   (How tall it stood in the river!)
Then drew the pith, like the heart of a man,
Steadily from the outside ring,
And notched the poor dry empty thing
   In holes, as he sat by the river.

" This is the way," laughed the great god Pan,
   (Laughed while he sat by the river,)
" The only way, since gods began
To make sweet music, they could succeed."
Then, dropping his mouth to a hole in the reed,
   He blew in power by the river.

Sweet, sweet, sweet, O Pan!
   Piercing sweet by the river!
Blinding sweet, O great god Pan!
The sun on the hill forgot to die,
And the lilies revived, and the dragon-fly
   Came back to dream on the river.

Yet half a beast is the great god Pan,
   To laugh as he sits by the river,
Making a poet out of a man:
The true gods sigh for the cost and pain, —
For the reed which grows nevermore again
   As a reed with the reeds in the river.

                 Elizabeth Barrett Browning

DREAM–PEDLARY

If there were dreams to sell,
   What would you buy?
Some cost a passing bell;
   Some a light sigh,
That shakes from Life's fresh crown
Only a rose-leaf down.

If there were dreams to sell,
Merry and sad to tell,
And the crier rang the bell,
   What would you buy?

A cottage lone and still,
   With bowers nigh,
Shadowy, my woes to still,
   Until I die.
Such pearl from Life's fresh crown
Fain would I shake me down.
Were dreams to have at will,
This would best heal my ill,
   This would I buy.

                 Thomas Lovell Beddoes

A BIRTHDAY

My heart is like a singing bird
    Whose nest is in a watered shoot; [1]
My heart is like an apple-tree
    Whose boughs are bent with thickest fruit.
My heart is like a rainbow shell
    That paddles in a halcyon sea;
My heart is gladder than all these
    Because my love is come to me.

Raise me a dais of silk and down;
    Hang it with vair [2] and purple dyes;
Carve it in doves and pomegranates,
    And peacocks with a hundred eyes;
Work it in gold and silver grapes,
    In leaves and silver fleurs-de-lys;
Because the birthday of my life
    Is come, my love is come to me.

Christina Georgina Rossetti

HOW DO I LOVE THEE?

How do I love thee? Let me count the ways.
I love thee to the depth and breadth and height
My soul can reach, when feeling out of sight
For the ends of Being and ideal Grace.
I love thee to the level of everyday's
Most quiet need, by sun and candle-light.
I love thee freely, as men strive for Right;
I love thee purely, as they turn from Praise.
I love thee with the passion put to use
In my old griefs, and with my childhood's faith.

[1] Watered shoot = a young branch which shoots out from the main stock.
[2] vair = "in heraldry, one of the furs composed of separate pieces, silver and blue, cut to resemble little shields or the flower of the campanula."

I love thee with a love I seemed to lose
With my lost saints, — I love thee with the breath,
Smiles, tears, of all my life!—and, if God choose,
I shall but love thee better after death.

Elizabeth Barrett Browning

BREAK, BREAK, BREAK

Break, break, break,
  On thy cold grey stones, O Sea!
And I would that my tongue could utter
  The thoughts that arise in me.

O well for the fisherman's boy,
  That he shouts with his sister at play!
O well for the sailor lad,
  That he sings in his boat on the bay!

And the stately ships go on
  To their haven under the hill;
But O for the touch of a vanished hand,
  And the sound of a voice that is still!

Break, break, break,
  At the foot of thy crags, O Sea!
But the tender grace of a day that is dead
  Will never come back to me.

Alfred Lord Tennyson

THE ODYSSEY

As one that for a weary space has lain
Lulled by the song of Circe and her wine
In gardens near the pale of Proserpine,
Where that Ææan Isle forgets the main,
And only the low lutes of love complain,

And only shadows of wan lovers pine,
As such an one were glad to know the brine
Salt on his lips, and the large air again, —
So gladly, from the songs of modern speech
Men turn, and see the stars, and feel the free
Shrill wind beyond the close of heavy flowers,
And, through the music of the languid hours,
They hear like ocean on a western beach
The surge and thunder of the Odyssey.

Andrew Lang

Come, read to me some poem,
  Some simple and heartfelt lay,
That shall soothe this restless feeling,
  And banish the thoughts of day.

Such songs have power to quiet
  The restless pulse of care,
And come like the benediction
  That follows after prayer.
— HENRY WADSWORTH LONGFELLOW

A TURKISH LEGEND

A certain pasha, dead five thousand years,
Once from his harem fled in sudden tears,

And had this sentence on the city's gate
Deeply engraven: " Only God is great."

So these four words above the city's noise
Hung like the accents of an angel's voice,

And evermore from the high barbican [1]
Saluted each returning caravan.

Lost is that city's glory. Every gust
Lifts with crisp leaves the unknown pasha's dust,

And all is ruin, save one wrinkled gate
Whereon is written, " Only God is great."
Thomas Bailey Aldrich

[1] barbican = a gate-house or a fortified tower at the entrance to a city.

ANNABEL LEE

It was many and many a year ago,
   In a kingdom by the sea
That a maiden there lived, whom you may know
   By the name of Annabel Lee;
And this maiden she lived with no other thought
   Than to love, and be loved by me.

I was a child and she was a child,
   In this kingdom by the sea;
But we loved with a love that was more than love,
   I and my Annabel Lee —
With a love that the wingèd seraphs of heaven
   Coveted her and me.

And this was the reason that, long ago,
   In this kingdom by the sea,
A wind blew out of a cloud, chilling
   My beautiful Annabel Lee;
So that her highborn kinsman came
   And bore her away from me,
To shut her up in a sepulchre
   In his kingdom by the sea.

The angels, not half so happy in heaven,
   Went envying her and me,
Yes! that was the reason (as all men know,
   In this kingdom by the sea)
That the wind came out of the cloud by night,
   Chilling and killing my Annabel Lee.

But our love it was stronger by far than the love
   Of those who were older than we,
   Of many far wiser than we:

And neither the angels in heaven above,
   Nor the demons down under the sea,
Can ever dissever my soul from the soul
   Of the beautiful Annabel Lee.

For the moon never beams without bringing me dreams
   Of the beautiful Annabel Lee,
And the stars never rise, but I feel the bright eyes
   Of the beautiful Annabel Lee;
And so, all the night-tide, I lie down by the side
Of my darling — my darling — my life and my bride,
   In the sepulchre there by the sea,
   In her tomb by the sounding sea.

                                Edgar Allan Poe

THE DEACON'S MASTERPIECE; OR THE WONDERFUL " ONE–HOSS SHAY "

Have you heard of the wonderful one-hoss shay,
That was built in such a logical way
It ran a hundred years to a day,
And then, of a sudden, it — ah, but stay,
I'll tell you what happened without delay,
Scaring the parson into fits,
Frightening people out of their wits, —
Have you ever heard of that, I say?

Seventeen hundred and fifty-five.
Georgius Secundus [2] was then alive, —
Snuffy old drone from the German hive.
That was the year when Lisbon-town
Saw the earth open and gulp her down,
And Braddock's army was done so brown,
Left without a scalp to its crown.
It was on the terrible Earthquake-day
That the Deacon finished the one-hoss shay.

  [2] *Georgius Secundus* = Even you who haven't studied Latin must know that this means King George the Second.

Now in building of chaises, I tell you what,
There is always *somewhere* a weakest spot, —
In hub, tire, felloe, in spring or thill,
In panel, or crossbar, or floor, or sill,
In screw, bolt, thoroughbrace, — lurking still,
Find it somewhere you must and will. —
Above or below, or within or without, —
And that's the reason, beyond a doubt,
That a chaise *breaks down*, but doesn't *wear out*.

But the Deacon swore (as Deacons do,
With an " I dew vum," or an " I tell *yeou* ")
He would build one shay to beat the taown
'N' the keounty 'n' all the kentry raoun';
It should be so built that it couldn't break daown:
" Fur," said the Deacon, " 't's mighty plain
Thut the weakes' place mus' stan' the strain;
'N' the way t' fix it, uz I maintain,
    Is only jest
'T make *that* place uz strong uz the rest."

So the Deacon inquired of the village folk
Where he could find the strongest oak,
That couldn't be split nor bent nor broke, —
That was for spokes and floors and sills;
He sent for lancewood to make the thills;
The crossbars were ash, from the straightest trees,
The panels of white-wood, that cuts like cheese,
But lasts like iron for things like these;
The hubs of logs from the " Settler's ellum," —
Last of its timber, — they couldn't sell 'em,
Never an axe had seen their chips,
And the wedges flew from between their lips,
Their blunt ends frizzled like celery-tips;
Step and prop-iron, bolt and screw,
Spring, tire, axle, and linchpin too,
Steel of the finest, bright and blue;

Thoroughbrace bison-skin, thick and wide;
Boot, top, dasher, from tough old hide
Found in the pit when the tanner died.
That was the way he " put her through."
" There! " said the Deacon, " Naow she'll dew! "
Do! I tell you, I rather guess
She was a wonder, and nothing less!
Colts grew horses, beards turned gray,
Deacon and deaconess dropped away,
Children and grandchildren — where were they?
But there stood the stout old one-hoss shay
As fresh as on Lisbon-earthquake-day!

Eighteen hundred; — it came and found
The Deacon's masterpiece strong and sound.
Eighteen hundred increased by ten; —
" Hahnsum kerridge " they called it then.
Eighteen hundred and twenty came; —
Running as usual; much the same.
Thirty and forty at last arrive,
And then come fifty, and fifty-five.

Little of all we value here
Wakes on the morn of its hundredth year
Without both feeling and looking queer.
In fact, there's nothing that keeps its youth,
So far as I know, but a tree and truth.
(This is a moral that runs at large;
Take it. — You're welcome. — No extra charge.)

First of November, — the Earthquake-day, —
There are traces of age in the one-hoss shay,
A general flavor of mild decay,
But nothing local, as one may say.
There couldn't be, — for the Deacon's art
Had made it so like in every part
That there wasn't a chance for one to start.

For the wheels were just as strong as the thills,
And the floor was just as strong as the sills,
And the panel just as strong as the floor.
And the whipple-tree neither less nor more,
And the black crossbar as strong as the fore.
And spring and axle and hub *encore*.[3]
And yet, *as a whole*, it is past a doubt
In another hour it will be *worn out!*

First of November, 'Fifty-five
This morning the parson takes a drive.
Now, small boys, get out of the way!
Here comes the wonderful one-hoss shay,
Drawn by a rat-tailed, ewe-necked bay.
" Huddup! " said the parson. — Off went they.
The parson was working his Sunday's text, —
Had got to *fifthly,* and stopped perplexed
At what the — Moses — was coming next.

All at once the horse stood still,
Close by the meet'n'-house on the hill.
First a shiver, and then a thrill,
Then something decidedly like a spill, —
And the parson was sitting upon a rock,
At half past nine by the meet'n'-house clock,—
Just the hour of the Earthquake shock!
What do you think the parson found,
When he got up and stared around?
The poor old chaise in a heap or mound,
As if it had been to the mill and ground!
You see, of course, if you're not a dunce,
How it went to pieces all at once. —
All at once, and nothing first, —
Just as bubbles do when they burst.

End of the wonderful one-hoss shay.
Logic is logic. That's all I say.

Oliver Wendell Holmes

[3] *encore* = the same.

BARBARA FRIETCHIE

Up from the meadows rich with corn,
Clear in the cool September morn,

The clustered spires of Frederick stand
Green-walled by the hills of Maryland.

Round about them orchards sweep,
Apple and peach-tree fruited deep,

Fair as a garden of the Lord
To the eyes of the famished rebel horde,

On that pleasant morn of the early fall
When Lee marched over the mountain wall, —

Over the mountains winding down,
Horse and foot, into Frederick town.

Forty flags with their silver stars,
Forty flags with their crimson bars,

Flapped in the morning wind: the sun
Of noon looked down, and saw not one.

Up rose old Barbara Frietchie then,
Bowed with her fourscore years and ten;

Bravest of all in Frederick town,
She took up the flag the men hauled down;

In her attic-window the staff she set,
To show that one heart was loyal yet.

Up the street came the rebel tread,
Stonewall Jackson riding ahead.

Under his slouched hat left and right
He glanced: the old flag met his sight.

" Halt! " — the dust-brown ranks stood fast.
" Fire! " — out blazed the rifle-blast.

It shivered the window, pane and sash;
It rent the banner with seam and gash.

Quick, as it fell, from the broken staff
Dame Barbara snatched the silken scarf;

She leaned far out on the window-sill,
And shook it forth with a royal will.

" Shoot if you must, this old gray head,
But spare your country's flag," she said.

A shade of sadness, a blush of shame,
Over the face of the leader came;

The nobler nature within him stirred
To life at that woman's deed and word:

" Who touches a hair of yon gray head
Dies like a dog!   March on! " he said.

All day long through Frederick street
Sounded the tread of marching feet:

All day long that free flag tost
Over the heads of the rebel host.

Ever its torn folds rose and fell
On the loyal winds that loved it well;

And through the hill-gaps sunset light
Shone over it with a warm good-night.

Barbara Frietchie's work is o'er,
And the Rebel rides on his raids no more.

Honor to her! and let a tear
Fall, for her sake, on Stonewall's bier.

Over Barbara Frietchie's grave
Flag of Freedom and Union, wave!

Peace and order and beauty draw
Round thy symbol of light and law;

And ever the stars above look down
On thy stars below in Frederick town!

John Greenleaf Whittier

SKIPPER IRESON'S RIDE [4]

Of all the rides since the birth of time,
Told in story or sung in rhyme, —
On Apuleius's Golden Ass,
Or one-eyed Calendar's horse of brass,
Witch astride of a human back,
Islam's prophet on Al-Borak, —
The strangest ride that ever was sped
Was Ireson's, out from Marblehead!
  Old Floyd Ireson, for his hard heart,
    Tarred and feathered and carried in a cart
      By the women of Marblehead!

Body of turkey, head of owl,
Wings a-droop like a rained-on fowl,
Feathered and ruffled in every part,
Skipper Ireson stood in the cart.
Scores of women, old and young,
Strong of muscle, and glib of tongue,

---

[4] After you have read this, compare the poem in answer to it on page 239.

Pushed and pulled up the rocky lane,
Shouting and singing the shrill refrain:
  " Here's Flud Oirson, fur his horrd horrt,
    Torr'd an' futherr'd an' corr'd in a corrt
      By the women o' Morble'ead! "

Wrinkled scolds with hands on hips,
Girls in bloom of cheek and lips,
Wild-eyed, free-limbed, such as chase
Bacchus round some antique vase,
Brief of skirt, with ankles bare,
Loose of kerchief and loose of hair,
With conch-shells' blowing and fish-horns' twang,
Over and over the Mænads sang:
  " Here's Flud Oirson, fur his horrd horrt,
    Torr'd an' futherr'd an' corr'd in a corrt
      By the women o' Morble'ead! "

Small pity on him! — He sailed away
From a leaking ship, in Chaleur Bay, —
Sailed away from a sinking wreck,
With his own town's-people on her deck!
" Lay by! lay by! " they called to him.
Back he answered, " Sink or swim!
Brag of your catch of fish again! "
And off he sailed through the fog and rain!
  Old Floyd Ireson, for his hard heart,
    Tarred and feathered and carried in a cart
      By the women of Marblehead!

Fathoms deep in dark Chaleur
That wreck shall lie forevermore,
Mother and sister, wife and maid,
Looked from the rocks of Marblehead
Over the moaning and rainy sea, —
Looked for the coming that might not be!

What did the winds and the sea-birds say
Of the cruel captain who sailed away? —
   Old Floyd Ireson, for his hard heart,
   Tarred and feathered and carried in a cart
      By the women of Marblehead!

Through the street, on either side,
Up flew windows, doors swung wide;
Sharp-tongued spinsters, old wives gray,
Treble lent the fish-horn's bray.
Sea-worn grandsires, cripple-bound,
Hulks of old sailors run aground,
Shook head, and fist, and hat, and cane,
And croaked with curses the hoarse refrain:
   " Here's Flud Oirson, fur his horrd horrt,
   Torr'd an' futherr'd an' corr'd in a corrt
      By the women o' Morble'ead! "

Sweetly along the Salem road
Bloom of orchard and lilac showed.
Little the wicked skipper knew
Of the fields so green and the sky so blue.
Riding there in his sorry trim,
Like an Indian idol glum and grim,
Scarcely he seemed the sound to hear
Of voices shouting far and near:
   " Here's Flud Oirson, fur his horrd horrt,
   Torr'd an' futherr'd an' corr'd in a corrt
      By the women o' Morble'ead! "

" Hear me, neighbors! " at last he cried, —
" What to me is this noisy ride?
What is the shame that clothes the skin
To the nameless horror that lives within?
Waking or sleeping, I see a wreck,
And hear a cry from a reeling deck!

Hate me and curse me, — I only dread
The hand of God and the face of the dead! "
　　Said old Floyd Ireson, for his hard heart,
　　Tarred and feathered and carried in a cart
　　　By the women of Marblehead!

Then the wife of the skipper lost at sea
Said, " God has touched him — why should we? "
Said an old wife mourning her only son,
" Cut the rogue's tether and let him run! "
So with soft relenting and rude excuse,
Half scorn, half pity, they cut him loose,
And gave him a cloak to hide him in,
And left him alone with his shame and sin.
　　Poor Floyd Ireson, for his hard heart,
　　Tarred and feathered and carried in a cart
　　　By the women of Marblehead!

John Greenleaf Whittier

ULYSSES

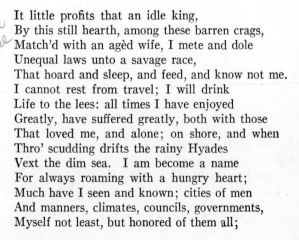

It little profits that an idle king,
By this still hearth, among these barren crags,
Match'd with an agèd wife, I mete and dole
Unequal laws unto a savage race,
That hoard and sleep, and feed, and know not me.
I cannot rest from travel; I will drink
Life to the lees: all times I have enjoyed
Greatly, have suffered greatly, both with those
That loved me, and alone; on shore, and when
Thro' scudding drifts the rainy Hyades
Vext the dim sea. I am become a name
For always roaming with a hungry heart;
Much have I seen and known; cities of men
And manners, climates, councils, governments,
Myself not least, but honored of them all;

And drunk delight of battle with my peers,
Far on the ringing plains of windy Troy.
I am a part of all that I have met;
Yet all experience is an arch wherethrough
Gleams that untravelled world, whose margin fades
For ever and for ever when I move.
How dull it is to pause, to make an end,
To rust unburnished, not to shine in use!
As tho' to breathe were life. Life piled on life
Were all too little, and of one to me
Little remains: but every hour is saved
From that eternal silence, something more,
A bringer of new things; and vile it were
For some three suns to store and hoard myself,
And this grey spirit yearning in desire
To follow knowledge like a sinking star,
Beyond the utmost bound of human thought.

   This is my son, mine own Telemachus,
To whom I leave the sceptre and the isle —
Well-loved of me, discerning to fulfil
This labor, by slow prudence to make mild
A rugged people, and thro' soft degrees
Subdue them to the useful and the good.
Most blameless is he, centred in the sphere
Of common duties, decent not to fail
In offices of tenderness, and pay
Meet adoration to my household gods,
When I am gone. He works his work, I mine.
   There lies the port: the vessel puffs her sail:
There gloom the dark broad seas. My mariners,
Souls that have toiled, and wrought, and thought with me —
That ever with a frolic welcome took
The thunder and the sunshine, and opposed
Free hearts, free foreheads — you and I are old;
Old age hath yet his honor and his toil;
Death closes all: but something ere the end,
Some work of noble note, may yet be done,

Not unbecoming men that strove with Gods.
The lights begin to twinkle from the rocks:
The long day wanes: the slow moon climbs: the deep
Moans round with many voices. Come, my friends,
'Tis not too late to seek a newer world.
Push off, and sitting well in order smite
The sounding furrows; for my purpose holds
To sail beyond the sunset, and the baths
Of all the western stars, until I die.
It may be that the gulfs will wash us down:
It may be we shall touch the Happy Isles,
And see the great Achilles, whom we knew.
Tho' much is taken, much abides; and tho'
We are not now that strength which in old days
Moved earth and heaven; that which we are, we are;
One equal temper of heroic hearts,
Made weak by time and fate, but strong in will
To strive, to seek, to find, and not to yield.

Alfred Lord Tennyson

THE LABORATORY

(*Ancien Régime* [5])

Now that I, tying thy glass-mask tightly,
May gaze thro' these faint smokes curling whitely,
As thou pliest thy trade in this devil's smithy —
Which is the poison to poison her, prithee?

He is with her; and they know that I know
Where they are, what they do; they believe my tears flow
While they laugh, laugh at me, at me fled to the drear
Empty church, to pray God in, for them! — I am here.

Grind away, moisten and mash up thy paste,
Pound at thy powder, — I am not in haste!

[5] The ancient or former order of things.

Better sit thus, and observe thy strange things,
Than go where men wait me and dance at the King's.

That in the mortar — you call it a gum?
Ah, the brave tree whence such gold oozings come!
And yonder soft phial, the exquisite blue,
Sure to taste sweetly, — is that poison too?

Had I but all of them, thee and thy treasures,
What a wild crowd of invisible pleasures!
To carry pure death in an earring, a casket,
A signet, a fan-mount, a filigree-basket!

Soon, at the King's, a mere lozenge to give
And Pauline should have just thirty minutes to live!
But to light a pastille, and Elise, with her head,
And her breast, and her arms, and her hands, should drop
    dead!

Quick — is it finished? The color's too grim!
Why not soft like the phial's, enticing and dim?
Let it brighten her drink, let her turn it and stir,
And try it and taste, ere she fix and prefer!

What a drop! She's not little, no minion like me —
That's why she ensnared him. This never will free
The soul from those strong, great eyes, say " no! "
To that pulse's magnificent come-and-go.

For only last night, as they whispered, I brought
My own eyes to bear on her so, that I thought
Could I keep them one half minute fixed, she would fall,
Shrivelled; she fell not; yet this does it all!

Not that I bid you spare her the pain!
Let death be felt and the proof remain;
Brand, burn up, bite into its grace —
He is sure to remember her dying face!

It is done? Take my mask off! Nay, be not morose,
It kills her, and this prevents seeing it close:
The delicate droplet, my whole fortune's fee —
If it hurts her, beside, can it ever hurt me?

Now, take all my jewels, gorge gold to your fill,
You may kiss me, old man, on my mouth if you will!
But brush this dust off me, lest horror it brings
Ere I know it — next moment I dance at the King's.

Robert Browning

THE BALLAD OF THE OYSTERMAN

It was a tall young oysterman lived by the river-side,
His shop was just upon the bank, his boat was on the tide;
The daughter of a fisherman, that was so straight and slim,
Lived over on the other bank, right opposite to him.

It was the pensive oysterman that saw a lovely maid,
Upon a moonlight evening, a-sitting in the shade;
He saw her wave her handkerchief, as much as if to say,
" I'm wide awake, young oysterman, and all the folks away."

Then up arose the oysterman, and to himself said he,
" I guess I'll leave the skiff at home, for fear that folks
    should see;
I read it in the story-book, that, for to kiss his dear,
Leander swam the Hellespont, — and I will swim this here."

And he has leaped into the waves, and crossed the shining
    stream,
And he has clambered up the bank, all in the moonlight
    gleam;
O there were kisses sweet as dew, and words as soft as
    rain, —
But they have heard her father's step, and in he leaps again!

Out spoke the ancient fisherman, — " O what was that, my
    daughter? "
" 'Twas nothing but a pebble, sir, I threw into the water."
" And what is that, pray tell me, love, that paddles off so
    fast? "
" It's nothing but a porpoise, sir, that's been a-swimming
    past."

Out spoke the ancient fisherman, — " Now bring me my
    harpoon!
I'll get into my fishing-boat, and fix the fellow soon."
Down fell that pretty innocent, as falls a snow-white lamb,
Her hair drooped round her pallid cheeks, like seaweed on
    a clam.

Alas for those two loving ones! she waked not from her
    swound,
And he was taken with the cramp, and in the waves was
    drowned;
But Fate has metamorphosed them, in pity 'of their woe,
And now they keep an oyster-shop for mermaids down
    below.

                        Oliver Wendell Holmes

THE DUEL

The gingham dog and the calico cat
Side by side on the table sat;
'Twas half-past twelve, and (what do you think!)
Nor one nor t'other had slept a wink!
    The old Dutch clock and the Chinese plate
    Appeared to know as sure as fate
There was going to be a terrible spat.
    (I wasn't there; I simply state
    What was told to me by the Chinese plate!)

The gingham dog went " bow-wow-wow! "
And the calico cat replied " mee-ow! "
The air was littered, an hour or so,
With bits of gingham and calico,
  While the old Dutch clock in the chimney-place
  Up with its hands before its face,
For it always dreaded a family row!
  (*Now mind: I'm only telling you
  What the old Dutch clock declares is true!*)

The Chinese plate looked very blue,
And wailed, " Oh, dear! what shall we do! "
But the gingham dog and the calico cat
Wallowed this way and tumbled that,
  Employing every tooth and claw
  In the awfullest way you ever saw —
And oh! how the gingham and calico flew!
  (*Don't fancy I exaggerate —
  I got my news from the Chinese plate!*)

Next morning, where the two had sat
They found no trace of a dog or cat;
And some folks think unto this day
That burglars stole that pair away!
  But the truth about the cat and pup
  Is this: they ate each other up!
Now what do you really think of that!
  (*The old Dutch clock it told me so,
  And that is how I came to know.*)

                                        Eugene Field

THE CAPTAIN AND THE MERMAIDS

  I sing a legend of the sea,
    So hard-a-port upon your lee!
      A ship on starboard tack!

She's bound upon a private cruise —
(This is the kind of spice I use
   To give a salt-sea smack).

Behold, on every afternoon
(Save in a gale or strong monsoon)
   Great Captain Capel Cleggs
(Great morally, though rather short)
Sat at an open weather-port
   And aired his shapely legs.

But Mermen didn't seem to care
Much time (as far as I'm aware)
   With Clegg's legs to spend;
Though Mermaids swam around all day
And gazed, exclaiming, " That's the way
   A gentleman should end!

" A pair of legs with well-cut knees,
And calves and ankles such as these,
   Which we in rapture hail,
Are far more eloquent, it's clear,
When clothed in silk and kerseymere,[6]
   Than any nasty tail."

At first the Mermen laughed a few,
But finally they jealous grew,
   And sounded loud recalls;
But vainly. So these fishy males
Declared they too would clothe their tails
   In silken hose and smalls.[7]

They set to work, these water-men,
And made their nether robes; but when
   They drew with dainty touch

6 kerseymere = a woolen cloth like cashmere. Some say that "kerseymere"
is actually cashmere, the word itself being only a corrupt pronunciation.
7 smalls = close-fitting knee-breeches.

The kerseymere upon their tails,
They found it scraped against their scales,
　　And hurt them very much.

So they designed another plan:
They sent their most seductive man
　　This note to him to show —
" Our Monarch sends to Captain Cleggs
His humble compliments, and begs
　　He'll join him down below;

" We've pleasant homes below the sea —
Besides, if Captain Cleggs should be
　　(As our advices say)
A judge of Mermaids, he will find
Our lady-fish of every kind
　　Inspection will repay."

The Mermen sank — the Captain too
Jumped overboard, and dropped from view
　　Like stone from catapult;
And when he reached the Mermen's lair
He certainly was welcomed there.
　　But, ah! with what result?

They didn't let him learn their law,
Or make a note of what he saw,
　　Or interesting mem.[8]:
The lady-fish he couldn't find,
But that, of course, he didn't mind —
　　He didn't come for them.

For though, when Captain Capel sank,
The Mermen drawn in double rank
　　Gave him a hearty hail;
Yet when secure of Captain Cleggs,
They cut off both his lovely legs,
　　And gave him *such* a tail!

[8] Memorandum, of course.

When Captain Cleggs returned aboard,
His blithesome crew convulsive roar'd
 To see him altered so
The Admiralty did insist
That he upon the Half-pay List
 Immediately should go.

In vain declared the poor old salt,
" It's my misfortune — not my fault,"
 With tear and trembling lip
In vain poor Capel begged and begged.
" A man must be completely legged
 Who rules a British ship."

So spake the stern First Lord aloud —
He was a wag, though very proud,
 And much rejoiced to say,
" You're only half a captain now —
And, so, my worthy friend, I vow
 You'll only get half-pay! "

        W. S. Gilbert

THE COWBOY'S DREAM

(*Sung to the air of " My bonnie lies over the ocean "*)

Last night as I lay on the prairie,
And looked at the stars in the sky,
I wondered if ever a cowboy
Would drift to that sweet by and by.

 Roll on, roll on;
 Roll on, little dogies,[9] *roll on, roll on,*
 Roll on, roll on;
 Roll on, little dogies, roll on.

     [9] *dogies* are young cattle.

The road to that bright happy region
Is a dim, narrow trail, so they say;
But the broad one that leads to perdition
Is posted and blazed all the way.

They say there will be a great round-up,
And cowboys, like dogies, will stand,
To be marked by the Riders of Judgment
Who are posted and know every brand.

I know that there's many a cowboy
Who'll be lost at the great, final sale,
When he might have gone in the green pastures
Had he known of the dim, narrow trail.

I wonder if ever a cowboy
Stood ready for that Judgment Day,
And could say to the Boss of the Riders,
" I'm ready, come drive me away."

For they, like the cows that are locoed,[10]
Stampede at the sight of a hand,
Are dragged with a rope to the round-up,
Or get marked with some crooked man's brand.

And I'm scared that I'll be a stray yearling, —
A maverick,[11] unbranded on high, —
And get cut in the bunch with the " rusties " [12]
When the Boss of the Riders goes by.

For they tell of another big owner
Who's ne'er overstocked, so they say,
But who always makes room for the sinner
Who drifts from the straight, narrow way.

[10] locoed = gone crazy.
[11] maverick = an unbranded animal, hence one that cannot be identified.
[12] "rusties" = the poor or useless stock.

They say he will never forget you,
That he knows every action and look;
So, for safety, you'd better get branded,
Have your name in the great Tally Book.

From Cowboy Ballads, collected by John A. Lomax

Haste thee, Nymph, and bring with thee
Jest and youthful Jollity,
Quips and Cranks, and wanton Wiles,
Nods, and Becks, and Wreathèd Smiles,
Such as hang on Hebe's cheek,
And love to live in dimple sleek;
Sport that wrinkled Care derides,
And Laughter holding both his sides.
Come, and trip it as ye go
On the light fantastic toe.

— JOHN MILTON

A NIGHTMARE

(*From "Iolanthe"*)

When you're lying awake with a dismal headache, and repose is taboo'd by anxiety,

I conceive you may use any language you choose to indulge in, without impropriety;

For your brain is on fire — the bedclothes conspire of usual slumber to plunder you:

First your counterpane goes and uncovers your toes, and your sheet slips demurely from under you;

Then the blanketing tickles — you feel like mixed pickles, so terribly sharp is the pricking,

And you're hot, and you're cross, and you tumble and toss till there's nothing 'twixt you and the ticking.

Then the bedclothes all creep to the ground in a heap, and you pick 'em all up in a tangle;

Next your pillow resigns and politely declines to remain at its usual angle!

Well, you get some repose in the form of a doze, with hot eye-balls and head ever aching,

But your slumbering teems with such horrible dreams that
you'd very much better be waking.

For you dream you are crossing the Channel, and tossing
about in a steamer from Harwich,[1]

Which is something between a large bathing machine and a
very small second-class carriage,

And you're giving a treat (penny ice and cold meat) to a
party of friends and relations —

They're a ravenous horde — and they all came on board at
Sloane Square and South Kensington Stations.

And bound on that journey you find your attorney (who
started that morning from Devon);

He's a bit undersized, and you don't feel surprised when he
tells you he's only eleven.

Well, you're driving like mad with this singular lad (by-the-
bye, the ship's now a four-wheeler),

And you're playing round games, and he calls you bad
names when you tell him that " ties pay the dealer ";

But this you can't stand, so you throw up your hand, and
you find you're as cold as an icicle,

In your shirt and your socks (the black silk with gold
clocks), crossing Salisbury Plain on a bicycle:

And he and the crew are on bicycles too — which they've
somehow or other invested in —

And he's telling the tars all the particu*lars* of a company
he's interested in —

It's a scheme of devices, to get at low prices, all goods from
cough mixtures to cables

(Which tickled the sailors) by treating retailers, as though
they were all vege*tables* —

You get a good spadesman to plant a small tradesman (first
take off his boots with a boot-tree),

And his legs will take root, and his fingers will shoot, and
they'll blossom and bud like a fruit tree —

From the greengrocer tree you get grapes and green pea,
cauliflower, pineapple and cranberries,

[1] Harwich is pronounced, as you can see from the next line, to rhyme with
"carriage."

While the pastry-cook plant, cherry brandy will grant, apple
    puffs, and three-corners, and banberries —
The shares are a penny, and ever so many are taken by
    Rothschild and Baring,
And just as a few are allotted to you, you awake with a
    shudder despairing —
You're a regular wreck, with a crick in your neck, and no
    wonder you snore, for your head's on the floor, and
    you've needles and pins from your soles to your shins,
    and your flesh is a-creep, for your left leg's asleep, and
    you've cramp in your toes, and a fly on your nose, and
    some fluff in your lung, and a feverish tongue, and a
    thirst that's intense, and a general sense that you
    haven't been sleeping in clover;
But the darkness has passed, and it's daylight at last, and
    the night has been long — ditto, ditto my song — and
    thank goodness they're both of them over!

W. S. Gilbert

TO THE TERRESTRIAL GLOBE

(*By a Miserable Wretch*)

Roll on, thou ball, roll on!
Through pathless realms of Space
        Roll on!
What, though I'm in a sorry case?
What, though I cannot meet my bills?
What, though I suffer toothache's ills?
What, though I swallow countless pills?
        Never *you* mind!
        Roll on!

Roll on, thou ball, roll on!
Through seas of inky air
        Roll on!
It's true I've got no shirts to wear;

It's true my butcher's bill is due;
It's true my prospects all look blue —
But don't let that unsettle you!
   Never *you* mind!
   Roll on!
     (It rolls on.)
       W. S. Gilbert

JEST 'FORE CHRISTMAS

Father calls me William, sister calls me Will,
Mother calls me Willie, but the fellers call me Bill!
Mighty glad I ain't a girl — ruther be a boy,
Without them sashes, curls, an' things that's worn by
  Fauntleroy!
Love to chawnk green apples an' go swimmin' in the lake —
Hate to take the castor-ile they give for belly-ache!
'Most all the time, the whole year round, there ain't no flies
  on me,
But jest 'fore Christmas I'm as good as I kin be!

Got a yeller dog named Sport, sick him on the cat;
First thing she knows she doesn't know where she is at!
Got a clipper sled, an' when us kids goes out to slide,
'Long comes the grocery cart, an' we all hook a ride!
But sometimes when the grocery man is worrited an' cross,
He reaches at us with his whip, an' larrups up his hoss,
An' then I laff an' holler, " Oh, ye never teched *me!* "
But jest 'fore Christmas I'm as good as I kin be!

Gran'ma says she hopes that when I git to be a man,
I'll be a missionarer like her oldest brother, Dan,
As was et up by the cannibuls that lives in Ceylon's Isle,
Where every prospeck pleases, an' only man is vile!
But gran'ma she has never been to see a Wild West show,
Nor read the Life of Daniel Boone, or else I guess she'd
  know

That Buff'lo Bill an' cow-boys is good enough for me!
Excep' jest 'fore Christmas, when I'm good as I kin be!

And then old Sport he hangs around, so solemn-like an' still,
His eyes they seem a-sayin': " What's the matter, little
    Bill? "
The old cat sneaks down off her perch an' wonders what's
    become
Of them two enemies of hern that used to make things hum!
But I am so perlite an' 'tend so earnestly to biz,
That mother says to father: " How improved our Willie
    is! "
But father, havin' been a boy hisself, suspicions me
When, jest 'fore Christmas, I'm as good as I kin be!

For Christmas, with its lots an' lots of candies, cakes an'
    toys,
Was made, they say, for proper kids, an' not for naughty
    boys;
So wash yer face an' bresh yer hair, an' mind yer p's
    and q's,
An' don't bust out yer pantaloons, and don't wear out yer
    shoes;
Say " Yessum " to the ladies, an' " Yessur " to the men,
An' when they's company, don't pass yer plate for pie again;
But, thinkin' of the things yer'd like to see upon that tree,
Jest 'fore Christmas be as good as yer kin be!

Eugene Field

THE MAN IN THE MOON [2]

Said The Raggedy Man, on a hot afternoon:
  My!
    Sakes!
      What a lot o' mistakes
Some little folks makes on The Man in the Moon!

[2] From *Rhymes of Childhood*, copyright 1890. Used by special permission of the publishers, The Bobbs-Merrill Company.

But people that's be'n up to *see* him, like *me,*
And calls on him frequent and intimuttly,
Might drop a few facts that would interest you
   Clean!
      Through!
         If you wanted 'em to —
Some *actual* facts that might interest you!

O The Man in the Moon has a crick in his back;
   Whee!
      Whimm!
         Ain't you sorry for him?
And a mole on his nose that is purple and black;
And his eyes are so weak that they water and run
If he dares to *dream* even he looks at the sun, —
So he jes' dreams of stars, as the doctors advise —
   My!
      Eyes!
         But isn't he wise —
To jes' dream of stars, as the doctors advise?

And The Man in the Moon has a boil on his ear —
   Whee!
      Whing!
         What a singular thing!
I know! but these facts are authentic, my dear, —
There's a boil on his ear; and a corn on his chin —
He calls it a dimple — but dimples stick in —
Yet it might be a dimple turned over, you know!
   Whang!
      Ho!
         Why, certainly so! —
It might be a dimple turned over, you know!

And The Man in the Moon has a rheumatic knee —
   Gee!
      Whizz!
         What a pity that is!

And his toes have worked round where his heels ought to
    be. —
So whenever he wants to go North he goes *South,*
And comes back with porridge-crumbs all round his mouth,
And he brushes them off with a Japanese fan,
   Whing!
      Whann!
         What a marvellous man!
    What a very remarkably marvellous man!

And The Man in the Moon, sighed The Raggedy Man,
   Gits!
      So!
         Sullonesome, you know, —
Up there by hisse'f sence creation began! —
That when I call on him and then come away,
He grabs me and holds me and begs me to stay, —
Till — *Well!* if it wasn't fer *Jimmy-cum-jim,*
   Dadd!
      Limb!
         I'd go pardners with him —
Jes' jump my job here and be pardners with *him!*
                    James Whitcomb Riley

THE WALRUS AND THE CARPENTER

(From " Through the Looking Glass ")

The sun was shining on the sea,
   Shining with all his might;
He did his very best to make
   The billows smooth and bright —
And this was odd, because it was
   The middle of the night.

The moon was shining sulkily,
   Because she thought the sun

Had got no business to be there
  After the day was done —
" It's very rude of him," she said,
  " To come and spoil the fun! "

The sea was wet as wet could be,
  The sands were dry as dry.
You could not see a cloud, because
  No cloud was in the sky:
No birds were flying overhead —
  There were no birds to fly.

The Walrus and the Carpenter
  Were walking close at hand:
They wept like anything to see
  Such quantities of sand:
" If this were only cleared away,"
  They said, " It would be grand! "

" If seven maids with seven mops
  Swept it for half a year,
Do you suppose," the Walrus said,
  " That they could get it clear? "
" I doubt it," said the Carpenter,
  And shed a bitter tear.

" O Oysters, come and walk with us! "
  The Walrus did beseech.
" A pleasant walk, a pleasant talk,
  Along the briny beach:
We cannot do with more than four,
  To give a hand to each."

The eldest Oyster looked at him,
  But never a word he said:
The eldest Oyster winked his eye,
  And shook his heavy head —
Meaning to say he did not choose
  To leave the oyster-bed.

But four young Oysters hurried up,
    All eager for a treat.
Their coats were brushed, their faces washed,
    Their shoes were clean and neat —
And this was odd, because, you know,
    They hadn't any feet.

Four other Oysters followed them,
    And yet another four;
And thick and fast they came at last,
    And more, and more, and more —
All hopping through the frothy waves,
    And scrambling to the shore.

The Walrus and the Carpenter
    Walked on a mile or so,
And then they rested on a rock
    Conveniently low:
And all the little Oysters stood
    And waited in a row.

" The time has come," the Walrus said,
    " To talk of many things:
Of shoes — and ships — and sealing-wax —
    Of cabbages — and kings —
And why the sea is boiling hot —
    And whether pigs have wings."

" But wait a bit," the Oysters cried,
    " Before we have our chat;
For some of us are out of breath,
    And all of us are fat."
" No hurry! " said the Carpenter.
    They thanked him much for that.

" A loaf of bread," the Walrus said,
    " Is what we chiefly need;

Pepper and vinegar besides
  Are very good indeed —
Now, if you're ready, Oysters dear,
  We can begin to feed."

" But not on us! " the Oysters cried,
  Turning a little blue,
" After such kindness, that would be
  A dismal thing to do! "
" The night is fine," the Walrus said.
  " Do you admire the view?

" It was so kind of you to come!
  And you are very nice! "
The Carpenter said nothing but
  " Cut us another slice.
I wish you were not quite so deaf —
  I've had to ask you twice! "

" It seems a shame," the Walrus said,
  " To play them such a trick.
After we've brought them out so far,
  And made them trot so quick! "
The Carpenter said nothing but
  " The butter's spread too thick! "

" I weep for you," the Walrus said:
  " I deeply sympathize."
With sobs and tears he sorted out
  Those of the largest size,
Holding his pocket-handkerchief
  Before his streaming eyes.

" O Oysters," said the Carpenter,
  " You've had a pleasant run!
Shall we be trotting home again? "
  But answer there came none —

And this was scarcely odd, because
They'd eaten every one.

Lewis Carroll

HOW DOTH THE LITTLE CROCODILE [3]

(*From " Alice in Wonderland "*)

How doth the little crocodile
    Improve his shining tail,
And pour the waters of the Nile
    On every golden scale!

How cheerfully he seems to grin,
    How neatly spreads his claws,
And welcomes little fishes in
    With gently smiling jaws!

Lewis Carroll

THE POBBLE WHO HAS NO TOES

The Pobble who has no toes
    Had once as many as we;
When they said, " Some day you may lose them all; "
    He replied, " Fish fiddle de-dee! "
And His Aunt Jobiska made him drink
Lavender-water tinged with pink;
For she said, " The World in general knows
There's nothing so good for a Pobble's toes! "

The Pobble who has no toes
    Swam across the British Channel:
But before he set out he wrapped his nose
    In a piece of scarlet flannel.

[3] For those who may not recognize it, this is a burlesque of Doctor Isaac
Watts' famous poem which begins:

> How doth the little busy bee
> Improve each shining hour,
> And gather honey all the day
> From every opening flower.

For his Aunt Jobiska said, " No harm
Can come to his toes if his nose is warm;
And it's perfectly known that a Pobble's toes
Are safe — provided he minds his nose."

The Pobble swam fast and well,
   And when boats or ships came near him,
He tinkledy-binkledy-winkled a bell
   So that all the world could hear him.
And all the Sailors and Admirals cried,
When they saw him nearing the further side, —
" He has gone to fish, for his Aunt Jobiska's
Runcible Cat with crimson whiskers! "

But before he touched the shore, —
   The shore of the Bristol Channel,
A sea-green Porpoise carried away
   His wrapper of scarlet flannel.
And when he came to observe his feet,
Formerly garnished with toes so neat,
His face at once became forlorn
On perceiving that all his toes were gone!

And nobody ever knew,
   From that dark day to the present,
Whoso had taken the Pobble's toes,
   In a manner so far from pleasant.
Whether the shrimps or crawfish gray,
Or crafty Mermaids stole them away,
Nobody knew; and nobody knows
How the Pobble was robbed of his twice five toes!

The Pobble who has no toes
   Was placed in a friendly Bark,
And they rowed him back, and carried him up
   To his Aunt Jobiska's Park.

And she made him a feast, at his earnest wish,
Of eggs and buttercups fried with fish;
And she said, " It's a fact the whole world knows,
That Pobbles are happier without their toes."

Edward Lear

"IN VAIN TO–DAY"

In vain to-day I scrape and blot:
    The nimble words, the phrases neat,
    Decline to mingle and to meet;
My skill is all forgone, forgot.

He will not canter, walk, or trot,
    My Pegasus; I spur, I beat
        In vain to-day.

And yet 'twere sure the saddest lot
    That I should fail to leave complete
    One poor . . . the rhyme suggests "conceit!"
Alas! 'tis all too clear I'm not
        In vein to-day.

Austin Dobson

JUNIPER JIM

(A Burlesque Parlor-Poem for the Use of the Young
Reciter)

(*Flick your right boot with the whip, and dash impetuously at the first line.*)

Yes! (*aggressively, as if somebody had just implied that it
    wasn't*) Steeple-chasing is stirring sport — and the most
    exciting events of all
Are at Purlingham Park, when the field is large, and the
    ditches deep and the fences tall,

And I for one shall never forget — till my brain is blurred
and my eyes are dim,
  (*Pass hand over eyes and blink, with just a suggestion of
  pathos.*)
The day that Dot and Go One was steered by an infant
hero — (*with a burst of candor*) Juniper Jim!
  (*Quieter explanatory manner for next two lines.*)

Robert Roper was down to ride, and we'd backed his mount,
for he knew the course,
And, gad! he'd have managed to romp in first if they put
him up on a rocking-horse!
But out of the paddock the horses filed — and a murmur
ran: ' It is Roper's *son!*
Why, where the dickens can Robert be, that he's not in
charge of Dot and Go One? '

And the devotees of ' The Ring and the Book ' said many a
swear as they saw the lad:
While some declared that the bets were off; and all considered the outlook bad.
For Dot and Go One — though a grand old gee [4] — was a
trifle groggy in wind and limb,
And we feared he would never run up to his form, with a
child on his back like Juniper Jim.
                    (*Shake your head apprehensively.*)

Now — Roper, it happened, was under a cloud, and the
Stewards had given him notice to quit,
For (*apologetically*) a little artistic ' arrangement in oils '
he'd endeavoured to paint on the favorite's bit.
' They might ha' waited! ' his trainer cried, ' and warned
him off when the race was run,
For where's the party to take his place, and perform as
pilot to Dot and Go One? '
                    (*Gaze round the room despairingly.*)

[4] A "gee" as, of course you know, is what we used to call a "geegee,"
which is nursery for 'horse."

(*Lower key.*) And the silence answered — for no one spoke,
till — (*brighten up here*) — just as the last faint hope
had gone —

Came (*in a tone of wondering pity*) a chit of seven, and
said: ' I'll try! (*pathetically*) I am only a child, but
(*with modest confidence*) — I *can* stick on!

See, I've donned my father's jacket and cap — his cords
encircle my legs so slim,

They are undersized (*with childish frankness*), I was nursed
on gin — which is why they call me Juniper Jim.

' But, in spite of my size and tender years, though I've
seldom been on a horse before,

I'll keep in the saddle, whatever befalls — and the finest
horseman can do no more!

And the simple boon that I crave of you, when the post is
passed and my duty done,

Is — my father's pardon! ' (*pause — then impulsively*) . . .
' A bargain, boy! ' (*second pause — then quietly*) So
they hoisted him up on Dot and Go One.

(*Historic present for following stanzas. Let your deliv-
ery be rapid, brilliant, illustrative, graphic, sporting AND
dramatic — and you can't possibly fail.*)

He has come into line with the pick of the field, with the
chestnut, the bay, and the strawberry roan,
> (*With an air of gradual identification*)
The Stiff'un, the Catsmeat, Polonia's Pride, and Titupping
Tommy, and Second Trombone.

Now they're off with a jump at the fall of the flag, and the
heather-topped hurdles (*Do mind your h's here, or
you may come a cropper over those hurdles*) they
airily skim.

But the boy! (*Bend forward and strain your eyes eagerly
— then with irrepressible enthusiasm*) Like a leech to

the pigskin he sticks! And we shout to him, ' Bravo, Juniper Jim! '

(' *Brio* ' *here if you can manage it and if you know what it is.*)

(*Lower your voice, intense anxiety, vivid facial expression, all your features working hard.*)
They are close at it now, and (*groan*) his stirrups are lost, and — merciful powers! what *is* he about?

    (*Agonized glance at front row of audience here.*)
There! what did I *tell* you? the pair of 'em in — and it's odds if a pair of 'em ever come out!
But (*pointing*) — wonder of wonders! look — Dot and Go One has scrambled out — and on top of him,
Damp and draggled, but sticking tight (*laugh here hysterically*), like a game little limpet is Juniper Jim!

And the gallant grey is galumphing on, like the scion true of a rare old stock,
(For isn't he brother to Creepie Stool and stable-companion to Golden Crock?).
There's a brook in front — but he plunges in and strikes out boldly — he's game to swim.
(*Not that horses DO strike out — in the water at least — but what does it matter in a Recitation?*)
And he's shaking himself on the opposite side — but he can't shake off young Juniper Jim!

There are only a couple ahead of him now, and he shambles up with his raking stride;
And the poor old Trombone's beginning to blow, as he pants in the rear of Polonia's Pride.
She is over the five-foot fence like a frog — but the Trombone's down, and out of the fun;
(*Put both hands to mouth and yell*) Now — *cram* him at it, Juniper Jim! (*Relieved*) Well, he's done it *somehow* on Dot and Go One!

There's a roar from the Ring, and a shout from the Stand,
    as they bucket by with a final burst;
For the mare is beaten by half a head, and the clever old
    grey is at home the first!
And the crowd are cheering the pallid child, as he capless
    sits in the burning sun,
' Hip, hip, hooray! for the infant pluck that has scored a
    win with Dot and Go One! '

But the boy replies with a gentle smile: (*keep this very
    sweet and modest*) ' I thank you all — I have done my
    part,
Now I claim the guerdon — a Father's name is dear indeed
    to his Offspring's heart! '
       (*Very tender and sympathetic for this next line.*)
And the very Stewards are softened now, and the unshed
    tears to their eyelids brim,
As they pardon Roper his little ruse, for the sake of their
    promise to Juniper Jim.

Then we all of us rush to embrace the lad, and to lift him
    down — (*In a tone of extreme surprise*) — But we
    strain our backs!
And the child explains with simple glee, that he's rubbed
    the saddle with cobbler's wax.
               (*Pause — then in challenge*)
' With such a precaution,' the cynic sneers, ' what danger
    was there — to seek or shun? '
  (*Affect to ponder over this objection for a moment, and
then dismiss it with a ringing inflection of good-humored
contempt.*)
Well — the answer to *that* is — Try it yourself — at Pur-
    lingham Park, on Dot and Go One!

  (*If you cannot bring the house down with this, you had
better give up reciting altogether and come out at a special
matinée as Hamlet.*)

                                F. Anstey

A thing of beauty is a joy forever;
Its loveliness increases; it will never
Pass into nothingness.

— JOHN KEATS

RABBI BEN EZRA

(*Condensed Version*)

Grow old along with me!
The best is yet to be,
The last of life, for which the first was made:
Our times are in His hand
Who saith ' A whole I planned,
Youth shows but half; trust God; see all, nor be afraid!

Not for such hopes and fears
Annulling youth's brief years,
Do I remonstrate: folly wide the mark!
Rather I prize the doubt
Low kinds exist without,
Finished and finite clods, untroubled by a spark.

Then welcome each rebuff
That turns earth's smoothness rough,
Each sting that bids nor sit nor stand but go!
Be our joys three-parts pain!
Strive, and hold cheap the strain;
Learn, nor account the pang; dare, never grudge the throe!

For thence, — a paradox
Which comforts while it mocks, —
Shall life succeed in that it seems to fail:

What I aspired to be,
And was not, comforts me;
A brute I might have been, but would not sink i' the scale.

What is he but a brute
Whose flesh hath soul to suit,
Whose spirit works lest arms and legs want play?
To man, propose this test —
Thy body at its best,
How far can that project thy soul on its lone way?

For pleasant is this flesh;
Our soul in its rose-mesh
Pulled ever to the earth, still yearns for rest:
Would we some prize might hold
To match those manifold
Possessions of the brute, — gain most, as we did best!

Let us not always say
'Spite of this flesh today
I strove, made head, gained ground upon the whole!'
As the bird wings and sings,
Let us cry 'All good things
Are ours, nor soul helps flesh more, now, than flesh helps
    soul!'

Therefore I summon age
To grant youth's heritage,
Life's struggle having so far reached its term:
Thence shall I pass, approved:
A man, for aye removed
From the developed brute, a God though in the germ.

For note, when evening shuts,
A certain moment cuts
The deed off, calls the glory from the grey:
A whisper from the west
Shoots — 'Add this to the rest,
Take it and try its worth: here dies another day.'

As it was better, youth
Should strive, through acts uncouth,
Toward making, than repose on aught found made:
So, better, age, exempt
From strife, should know, than tempt
Further. Thou waitedest age; wait death nor be afraid!

Thoughts hardly to be packed
Into a narrow act,
Fancies that broke through language and escaped;
All I could never be,
All, men ignored in me,
This, I was worth to God, whose wheel the pitcher shaped.

Aye, note that Potter's wheel,
That metaphor! and feel
Why time spins fast, why passive lies our clay, —
Thou, to whom fools propound,
When the wine makes its round,
' Since life fleets, all is change; the Past gone, seize today! '

Fool! All that is, at all,
Lasts ever, past recall;
Earth changes, but thy soul and God stand sure:
What entered into thee,
That was, is, and shall be:
Time's wheel runs back or stops; Potter and clay endure.

Look not thou down but up!
To uses of a cup,
The festal board, lamp's flash and trumpet's peal,
The new wine's foaming flow,
The Master's lips aglow!
Thou, heaven's consummate cup, what needst thou with
    earth's wheel?

But I need, now as then,
Thee, God, who mouldest men;

And since, not even while the whirl was worst,
Did I, — to the wheel of life
With shapes and colors rife
Bound dizzily, — mistake my end, to slake Thy thirst:

So, take and use Thy work!
Amend what flaws may lurk,
What strain o' the stuff, what warpings past the aim!
My times be in Thy hand!
Perfect the cup as planned!
Let age approve of youth, and death complete the same!

Robert Browning

GOOD–BYE

Good-bye, proud world! I'm going home:
Thou art not my friend, and I'm not thine.
Long through thy weary crowds I roam;
A river-ark on the ocean brine,
Long I've been tossed like the driven foam;
But now, proud world! I'm going home.
Good-bye to Flattery's fawning face;
To grandeur with his wise grimace;
To upstart Wealth's averted eye;
To supple Office, low and high;
To crowded halls, to court and street;
To frozen hearts and hasting feet;
To those who go, and those who come;
Good-bye, proud world! I'm going home.

I am going to my own hearth-stone,
Bosomed in yon green hills alone, —
A secret nook in a pleasant land,
Whose groves the frolic fairies planned;
Where arches green, the livelong day,
Echo the blackbird's roundelay,
And vulgar feet have never trod
A spot that is sacred to thought and God.

O, when I am safe in my sylvan home,
I tread on the pride of Greece and Rome;
And when I am stretched beneath the pines,
Where the evening star so holy shines,
I laugh at the lore and the pride of man,
At the sophist schools, and the learned clan;
For what are they all, in their high conceit,
When man in the bush with God may meet?

Ralph Waldo Emerson

FORBEARANCE

Hast thou named all the birds without a gun?
Loved the wood-rose, and left it on its stalk?
At rich men's tables eaten bread and pulse?
Unarmed, faced danger with a heart of trust?
And loved so well a high behaviour,
In man or maid, that thou from speech refrained,
Nobility more nobly to repay?
O, be my friend, and teach me to be thine!

Ralph Waldo Emerson

THE RUBAIYAT OF OMAR KHAYYAM

(*Selected Stanzas*)

A Book of Verses underneath the Bough,
A Jug of Wine, a Loaf of Bread — and Thou
    Beside me singing in the Wilderness —
Oh, Wilderness were Paradise enow!

I sometimes think that never blows so red
The Rose as where some buried Caesar bled;
    That every Hyacinth the Garden wears
Dropt in her Lap from some once lovely Head.

And this reviving Herb whose tender Green
Fledges the River-Lip on which we lean —
    Ah, lean upon it lightly! for who knows
From what once lovely Lip it springs unseen!

Why, if the Soul can fling the Dust aside,
And naked on the Air of Heaven ride,
    Were't not a Shame — were't not a Shame indeed
In this clay carcass crippled to abide?

We are no other than a moving row
Of Magic Shadow-shapes that come and go
    Round with the Sun-illumined Lantern held
In Midnight by the Master of the Show.

The Ball no question makes of Ayes and Noes,
But Here or There as strikes the Player goes;
    And He that toss'd you down into the Field,
He knows about it all — HE knows — HE knows!

The Moving Finger writes; and, having writ,
Moves on: nor all your Piety nor Wit
    Shall lure it back to cancel half a Line,
Nor all your Tears wash out a Word of it.

And that inverted Bowl they call the Sky,
Whereunder crawling coop'd we live and die,
    Lift not your hands to *It* for help — for It
As impotently moves as you or I.

Yet Ah, that Spring should vanish with the Rose!
That Youth's sweet-scented manuscript should close!
    The Nightingale that in the branches sang,
Ah whence, and whither flown again, who knows!

Ah Love! could you and I with Him conspire
To grasp this sorry Scheme of Things entire,
    Would not we shatter it to bits — and then
Re-mould it nearer to the Heart's Desire!

Yon rising Moon that looks for us again —
How oft hereafter will she wax and wane;
    How oft hereafter rising look for us
Through this same Garden — and for *one* in vain!

And when like her, oh Sáki,[1] you shall pass
Among the Guests Star-scatter'd on the Grass,
  And in your joyous errand reach the spot
Where I made One — turn down an empty Glass!
                              Edward Fitzgerald

" UNDER THE SUN "

      Under the sun
        There's nothing new;
      Poem or pun,
      Under the sun,
      Said Solomon,
        And he said true.
      Under the sun
        There's nothing new.
                    Henry Charles Beeching

THE POTTER'S SONG

(*From " Kéramos "*)

Turn, turn, my wheel! Turn round and round
Without a pause, without a sound:
  So spins the flying world away!
This clay, well mixed with marl and sand,
Follows the motion of my hand;
For some must follow, and some command,
  Though all are made of clay!

Turn, turn, my wheel! All things must change
To something new, to something strange;
  Nothing that is can pause or stay;
The moon will wax, the moon will wane,
The mist and cloud will turn to rain,
The rain to mist and cloud again,
  To-morrow be to-day,

---

[1] Sáki is the cup-bearer.

Turn, turn, my wheel!   All life is brief;
What now is bud will soon be leaf,
    What now is leaf will soon decay;
The wind blows east, the wind blows west;
The blue eggs in the robin's nest
Will soon have wings and beak and breast,
    And flutter and fly away.

Turn, turn, my wheel!   This earthen jar
A touch can make, a touch can mar;
    And shall it to the Potter say,
What makest thou?   Thou hast no hand?
As men who think to understand
A world by their Creator planned,
    Who wiser is than they.

Turn, turn, my wheel!   'Tis nature's plan
The child should grow into the man,
    The man grow wrinkled, old, and gray;
In youth the heart exults and sings,
The pulses leap, the feet have wings;
In age the cricket chirps, and brings
    The harvest-home of day.

Turn, turn, my wheel!   The human race,
Of every tongue, of every place,
    Caucasian, Coptic, or Malay,
All that inhabit this great earth,
Whatever be their rank or worth,
Are kindred and allied by birth,
    And made of the same clay.

Turn, turn, my wheel!   What is begun
At daybreak must at dark be done,
    To-morrow will be another day;
To-morrow the hot furnace flame
Will search the heart and try the frame,
And stamp with honor or with shame
    These vessels made of clay.

Stop, stop, my wheel!   Too soon, too soon,
The noon will be the afternoon,
   Too soon to-day be yesterday;
Behind us in our path we cast
The broken potsherds [2] of the past,
And all are ground to dust at last,
   And trodden into clay!

Henry Wadsworth Longfellow

ALOOF

The irresponsive silence of the land,
The irresponsive sounding of the sea,
Speak both one message of one sense to me: —
Aloof, aloof, we stand aloof, so stand
Thou too aloof, bound with the flawless band
Of inner solitude; we bind not thee;
But who from thy self-chain shall set thee free?
What heart shall touch thy heart?   What hand thy hand?

And I am sometimes proud and sometimes meek,
And sometimes I remember days of old
When fellowship seem'd not so far to seek,
And all the world and I seem'd much less cold,
And at the rainbow's foot lay surely gold,
And hope felt strong, and life itself not weak.

Christina Georgina Rossetti

[2] potsherds = shards (broken pieces or fragments) of the pot.

Sunset and evening star,
 And one clear call for me!
And may there be no moaning of the bar
 When I put out to sea.

      — ALFRED LORD TENNYSON

PROSPICE [1]

Fear death? — to feel the fog in my throat,
 The mist in my face,
When the snows begin, and the blasts denote
 I am nearing the place,
The power of the night, the press of the storm,
 The post of the foe;
Where he stands, the Arch Fear in a visible form,
 Yet the strong man must go;
For the journey is done and the summit attained,
 And the barriers fall,
Though a battle's to fight ere the guerdon be gained,
 The reward of it all.
I was ever a fighter, so — one fight more,
 The best and the last!
I would hate that death bandaged my eyes, and forbore,
 And bade me creep past,
No! let me taste the whole of it, fare like my peers
 The heroes of old.
Bear the brunt, in a minute pay glad life's arrears
 Of pain, darkness and cold.
For sudden the worst turns the best to the brave,
 The black minute's at end,

[1] Prospice = Look forward.

And the elements' rage, the fiend-voices that rave,
   Shall dwindle, shall blend,
Shall change, shall become first a peace, then a joy,
   Then a light, then thy breast,
O thou soul of my soul! I shall clasp thee again,
   And with God be the rest!

Robert Browning

FROM " THANATOPSIS "

Earth, that nourished thee, shall claim
Thy growth, to be resolved to earth again,
And, lost each human trace, surrendering up
Thine individual being, shalt thou go
To mix forever with the elements,
To be a brother to the insensible rock
And to the sluggish clod, which the rude swain
Turns with his share and treads upon. The oak
Shall send his roots abroad, and pierce thy mould.
Yet not to thine eternal resting-place
Shalt thou retire alone — nor couldst thou wish
Couch more magnificent. Thou shalt lie down
With patriarchs of the infant world — with kings,
The powerful of the earth — the wise, the good,
Fair forms, and hoary seers of ages past,
All in one mighty sepulchre. — The hills
Rock-ribbed and ancient as the sun, — the vales
Stretching in pensive quietness between;
The venerable woods — rivers that move
In majesty, and the complaining brooks
That make the meadows green; and, poured round all,
Old ocean's gray and melancholy waste —
Are but the solemn decorations all
Of the great tomb of man. . . .

. . . .

So live, that when thy summons comes to join
The innumerable caravan, that moves

To that mysterious realm, where each shall take
His chamber in the silent halls of death,
Thou go not, like the quarry-slave at night,
Scourged to his dungeon, but, sustained and soothed
By an unfaltering trust, approach thy grave,
Like one who wraps the drapery of his couch
About him, and lies down to pleasant dreams.

William Cullen Bryant

THE OLD

They are waiting on the shore
    For the bark to take them home:
They will toil and grieve no more;
    The hour for release hath come.

All their long life lies behind
    Like a dimly blending dream:
There is nothing left to bind
    To the realms that only seem.

They are waiting for the boat;
    There is nothing left to do;
What was near them grows remote,
    Happy silence falls like dew;
Now the shadowy bark is come,
    And the weary may go home.

By still water they would rest
    In the shadow of the tree:
After battle sleep is best,
    After noise, tranquillity.

Roden Noel

O CAPTAIN! MY CAPTAIN!

O Captain! My Captain! our fearful trip is done,
The ship has weather'd every rack, the prize we sought
is won,
The port is near, the bells I hear, the people all exulting,
While follow eyes the steady keel, the vessel grim and
daring;
  But O heart! heart! heart!
    O the bleeding drops of red,
      Where on the deck my Captain lies,
      Fallen cold and dead.

O Captain! My Captain! rise up and hear the bells;
Rise up — for you the flag is flung — for you the bugle
trills,
For you bouquets and ribbon'd wreaths — for you the
shores a-crowding,
For you they call, the swaying mass, their eager faces
turning;
  Here Captain! dear father!
    This arm beneath your head!
      It is some dream that on the deck,
      You've fallen cold and dead.

My Captain does not answer, his lips are pale and still,
My father does not feel my arm, he has no pulse nor will,
The ship is anchor'd safe and sound, its voyage closed and
done,
From fearful trip the victor ship comes in with object won;
  Exult O shores, and ring O bells!
    But I with mournful tread,
      Walk the deck my Captain lies,
      Fallen cold and dead.

Walt Whitman

WHEN LILACS LAST IN THE DOORYARD BLOOM'D

(*Condensed Version*)

1

When lilacs last in the dooryard bloom'd,
And the great star early droop'd in the western sky in the
    night,
I mourn'd, and yet shall mourn with ever-returning spring.
Ever-returning spring, trinity sure to me you bring:
Lilac blooming perennial and drooping star in the west,
And thought of him I love.

2

O powerful western fallen star!
O shades of night — O moody, tearful night!
O great star disappear'd — O the black murk that hides
    the star!
O cruel hands that hold me powerless —
O helpless soul of me!
O harsh surrounding cloud that will not free my soul.

3

In the dooryard fronting an old farm-house near the white-
    wash'd palings,
Stands the lilac-bush tall-growing with heart-shaped leaves
    of rich green,
With many a pointed blossom rising delicate, with the
    perfume strong I love,
With every leaf a miracle — and from this bush in the
    dooryard,
With delicate-color'd blossoms and heart-shaped leaves of
    rich green,
A sprig with its flower I break.

4

In the swamp in secluded recesses,
A shy and hidden bird is warbling a song.
Solitary the thrush,
The hermit withdrawn to himself, avoiding the settlements,
Sings by himself a song.
Song of the bleeding throat,
Death's outlet song of life, (for well, dear brother, I know,
If thou wast not granted to sing thou would'st surely die.)

5

Over the breast of the spring, the land, amid cities,
Amid lanes and through old woods, where lately the violets
    peep'd from the ground, spotting the gray debris,
Amid the grass in the fields each side of the lanes, passing
    the endless grass,
Passing the yellow-spear'd wheat, every grain from its
    shroud in the dark-brown fields uprisen,
Passing the apple-tree blows of white and pink in the
    orchards,
Carrying a corpse to where it shall rest in the grave,
Night and day journeys a coffin.

6

Coffin that passes through lanes and streets,
Through day and night with the great cloud darkening
    the land,
With the pomp of the inloop'd flags with the cities draped
    in black,
With the show of the States themselves as of crape-veil'd
    women standing,
With processions long and winding and the flambeaus of
    the night,
With the countless torches lit, with the silent sea of faces
    and the unbared heads,

With the waiting depot, the arriving coffin, and the sombre
    faces,
With dirges through the night, with the thousand voices
    rising strong and solemn,
With all the mournful voices of the dirges pour'd around
    the coffin,
The dim-lit churches and the shuddering organs — where
    amid these you journey,
With the tolling, tolling bell's perpetual clang,
Here, coffin that slowly passes,
I give you my sprig of lilac.

7

(Not for you, for one alone,
Blossoms and branches green to coffins all I bring,
For fresh as the morning, thus would I chant a song for
    you, O sane and sacred death.
All over bouquets of roses,
O death, I cover you over with roses and early lilies,
But mostly and now the lilac that blooms the first,
Copious I break, I break the sprigs from the bushes,
With loaded arms I come, pouring for you,
For you and the coffins all of you, O death.)

8

Sing on there in the swamp,
O singer bashful and tender, I hear your notes, I hear your
    call,
I hear, I come presently, I understand you,
But a moment I linger, for the lustrous star has detain'd
    me,
The star my departing comrade holds and detains me.

9

O how shall I warble myself for the dead one there I
    loved?
And how shall I deck my song for the large sweet soul that
    has gone?

And what shall my perfume be for the grave of him I
    love?
Sea-winds blown from east and west,
Blown from the Eastern sea and blown from the Western
    sea, till there on the prairies meeting,
These and with these and the breath of my chant,
I'll perfume the grave of him I love.

10

Sing on, sing on, you gray-brown bird,
Sing from the swamps, the recesses, pour your chant from
    the bushes,
Limitless out of the dusk, out of the cedars and pines.
Sing on, dearest brother, warble your reedy song,
Loud human song, with voice of uttermost woe.
O liquid and free and tender!
O wild and loose to my soul — O wondrous singer!
You only I hear — yet the star holds me, (but will soon
    depart,)
Yet the lilac with mastering odor holds me.

11

Then with the knowledge of death as walking one side of
    me,
And the thought of death close-walking the other side of
    me,
And I in the middle as with companions, and as holding the
    hands of companions,
I fled forth to the hiding, receiving night that talks not,
Down to the shores of the water, the path by the swamp in
    the dimness,
To the solemn shadowy cedars and ghostly pines so still.
And the singer so shy to the rest receiv'd me,
The gray-brown bird I know receiv'd us comrades three,
And he sang the carol of death, and a verse for him I love.
From deep secluded recesses,
From the fragrant cedars and the ghostly pines so still,

Came the carol of the bird.
And the charm of the carol rapt me,
As I held as if by their hands my comrades in the night,
And the voice of my spirit tallied the song of the bird.

(Death Chant)

Come, lovely and soothing death,
Undulate round the world, serenely arriving, arriving,
In the day, in the night, to all, to each,
Sooner or later, delicate death.
Prais'd be the fathomless universe,
For life and joy, and for objects and knowledge curious,
And for love, sweet love — but praise! praise! praise!
For the sure-enwinding arms of cool-enfolding death.
Dark mother always gliding near with soft feet,
Have none chanted for thee a chant of fullest welcome?
Then I chant it for thee, I glorify thee above all,
I bring thee a song that when thou must indeed come, come
*   unfalteringly.*
Approach, strong deliveress,
When it is so, when thou hast taken them I joyously sing
*   the dead,*
Lost in the loving floating ocean of thee,
Laved in the flood of thy bliss, O death.
From me to thee, glad serenades,
Dances for thee I propose saluting thee, adornments and
*   feastings for thee,*
And the sights of the open landscape and the high-spread
*   sky are fitting,*
And life and the fields, and the huge and thoughtful night.
The night in silence under many a star,
The ocean shore and the husky whispering wave whose
*   voice I know,*
And the soul turning to thee, O vast and well-veil'd death,
And the body gratefully nestling close to thee.
Over the tree-tops I float thee a song,

*Over the rising and sinking waves, over the myriad fields
   and the prairies wide,*
*Over the dense-pack'd cities all and the teeming wharves
   and ways,*
I float this carol with joy, with joy to thee, O death.

12

To the tally of my soul,
Loud and strong kept up the gray-brown bird,
With pure deliberate notes, spreading, filling the night.
Loud in the pines and cedars dim.
Clear in the freshness moist and the swamp-perfume,
And I with my comrades there in the night.
While my sight that was bound in my eyes unclosed,
As to long panoramas of visions.
And I saw askant the armies,
I saw as in noiseless dreams hundreds of battle-flags,
Borne through the smoke of the battles and pierc'd with
   missiles I saw them,
And carried hither and yon through the smoke, and torn
   and bloody,
And at last but a few shreds left on the staffs, (and all in
   silence),
And the staffs all splinter'd and broken.

13

Passing the visions, passing the night,
Passing, unloosing the hold of my comrades' hands,
Passing the song of the hermit bird and the tallying song
   of my soul,
Victorious song, death's outlet song, yet varying ever-al-
   tering song,
As low and wailing, yet clear the notes, rising and falling,
   flooding the night,
Sadly sinking and fainting, as waning and waning, and yet
   again bursting with joy,
Covering the earth and filling the spread of the heaven,

As that powerful psalm in the night I heard from recesses,
Passing, I leave thee lilac with heart-shaped leaves,
I leave thee there in the dooryard, blooming, returning with
    spring.

I cease from my song for thee,
From my gaze on thee in the west, communing with thee,
O comrade lustrous with silver face in the night.
The song, the wondrous chant of the gray-brown bird,
And the tallying chant, the echo arous'd in my soul,
With the lustrous and drooping star with the countenance
    full of woe,
With the holders holding my hand nearing the call of the
    bird,
Comrades mine and I in the midst, and their memory ever
    to keep, for the dead I loved so well,
For the sweetest, wisest soul of all my days and lands —
    and this for his dear sake,
Lilac and star and bird twined with the chant of my soul,
There in the fragrant pines and the cedars dusk and dim.
                             Walt Whitman

AFTERWARDS

When the Present has latched its postern [2] behind my
    tremulous stay,
  And the May month flaps its glad green leaves like
    wings,
Delicate-filmed as new-spun silk, will the neighbors say,
  " He was a man who used to notice such things " ?

If it be in the dusk when, like an eyelid's soundless blink,
  The dewfall-hawk comes crossing the shades to alight
Upon the wind-warped upland thorn, a gazer may think,
  " To him this must have been a familiar sight."

          [2] postern = a back door or gate.

If I pass during some nocturnal blackness, mothy and warm,
  When the hedgehog travels furtively over the lawn,
One may say, "He strove that such innocent creatures
    should come to no harm,
  But he could do little for them; and now he is gone."

If, when hearing that I have been stilled at last, they stand
    at the door,
  Watching the full-starred heavens that winter sees,
Will this thought rise on those who will meet my face no
    more,
  "He was one who had an eye for such mysteries"?

And will any say when my bell of quittance is heard in
    the gloom,
  And a crossing breeze cuts a pause in its outrollings,
Till they rise again, as they were a new bell's boom,
  "He hears it not now, but used to notice such things"?
                         Thomas Hardy

REQUIEM

Under the wide and starry sky
Dig the grave and let me lie:
Glad did I live and gladly die,
  And I laid me down with a will.

This be the verse you 'grave for me:
Here he lies where he long'd to be;
Home is the sailor, home from the sea,
  And the hunter home from the hill.
                 Robert Louis Stevenson

Sound, sound the clarion, fill the fife!
  To all the sensual world proclaim,
One crowded hour of glorious life
  Is worth an age without a name.

— WALTER SCOTT

INVICTUS [1]

Out of the night that covers me,
  Black as the Pit from pole to pole,
I thank whatever gods may be
  For my unconquerable soul.

In the fell clutch of circumstance
  I have not winced nor cried aloud.
Under the bludgeonings of chance
  My head is bloody, but unbowed.

Beyond this place of wrath and tears
  Looms but the horror of the shade,
And yet the menace of the years
  Finds, and shall find me, unafraid.

It matters not how strait the gate,
  How charged with punishments the scroll,
I am the master of my fate:
  I am the captain of my soul.

William Ernest Henley

[1] Invincible.

ENGLAND, MY ENGLAND

What have I done for you,
  England, my England?
What is there I would not do,
  England, my own?
With your glorious eyes austere,
As the Lord were walking near,
Whispering terrible things and dear
  As the Song on your bugles blown,
    England —
  Round the world on your bugles blown!

Where shall the watchful Sun,
  England, my England,
Match the master-work you've done,
  England, my own?
When shall he rejoice again
Such a breed of mighty men
As come forward, one to ten,
  To the Song on your bugles blown,
    England —
  Down the years on your bugles blown?

Ever the faith endures,
  England, my England: —
' Take and break us: we are yours,
  ' England, my own!
' Life is good, and joy runs high
' Between English earth and sky:
' Death is death; but we shall die
  ' To the Song on your bugles blown,
    ' England —
  ' To the stars on your bugles blown! '

They call you proud and hard,
  England, my England:

You with worlds to watch and ward,
   England, my own!
You whose mailed hand keeps the keys
Of such teeming destinies
You could know nor dread nor ease
   Were the Song on your bugles blown,
     England,
   Round the Pit on your bugles blown!

Mother of Ships whose might,
   England, my England,
Is the fierce old Sea's delight,
   England, my own,
Chosen daughter of the Lord,
Spouse-in-Chief of the ancient sword,
There's the menace of the Word
   In the Song on your bugles blown,
     England —
   Out of heaven on your bugles blown!

                   William Ernest Henley

MARCHING ALONG

(*A Cavalier Tune*)

Kentish Sir Byng stood for his King,
Bidding the crop-headed Parliament swing:
And, pressing a troop unable to stoop
And see the rogues flourish and honest folk droop,
Marched them along, fifty-score strong,
Great-hearted gentlemen, singing this song.

God for King Charles!   Pym and such carles [2]
To the Devil that prompts 'em their treasonous parles! [3]
Cavaliers, up!   Lips from the cup,

---

[2] carles = common fellows.
[3] parles = parleyings, dealings.

Hands from the pasty, nor bite take nor sup
Till you're (*Chorus*) *Marching along, fifty-score strong,*
        Great-hearted gentlemen, singing this song.

Hampden to Hell, and his obsequies' knell
Serve Hazelrig, Fiennes, and young Harry as well! '
England, good cheer!   Rupert is near! [5]
Kentish and loyalists, keep we not here
    (*Cho.*) *Marching along, fifty-score strong,*
        Great-hearted gentlemen, singing this song.

Then, God for King Charles!   Pym and his snarls
To the Devil that pricks on such pestilent carles!
Hold by the right, you double your might;
So, onward to Nottingham, fresh for the fight,
    (*Cho.*) *Marching along, fifty-score strong,*
        Great-hearted gentlemen, singing this song.

                  Robert Browning

EINAR TAMBERSKELVER

(*From "The Saga of King Olaf"*)

  It was Einar Tamberskelver
    Stood beside the mast;
  From his yew bow, tipped with silver,
    Flew the arrows fast;
  Aimed at Eric unavailing,
    As he sat concealed,
  Half behind the quarter-railing,
    Half behind his shield.

  First an arrow struck the tiller,
    Just above his head;
  " Sing, O Eyvind Skaldaspiller,"
    Then Earl Eric said.

---

[4] These were opponents of the King.
[5] Prince of Bavaria who sided with his uncle, Charles I.

" Sing the song of Hakon dying,
   Sing the funeral wail! "
And another arrow flying
   Grazed his coat of mail.

Turning to a Lapland yeoman,
   As the arrow passed,
Said Earl Eric, " Shoot that bowman
   Standing by the mast."
Sooner than the word was spoken
   Flew the yeoman's shaft;
Einar's bow in twain was broken,
   Einar only laughed.

" What was that? " said Olaf, standing
   On the quarter-deck.
" Something heard I like the stranding
   Of a shattered wreck."
Einar then, the arrow taking
   From the loosened string,
Answered, " That was Norway breaking
   From thy hand, O king! "

" Thou art but a poor diviner,"
   Straightway Olaf said;
" Take my bow, and swifter, Einar,
   Let thy shafts be sped."
Of his bows the fairest choosing,
   Reached he from above;
Einar saw the blood-drops oozing
   Through his iron glove.

But the bow was thin and narrow;
   At the first assay,
O'er its head he drew the arrow,
   Flung the bow away;
Said, with hot and angry temper
   Flushing in his cheek,

" Olaf! for so great a Kämper [6]
 Are thy bows too weak! "

Then, with smile of joy defiant
   On his beardless lip,
Scaled he, light and self-reliant,
   Eric's dragon-ship.
Loose his golden locks were flowing,
   Bright his armor gleamed;
Like Saint Michael overthrowing
   Lucifer he seemed.

                    Henry Wadsworth Longfellow

CONCORD HYMN [7]

By the rude bridge that arched the flood,
   Their flag to April's breeze unfurled,
Here once the embattled farmers stood
   And fired the shot heard round the world.

The foe long since in silence slept;
   Alike the conqueror silent sleeps;
And Time the ruined bridge has swept
   Down the dark stream which seaward creeps.

On this green bank, by this soft stream,
   We set today a votive stone;
That memory may their deeds redeem,
   When, like our sires, our sons are gone.

Spirit, that made those heroes dare
   To die, and leave their children free,
Bid Time and Nature gently spare
   The shaft we raise to them and thee.

                    Ralph Waldo Emerson

[6] Kämper = warrior.
[7] Sung at the completion of the battle monument, July 4, 1837.

THE DESERTER FROM THE CAUSE

He is gone: better so.   We should know who stand under
  Our Banner: let none but the trusty remain!
For there's stern work at hand, and the time comes shall
    sunder
  The shell from the pearl, and the chaff from the grain!
And the heart that thro' danger and death will be dutiful —
  Soul that with Cranmer in fire would shake hands;
With a Life, like a palace-home built for the Beautiful;
  Freedom of all her Belovèd demands!

He is gone from us!   Yet shall we march on victorious,
  Hearts burning like Beacons — eyes fixt on the Goal!
And if we fall fighting, we fall like the Glorious;
  With face to the Stars, and all heaven in the soul!
And aye for the brave stir of battle we'll barter
  The sword of life sheathed in the peace of the grave:
And better the fieriest fate of the Martyr,
  Than live like the Coward, and die like the Slave!

Gerald Massey

THE OLD STOIC

Riches I hold in light esteem,
  And Love I laugh to scorn;
And lust of fame was but a dream
  That vanished with the morn;

And if I pray, the only prayer
  That moves my lips for me
Is, " Leave the heart that now I bear,
  And give me liberty! "

Yes, as my swift days near their goal,
  'Tis all that I implore:
In life and death a chainless soul,
  With courage to endure.

Emily Brontë

SO NIGH IS GRANDEUR

In an age of fops and toys,
Wanting wisdom, void of right,
Who shall nerve heroic boys
To hazard all in Freedom's fight, —
Break sharply off their jolly games,
Forsake their comrades gay
And quit proud homes and youthful dames
For famine, toil and fray?
Yet on the nimble air benign
Speed nimbler messages,
That waft the breath of grace divine
To hearts in sloth and ease.
So nigh is grandeur to our dust,
So near is God to man,
When Duty whispers low, *Thou must,*
The youth replies, *I can.*

Ralph Waldo Emerson

ELDORADO

Gayly bedight,
A gallant knight,
In sunshine and in shadow,
Had journeyed long,
Singing a song,
In search of Eldorado.

But he grew old,
This knight so bold,
And o'er his heart a shadow
Fell as he found
No spot of ground
That looked like Eldorado.

And, as his strength
Failed him at length,
He met a pilgrim shadow:
" Shadow," said he,
"Where can it be,
This land of Eldorado? "

" Over the Mountains
Of the Moon,
Down the Valley of the Shadow,
Ride, boldly ride,"
The shade replied,
" If you seek for Eldorado! "

Edgar Allan Poe

COLUMBUS [8]

Behind him lay the grey Azores,
    Behind the Gates of Hercules;
Before him not the ghost of shores,
    Before him only shoreless seas.
The good mate said: " Now must we pray,
    For lo! the very stars are gone.
Brave Admiral, speak, what shall I say? "
    " Why, say ' Sail on! sail on! and on! ' "

" My men grow mutinous day by day;
    My men grow ghastly wan and weak."
The stout mate thought of home; a spray
    Of salt wave washed his swarthy cheek.
" What shall I say, brave Admiral, say,
    If we sight naught but seas at dawn? "
" Why, you shall say at break of day,
    ' Sail on! sail on! sail on! and on! ' "

[8] Permission to reprint this poem granted by Harr Wagner Publishing Company, publishers of the Complete Poetical Works of Joaquin Miller.

They sailed and sailed, as winds might blow,
    Until at last the blanched mate said,
" Why, now not even God would know
    Should I and all my men fall dead.
These very winds forget their way,
    For God from these dread seas is gone.
Now speak, brave Admiral, speak and say " —
    He said: " Sail on! sail on! and on! "

They sailed. They sailed. Then spake the mate:
    " This mad sea shows his teeth to-night.
He curls his lip, he lies in wait,
    With lifted teeth, as if to bite!
Brave Admiral, say but one good word:
    What shall we do when hope is gone? "
The words leapt like a leaping sword:
    " Sail on! sail on! sail on! and on! "

Then, pale and worn, he kept his deck,
    And peered through darkness. Ah, that night
Of all dark nights! And then a speck —
    A light! a light! a light! a light!
It grew, a starlit flag unfurled!
    It grew to be Time's burst of dawn.
He gained a world; he gave that world
    Its grandest lesson: " On! sail on! "

Joaquin Miller

TODAY

Selections from contemporary poets, born since 1850

The commonplace I sing:
How cheap is health!   How cheap nobility!
The open air I sing; freedom, toleration:
The common day and night, the common earth and waters,
Your farm, your work, life, occupation —
The democratic wisdom underneath, like solid ground for all.

— WALT WHITMAN

THERE'S NOTHING LIKE THE SUN

There's nothing like the sun as the year dies,
Kind as it can be, this world being made so,
To stones and men and beasts and birds and flies,
To all things that it touches except snow,
Whether on mountain side or street of town.
The south wall warms me: November has begun,
Yet never shone the sun as fair as now
While the sweet last-left damsons from the bough
With spangles of the morning's storm drop down
Because the starling shakes it, whistling what
Once swallows sang.   But I have not forgot
That there is nothing, too, like March's sun,
Like April's, or July's, or June's, or May's,
Or January's, or February's great days:
And August, September, October, and December
Have equal days, all different from November.
No day of any month but I have said —
Or, if I could live long enough, should say —
" There's nothing like the sun that shines to-day."
There's nothing like the sun till we are dead.

Edward Thomas

139

A GREAT TIME

Sweet Chance, that led my steps abroad,
   Beyond the town, where wild flowers grow —
A rainbow and a cuckoo, Lord!
   How rich and great the times are now!
     Know, all ye sheep
     And cows, that keep
On staring that I stand so long
   In grass that's wet from heavy rain —
A rainbow and a cuckoo's song
   May never come together again;
     May never come
     This side the tomb.
                  W. H. Davies

WEEK–END

The train!   The twelve o'clock for paradise.
   Hurry, or it will try to creep away.
Out in the country everyone is wise!
   We can be only wise on Saturday.
There you are waiting, little friendly house:
   Those are your chimney-stacks with you between,
Surrounded by old trees and strolling cows,
   Staring through all your windows at the green.
Your homely floor is creaking for our tread;
   The smiling tea-pot with contented spout
Thinks of the boiling water, and the bread
   Longs for the butter.   All their hands are out
     To greet us, and the gentle blankets seem
     Purring and crooning: " Lie in us, and dream."

The key will stammer, and the door reply,
   The hall wake, yawn, and smile; the torpid stair
Will grumble at our feet, the table cry:
   " Fetch my belongings for me; I am bare."

A clatter!   Something in the attic falls.
   A ghost has lifted up his robes and fled.
The loitering shadows move along the walls;
   Then silence very slowly lifts his head.
The starling with impatient screech has flown
   The chimney, and is watching from the tree.
They thought us gone for ever: mouse alone
   Stops in the middle of the floor to see.
     Now all you idle things, resume your toil.
     Hearth, put your flames on.   Sulky kettle, boil.

Contented evening; comfortable joys;
   The snoozing fire, and all the fields are still:
Tranquil delight, no purpose, and no noise —
   Unless the slow wind flowing round the hill.
" Murry " (the kettle) dozes; little mouse
   Is rambling prudently about the floor.
There's lovely conversation in this house:
   Words become princes that were slaves before.
What a sweet atmosphere for you and me
   The people that have been here left behind . . .
Oh, but I fear it may turn out to be
   Built of a dream erected in the mind:
     So if we speak too loud, we may awaken
     To find it vanished, and ourselves mistaken.

Morning!   Wake up!   Awaken!   All the boughs
   Are rippling on the air across the green.
The youngest birds are singing to the house.
   Blood of the world! — and is the country clean?
Disturb the precinct.   Call it with a shout.
   Sing as you trundle down to light the fire.
Turn the encumbering shadows tumbling out,
   And fill the chambers with a new desire.
Life is no good, unless the morning brings
   White happiness and quick delight of day.
These half-inanimate domestic things

Must all be useful, or must go away.
Coffee, be fragrant. Porridge in my plate,
Increase the vigour to fulfill my fate!

Harold Monro

BREAD AND MUSIC

Music I heard with you was more than music,
And bread I broke with you was more than bread;
Now that I am without you, all is desolate;
All that was once so beautiful is dead.

Your hands once touched this table and this silver,
And I have seen your fingers hold this glass.
These things do not remember you, belovèd,
And yet your touch upon them will not pass.

For it was in my heart you moved among them,
And blessed them with your hands and with your eyes;
And in my heart they will remember always, —
They knew you once, O beautiful and wise.

Conrad Aiken

THE CODE

There were three in the meadow by the brook
Gathering up windrows,[1] piling cocks of hay,
With an eye always lifted toward the west
Where an irregular sun-bordered cloud
Darkly advanced with a perpetual dagger
Flickering across its bosom. Suddenly
One helper, thrusting pitchfork in the ground,
Marched himself off the field and home. One stayed.
The town-bred farmer failed to understand.

[1] windrows = rows of hay raked together to be piled into cocks or heaps.

" What is there wrong? "
          " Something you just now said."
" What did I say? "
          " About our taking pains."

" To cock the hay? — because it's going to shower?
I said that more than half an hour ago.
I said it to myself as much as you."

" You didn't know.   But James is one big fool.
He thought you meant to find fault with his work.
That's what the average farmer would have meant.
James would take time, of course, to chew it over
Before he acted.   He's just got round to act."

" He is a fool if that's the way he takes me."

" Don't let it bother you.   You've found out something.
The hand that knows his business won't be told
To do work better or faster — those two things.
I'm as particular as anyone:
Most likely I'd have served you just the same.
But I know you don't understand our ways.
You were just talking what was in your mind,
What was in all our minds, and you weren't hinting.

Tell you a story of what happened once:
I was up here in Salem at a man's
Named Sanders with a gang of four or five
Doing the haying.   No one liked the boss.
He was one of the kind sports call a spider,
All wiry arms and legs that spread out wavy
From a humped body nigh as big's a biscuit.
But work! that man could work, especially
If by so doing he could get more work
Out of his hired help.   I'm not denying

He was hard on himself. I couldn't find
That he kept any hours — not for himself.
Daylight and lantern-light were one to him:
I've heard him pounding in the barn all night.
But what he liked was someone to encourage.
Them that he couldn't lead, he'd get behind
And drive, the way you can, you know, in mowing —
Keep at their heels and threaten to mow their legs off.
I'd seen about enough of his bulling tricks
(We call that bulling). I'd been watching him.
So when he paired off with me in the hayfield
To load the load, thinks I, 'Look out for trouble.'
I built the load and topped it off; old Sanders
Combed it down with a rake and says, ' O. K.'
Everything went well till we reached the barn
With a big catch to empty in a bay.
You understand that meant the easy job
For the man up on top of throwing *down*
The hay and rolling it off wholesale,
Where on a mow it would have been slow lifting.
You wouldn't think a fellow'd need much urging
Under these circumstances, would you now?
But the old fool seizes his fork in both hands,
And looking up bewhiskered out of the pit,
Shouts like an army captain, ' Let her come! '
Thinks I, D'ye mean it? ' What was that you said? '
I asked out loud, so's there'd be no mistake,
' Did you say, Let her come? ' ' Yes, let her come.'
He said it over, but he said it softer.
Never you say a thing like that to a man,
Not if he values what he is.   God, I'd as soon
Murdered him as left out his middle name.
I'd built the load and knew right where to find it.
Two or three forkfuls I picked lightly round for
Like meditating, and then I just dug in
And dumped the rackful on him in ten lots,
I looked over the side once in the dust

And caught sight of him treading-water-like,
Keeping his head above. ' Damn ye,' I says,
' That gets ye! ' He squeaked like a squeezed rat.
That was the last I saw or heard of him.
I cleaned the rack and drove out to cool off.
As I sat mopping hayseed from my neck,
And sort of waiting to be asked about it,
One of the boys sings out, ' Where's the old man? '
' I left him in the barn under the hay.
If ye want him, ye can go and dig him out.'
They realized from the way I swobbed my neck
More than was needed something must be up.
They headed for the barn; I stayed where I was.
They told me afterward. First they forked the hay,
A lot of it, out into the barn floor.
Nothing! They listened for him. Not a rustle.
I guess they thought I'd spiked him in the temple
Before I buried him, or I couldn't have managed.
They excavated more. ' Go keep his wife
Out of the barn.' Someone looked in a window,
And curse me if he wasn't in the kitchen
Slumped way down in a chair, with both his feet
Stuck in the oven, the hottest day that summer.
He looked so clean disgusted from behind
There was no one that dared to stir him up,
Or let him know that he was being looked at.
Apparently I hadn't buried him
(I may have knocked him down); but my just try-
    ing
To bury him had hurt his dignity.
He had gone to the house so's not to meet me.
He'd kept away from us all afternoon.
We tended to his hay. We saw him out
After a while picking peas in his garden:
He couldn't keep away from doing something."

"Weren't you relieved to find he wasn't dead? "

" No! and yet I don't know — it's hard to say.
I went about to kill him fair enough."

" You took an awkward way. Did he discharge you? "

" Discharge me? No! He knew I did just right."

Robert Frost

THE WOOD–PILE

Out walking in the frozen swamp one grey day
I paused and said, " I will turn back from here.
No, I will go on farther — and we shall see."
The hard snow held me, save where now and then
One foot went down. The view was all in lines
Straight up and down of tall slim trees
Too much alike to mark or name a place by
So as to say for certain I was here
Or somewhere else; I was just far from home.
A small bird flew before me. He was careful
To put a tree between us when he 'lighted,
And say no word to tell me who he was
Who was so foolish as to think what *he* thought.
He thought that I was after him for a feather —
The white one in his tail; like one who takes
Everything said as personal to himself.
One flight out sideways would have undeceived him.
And then there was a pile of wood for which
I forgot him and let his little fear
Carry him off the way I might have gone,
Without so much as wishing him good-night.
He went behind it to make his last stand.
It was a cord of maple, cut and split
And piled and measured, four by four by eight.
And not another like it could I see.
No runner tracks in this year's snow looped near it.

And it was older sure than this year's cutting,
Or even last year's or the year's before.
The wood was grey and the bark warping off it
And the pile somewhat sunken. Clematis
Had wound strings round and round it like a bundle.
What held it though on one side was a tree
Still growing, and on one a stake and prop,
These latter about to fall. I thought that only
Someone who lived in turning to fresh tasks
Could so forget his handiwork on which
He spent himself, the labor of his axe,
And leave it there far from a useful fireplace
To warm the frozen swamp as best it could
With the slow smokeless burning of decay.

Robert Frost

THE COVERED BRIDGE

There, from its entrance, lost in matted vines, —
Where in the valley foams a water-fall, —
Is glimpsed a ruined mill's remaining wall;
Here, by the road, the oxeye daisy mines
Hot brass and bronze; the trumpet-trailer shines
Red as the plumage of the cardinal.
Faint from the forest comes the rain-crow's call
Where dusty Summer dreams among the pines.
This is the spot where Spring writes wildflower verses
In primrose pink, while, drowsing o'er his reins,
The ploughman, all unnoticing, plods along:
And where the Autumn opens weedy purses
Of sleepy silver, while the corn-heaped wains [2]
Rumble the bridge like some deep throat of song.

Madison Cawein

[2] wains = heavy wagons.

LAMP POSTS

What kind of trees
Are these
With slender straight trunks of gray?
No branches or leaves have they,
Growing along the edges of the walk;
Only a single stalk
Bearing a magic flower with heart of flame.
What is your name,
Mysterious soft bloom?
I see your clusters in the gloom,

And over the flower beds
Your brightly-petaled heads,
And by the dark curve of the lagoon,
Moon after moon —
Gem after gem
Hanging from your invisible stem!

Helen Hoyt

THE PRETTIEST THINGS

The prettiest things there are must lie
Unused, unheeded utterly,

As where the lorries drop bright oil
Weed-shaped, to turn our highways' soil

As lovely as the ocean-bed,
Blue branching green, gold branching red,

And all the little friendly words
In secret nests of mice and birds,

And window missal-scrolls of frost
Unnumbered times achieved and lost,

And songs that fill the blackbird's head
In March, that August finds unsaid,

And tales we dreamt at five years old
That by no later skill are told,

While towns and faces dull as clay
Are praised and copied every day.

Camilla Doyle

FOR A DEWDROP

Small shining drop, no lady's ring
Holds so beautiful a thing.
At sun-up in the early air
The sweetness of the world you snare.
Within your little mirror lie
The green grass and the wingèd fly,
The lowest flower, the tallest tree
In your crystal I can see,
Why, in your tiny globe you hold
The sun himself, a midge of gold.
It makes me wonder if the world
In which so many things are curled,
The world which all men real call,
Is not the real world at all,
But just a drop of dew instead
Swinging on a spider's thread.

Eleanor Farjeon

CARGOES [3]

Quinquereme [4] of Nineveh from distant Ophir,
Rowing home to haven in sunny Palestine,
With a cargo of ivory,
And apes and peacocks,
Sandalwood, cedarwood, and sweet white wine.

[3] From *Story of a Round House* by John Masefield. Reprinted by special arrangement with The Macmillan Company, Publishers.
[4] quinquereme = a galley (ship) having five banks of oars.

Stately Spanish galleon coming from the Isthmus,
Dipping through the Tropics by the palm-green shores,
With a cargo of diamonds,
Emeralds, amethysts,
Topazes, and cinnamon, and gold moidores.[5]

Dirty British coaster with a salt-caked smoke stack,
Butting through the Channel in the mad March days,
With a cargo of Tyne coal,
Road-rails, pig-lead,
Firewood, iron-ware, and cheap tin trays.

                                    John Masefield

SMOKE ROSE–GOLD

The dome of the Capitol looks to the Potomac river,
    Out of haze over the sunset,
    Out of a smoke rose-gold:
One star shines over the sunset.
Night takes the dome and the river, the sun and the smoke
    rose-gold,
The haze changes from sunset to star.
The pour of a thin silver struggles against the dark.
A star might call: It's a long way across.

                                    Carl Sandburg

MY DESK

        All that I ask
        is a desk —
        with blotting paper white
        changed every night;
        no litter but the good
        company of cool wood;
        a glass inkpot so clean
        my pen can wade therein

        [5] moidore = a gold coin.

up to her waist and not
be liable to blot —
also laid in her place
a crystal pencil-case;
and in that glassy bed —
pencils new sharpenèd;
nothing to vex the soul
in the neat pigeon-hole;
and finally there must
be not a speck of dust.

And I would have the wall
austerely virginal,
with nothing to intervene
(above my desk) between
the thing I try to see
and me.

There let me sit
and write at it —
content with this
slim doorway to infinities.

Humbert Wolfe

SMELLS

Why is it that the poets tell
So little of the sense of smell?
These are the odors I love well:

The smell of coffee freshly ground;
Or rich plum pudding, holly crowned;
Or onions fried and deeply browned.

The fragrance of a fumy pipe;
The smell of apples, newly ripe;
And printer's ink on leaden type.

Woods by moonlight in September
Breathe most sweet; and I remember
Many a smoky camp-fire ember.

Camphor, turpentine, and tea,
The balsam of a Christmas tree,
These are whiffs of gramarye.[6] . . .
A ship smells best of all to me!

Christopher Morley

BUNS FOR TEA

When I buy a bun
I buy a shadowed world,
Lit by sunlight,
Dark with shadowed sunlight.

Wavering corn I buy,
Bushes of green currants,
Tall cane and spices,
Butter from bright fields.

I see the gathering
Gold corn and purple berries,
Dark spices, syrup crystals,
Cream in the pan.

Dark holds of ships,
Seething souls of toilers,
Darkness of the town night
Around the bakery.

Beetles, and the soft
Death-dealing
Dust of fine flour,
Stealthily streaming,

---

6 gramarye = an ancient word meaning "magic."

Into the life-breath
Of the baker.
When I buy a bun
I buy a world, sun-shadowed.

Dorothy M. Richardson

THE FLATHOUSE ROOF

I linger on the flathouse roof, the moonlight is divine.
But my heart is all a-flutter like the washing on the line.

I long to be a heroine, I long to be serene,
But my feet, they dance in answer to a distant tambourine.

And, oh! the dreams of ecstasy. Oh! Babylon and Troy.
I've a hero in the basement, he's the janitor's red-haired
boy.

There's the music of his mallet and the jigging of his saw;
I wonder what he's making on that lovely cellar floor?

He loves me, for he said it when we met upon the stair,
And that is why I'm on the roof to get a breath of air.

He said it! Oh! He said it! And the only thing I said
Was, " Roger Jones, I like you, for your hair is very red."

We parted when intruders came a-tramping through the
hall;
He's got my pocket handkerchief and I have got his ball.

And so it is I'm on the roof. Oh! Babylon and Troy!
I'm very sure that I'm in love with someone else's boy.

Alone, upon the starry heights, I'm dancing on a green,
To the jingling and the jangling of a distant tambourine.

To the stamping of a hammer and the jigging of a saw,
And the secret sort of feeling I'm in love forevermore.

Do you think it's any wonder, with the moonlight so divine,
That my heart is all a-flutter, like the washing on the line?

Nathalia Crane

THE SHELL

And then I pressed the shell
Close to my ear
And listened well,
And straightway like a bell
Came low and clear
The slow, sad murmur of far distant seas,
Whipped by an icy breeze
Upon a shore
Wind-swept and desolate.
It was a sunless strand that never bore
The footprint of a man,
Nor felt the weight
Since time began
Of any human quality or stir
Save what the dreary winds and waves incur.
And in the hush of waters was the sound
Of pebbles rolling round,
For ever rolling with a hollow sound.
And bubbling sea-weeds as the waters go
Swished to and fro
Their long cold tentacles of slimy grey.
There was no day,
Nor ever came a night
Setting the stars alight
To wonder at the moon:
Was twilight only and the frightened croon,
Smitten to whimpers, of the dreary wind
And waves that journeyed blind . . .
And then I loosed my ear — O, it was sweet
To hear a cart go jolting down the street.

James Stephens

THE GOOD GROUND

O good gigantic smile o' the brown old earth,
  This autumn morning!   How he sets his bones
To bask i' the sun, and thrusts out knees and feet
For the ripple to run over in its mirth;
  Listening the while, where on the heap of stones
The white breast of the sea-lark twitters sweet.

— ROBERT BROWNING

GOD'S WORLD *

O world, I cannot hold thee close enough!
  Thy winds, thy wide grey skies!
  Thy mists that roll and rise!
Thy woods, this autumn day, that ache and sag
And all but cry with color!   That gaunt crag
To crush!   To lift the lean of that black bluff!
World, World, I cannot get thee close enough!

Long have I known a glory in it all,
  But never knew I this;
  Here such passion is
As stretcheth me apart.   Lord, I do fear
Thou'st made the world too beautiful this year.
My soul is all but out of me, — let fall
No burning leaf; prithee, let no bird call.

Edna St. Vincent Millay

THE GOOD GROUND

I fling myself against the ground,
My body downward.   Not a sound
Escapes my fingers tho they tear
The new-cut timothy in fear

---

* From *Renascence and Other Poems*, published by Harper & Brothers, copyright 1917 by Edna St. Vincent Millay.

Lest I should not turn into hay
And hay into myself. Today
I will be more by being less
Than what I was! O body, press
Against the earth! O open door
Of my wide nostril, open more,
So that below your lintel may
Step the honest smell of hay!
Somewhere, in some far field, jackdaws
Are propagating with their caws
Unkindred and peculiar gall —
O Earth, it does not matter at all!
It does not matter if the birds,
And men, and bricks, and even words,
Are marshalled, clever and morose,
Against us here — ourselves cleave close!
From you they sprung, and more than they,
Since greater gods are made of clay,
And chipmunks, and a row of beans,
And little stubby evergreens
Defying frost, and rain, and rocks,
And the uncomprehending ox.
They will return at last to you,
When rocks are powder and rains are through
Spilling upon the heads of men
Who will grow lichenous again
And full of soil. O Earth, I hold
All things — their germ, their ultimate mould —
In holding you! Is it so strange
That you and I should interchange
Identity, or strange that I
Should weep, and not remember why?
As long as finity is brief,
Spasmodically my decent grief,
My laughter and my fist will pound
Against the brown ribs of the ground!

Virginia Moore

AMENDS TO NATURE

I have loved colors, and not flowers;
Their motion, not the swallow's wings;
And wasted more than half my hours
Without the comradeship of things.

How is it, now, that I can see,
With love and wonder and delight,
The children of the hedge and tree,
The little lords of day and night.

How is it that I see the roads,
No longer with usurping eyes,
A twilight meeting-place for toads,
A mid-day mart [1] for butterflies?

I feel, in every midge that hums,
Life, fugitive and infinite,
And suddenly the world becomes
A part of me and I of it.

Arthur Symons

A WIND OF FALL

A wind went forth a little after dawn,
And sounded his thin horn above the trees,
And there was sudden stilling of those bells
On which the tree-toads rang quaint harmonies.

The languid mists upon the morning hills
Melted beneath that wind's swift icy breath;
Each tree took on a loveliness more keen
To taste the rare bright atmosphere of death.

[1] mart = market or place of traffic.

Each leaf was as a gallant banner flown
For that far runner the wind heralded.
Would they not know the outflung delicate locks
Down all the ways the silver-limbed had fled?

Before the joy of that clear visioning
They had no sorrow, leaf and leaf, to part.
I cry the wind from out the clouds to blow
Through all the dusty summer of my heart.

Léonie Adams

AN ENGLISH WOOD

This valley wood is hedged
With the set shape of things.
Here sorrows come not edged,
Here are no harpies [2] fledged,
No roc has clapped his wings,
No gryphons wave their stings;
Here, poised in quietude
Calm elementals brood
On the set shape of things;
They fend away alarms
From this green wood.
Here nothing is that harms,
No bull with lungs of brass,
No toothed or spiny grass,
No tree whose clutching arms
Drink blood when travellers pass,
No Mount of Glass.
No bardic tongues unfold
Satires or charms.
Only the lawns are soft,
The tree-stems, grave and old.

[2] harpies, rocs and gryphons are fabled animals.

Slow branches sway aloft,
The evening air comes cold,
The sunset scatters gold.
Small grasses toss and bend,
Small pathways idly tend
Towards no certain end.

Robert Graves

MOWING

There was never a sound beside the wood but one,
And that was my long scythe whispering to the ground.
What was it it whispered?   I knew not well myself;
Perhaps it was something about the heat of the sun,
Something, perhaps, about the lack of sound —
And that was why it whispered and did not speak.
It was no dream of the gift of idle hours,
Or easy gold at the hand of fay or elf:
Anything more than the truth would have seemed too weak
To the earnest love that laid the swale in rows,
Not without feeble-pointed spikes of flowers
(Pale orchises), and scared a bright green snake.
The fact is the sweetest dream that labor knows,
My long scythe whispered and left the hay to make.

Robert Frost

A BALLADE OF SPRING'S UNREST

Up in the woodland where Spring
Comes as a laggard, the breeze
Whispers the pines that the King,
Fallen, has yielded the keys
To his White Palace and flees
Northward o'er mountain and dale.
Speed then the hour that frees!
Ho, for the pack and the trail!

Northward my fancy takes wing,
Restless am I, ill at ease.
Pleasures the city can bring
Lose now their power to please.
Barren, all barren, are these,
Town life's a tedious tale;
That cup is drained to the lees —
Ho, for the pack and the trail!

Ho, for the morning I sling
Pack at my back, and with knees
Brushing a thoroughfare, fling
Into the green mysteries:
One with the birds and the bees,
One with the squirrel and quail,
Night, and the stream's melodies —
Ho, for the pack and the trail!

Envoy

Pictures and music and teas,
Theaters — books even — stale.
Ho, for the smell of the trees!
Ho, for the pack and the trail!

Bert Leston Taylor

SPRING SONG

Make me over, mother April,
When the sap begins to stir!
When thy flowery hand delivers
All the mountain-prisoned rivers,
And thy great heart beats and quivers
To revive the days that were,
Make me over, mother April,
When the sap begins to stir!

Take my dust and all my dreaming,
Count my heart-beats one by one,
Send them where the winters perish;
Then some golden noon recherish
And restore them in the sun,
Flower and scent and dust and dreaming
With their heart-beats every one!

Set me in the urge and tide-drift
Of the streaming hosts a-wing!
Breast of scarlet, throat of yellow,
Raucous challenge, wooings mellow —
Every migrant is my fellow,
Making northward with the Spring.
Loose me in the urge and tide-drift
Of the streaming hosts a-wing!

Make me of thy seed to-morrow,
When the sap begins to stir!
Tawny light-foot, sleepy bruin,
Bright-eyes in the orchard ruin,
Gnarl the good life goes askew in,
Whiskey-jack, or tanager, —
Make me anything to-morrow,
When the sap begins to stir!

Give me the old clue to follow,
Through the labyrinth of night!
Clod of clay with heart of fire,
Things that burrow and aspire,
With the vanishing desire,
For the perishing delight, —
Only the old clue to follow,
Through the labyrinth of night!

Make me over in the morning
From the rag-bag of the world!

Scraps of dream and duds of daring,
Home-brought stuff from far sea-faring,
Faded colors once so flaring,
Shreds of banners long since furled!
Hues of ash and glints of glory,
In the rag-bag of the world!

Only make me over, April,
When the sap begins to stir!
Make me man or make me woman,
Make me oaf or ape or human,
Cup of flower or cone of fir;
Make me anything but neuter
When the sap begins to stir!

Bliss Carman

THE ELEMENTS

No house of stone
    Was built for me;
When the Sun shines —
    I am a bee.

No sooner comes
    The Rain so warm,
I come to light —
    I am a worm.

When the Winds blow,
    I do not strip,
But set my sails —
    I am a ship.

When Lightning comes,
    It plays with me
And I with it —
    I am a tree.

When drowned men rise
At Thunder's word,
Sings Nightingale —
I am a bird.   *W. H. Davies*

MAY IS BUILDING HER HOUSE

May is building her house. With apple blooms
  She is roofing over the glimmering rooms;
Of the oak and the beech hath she builded its beams,
  And, spinning all day at her secret looms,
With arras [3] of leaves each wind-sprayed wall
She pictureth over, and peopleth it all
  With echoes and dreams,
  And singing of streams.

May is building her house. Of petal and blade,
Of the roots of the oak, is the flooring made,
  With a carpet of mosses and lichen and clover,
  Each small miracle over and over,
And tender, traveling green things strayed.

Her windows, the morning and evening star,
And her rustling doorways, ever ajar
  With the coming and going
  Of fair things blowing,
The thresholds of the four winds are.

May is building her house. From the dust of things
She is making the songs and the flowers and the wings;
  From October's tossed and trodden gold
  She is making the young year out of the old;
    Yea: out of winter's flying sleet
    She is making all the summer sweet,
    And the brown leaves spurned of November's feet
She is changing back again to spring's.
               Richard Le Gallienne

[3] arras = a hanging tapestry.

END OF SUMMER

There were sights to be seen at the flaming end of summer
As we sped over the land like a flying scarf:
The kindled braziers of the mountain-ash
Swinging their wild greetings from tame door-yards;
Gypsy-dressed zinnias, spinsters in masquerade;
The tidy farmer, raking his first brush-fire,
Himself an angular shadow beside its supple aliveness;
Obliging cows, arranging themselves in pleasing groups
Over the stone-sprinkled meadows;
Sun-bleached spread of a hill
And sun-dyed tapestry of an apple-tree;
Obsequious sun himself, Summer's gifted servant —
All these came running to the roadside
With mocking gestures of farewell.

Jean Starr Untermeyer

AN INDIAN SUMMER DAY ON
THE PRAIRIE [4]

In the Beginning

The sun is a huntress young,
The sun is a red, red joy,
The sun is an Indian girl,
Of the tribe of the Illinois.

Mid-Morning

The sun is a smoldering fire,
That creeps through the high gray plain,
And leaves not a bush of cloud
To blossom with flowers of rain.

[4] From *Collected Poems* by Vachel Lindsay. Reprinted by special arrangement with The Macmillan Company, Publishers.

Noon

The sun is a wounded deer,
That treads pale grass in the skies,
Shaking his golden horns,
Flashing his baleful eyes.

Sunset

The sun is an eagle old,
There in the windless west,
Atop of the spirit-cliffs
He builds him a crimson nest.

Vachel Lindsay

ABANDONED

The hornets build in plaster-dropping rooms,
And on its mossy porch the lizard lies;
Around its chimneys slow the swallow flies,
And on its roof the locusts snow their blooms.
Like some sad thought that broods here, old perfumes
Haunt its dim stairs; the cautious zephyr tries
Each gusty door, like some dead hand, then sighs
With ghostly lips among the attic glooms.
And now a heron, now a kingfisher,
Flits in the willows where the riffle [5] seems
At each faint fall to hesitate to leap,
Fluttering the silence with a little stir.
Here Summer seems a placid face asleep,
And the near world a figment of her dreams.

Madison Cawein

THE SHEAVES [6]

Where long the shadows of the wind had rolled,
Green wheat was yielding to the change assigned;
And as by some vast magic undivined
The world was turning slowly into gold.

[5] riffle = a little spurt of water making the ripple.
[6] From *Dionysus in Doubt* by Edwin Arlington Robinson. Reprinted by special arrangement with The Macmillan Company, Publishers.

Like nothing that was ever bought or sold
It waited there, the body and the mind;
And with a mighty meaning of a kind
That tells the more the more it is not told.

So in a land where all days are not fair,
Fair days went on till on another day
A thousand golden sheaves were lying there,
Shining and still, but not for long to stay —
As if a thousand girls with golden hair
Might rise from where they slept and go away.

Edwin Arlington Robinson

THE FIRST AUTUMN

Where God had walked
The goldenrod
Sprang like fire
From the burning sod.

The purple asters,
When He spoke,
Rose up beautifully
Like smoke,

And shouting glory
To the sky,
The maple trees
Where He passed by!

But when God blessed
The last bright hill
The holy world
Grew white and still.

Marshall Schacht

TREES

I think that I shall never see
A poem lovely as a tree.

A tree whose hungry mouth is prest
Against the earth's sweet flowing breast;

A tree that looks at God all day,
And lifts her leafy arms to pray;

A tree that may in summer wear
A nest of robins in her hair;

Upon whose bosom snow has lain;
Who intimately lives with rain.

Poems are made by fools like me,
But only God can make a tree.

Joyce Kilmer

SUMACH AND BIRDS

If you never came with a pigeon rainbow purple
Shining in the six o'clock September dusk:
If the red sumach on the autumn roads
Never danced on the flame of your eyelashes:
If the red-haws never burst in a million
Crimson fingertwists of your heartcrying:
If all this beauty of yours never crushed me
Then there are many flying acres of birds for me,
Many drumming gray wings going home I shall see,
Many crying voices riding the north wind.

Carl Sandburg

BUTTERCUPS

Buttercups, buttercups,
　What do you hold?
Buttercups, buttercups,
　Minting your gold.

How do your rootlets
　Filch from the mire
The sunken sunbeams
　To fountains of fire?

What bosoms have crumbled
　To lift you there, —
Golden *Amens*
　To Beauty's prayer.

You tip-toe and listen
　To birds that rejoice, —
Those bits of a rainbow,
　Blessed with a voice.

I also am hearing
　Your golden words,
O buttercups, buttercups, —
　Rooted birds!

Louis Ginsberg

THE GARDEN BY MOONLIGHT

A black cat among roses,
Phlox, lilac-misted under a first-quarter moon,
The sweet smells of heliotrope and night-scented stock.
The garden is very still,
It is dazed with moonlight,
Contented with perfume,
Dreaming the opium dreams of its folded poppies.

Firefly-lights open and vanish
High as the tip buds of the golden glow,
Low as the sweet alyssum flowers at my feet.
Moon-shimmer on leaves and trellises,
Moon-spikes shafting through the snow-ball bush.
Only the little faces of the ladies' delight are alert and
    staring,
Only the cat, padding between the roses,
Shakes a branch and breaks the chequered pattern
As water is broken by the falling of a leaf.
Then you come,
And you are quiet like the garden,
And white like the alyssum flowers,
And beautiful as the silent sparks of the fireflies.
Ah, Belovèd, do you see those orange lilies?
They knew my mother,
But who belonging to me will they know
When I am gone? *Amy Lowell*

MAGDALEN WALKS

The little white clouds are racing over the sky,
    And the fields are strewn with the gold of the flower of
      March,
    The daffodil breaks under foot, and the tasselled larch
Sways and swings as the thrush goes hurrying by.

A delicate odor is borne on the wings of the morning breeze,
    The odor of deep wet grass, and of brown new-furrowed
      earth,
    The birds are singing for joy of the Spring's glad birth,
Hopping from branch to branch on the rocking trees.

And all the woods are alive with the murmur and sound of
    Spring,
    And the rosebud breaks into pink on the climbing briar,
    And the crocus-bed is a quivering moon of fire
Girdled round with the belt of an amethyst ring.

And the plane [7] to the pine-tree is whispering some tale of
   love
  Till it rustles with laughter and tosses its mantle of green,
  And the gloom of the wych-elm's hollow is lit with the
     iris sheen
Of the burnished rainbow throat and the silver breast of a
   dove.

See! the lark starts up from his bed in the meadow there,
  Breaking the gossamer threads and the nets of dew,
  And flashing a-down the river, a flame of blue!
The kingfisher flies like an arrow, and wounds the air.

Oscar Wilde

THE LAKE ISLE OF INNISFREE

I will arise and go now, and go to Innisfree,
And a small cabin build there, of clay and wattles made;
Nine bean rows will I have there, a hive for the honey bee,
And live alone in the bee-loud glade.

And I shall have some peace there, for peace comes dropping
   slow,
Dropping from the veils of the morning to where the cricket
   sings;
There midnight's all a glimmer, and noon a purple glow,
And evening full of the linnet's wings.

I will arise and go now, for always night and day
I hear lake water lapping with low sounds by the shore;
While I stand on the roadway, or on the pavements gray,
I hear it in the deep heart's core.

William Butler Yeats

[7] Here the word "plane" refers to the English plane-tree.

ON THE SOUTH DOWNS

Over the downs there were birds flying,
  Far off glittered the sea,
And toward the north the weald [8] of Sussex
  Lay like a kingdom under me.

I was happier than the larks
  That nest on the downs and sing to the sky —
Over the downs the birds flying
  Were not so happy as I.

It was not you, though you were near,
  Though you were good to hear and see;
It was not earth, it was not heaven,
  It was myself that sang in me.

Sara Teasdale

A DECEMBER DAY

Dawn turned on her purple pillow,
  And late, late, came the winter day;
Snow was curved to the boughs of the willow,
  The sunless world was white and grey.
At noon we heard a blue-jay scolding,
  At five the last cold light was lost
From blackened windows faintly holding
  The feathery filigree of frost.

Sara Teasdale

WIND SONG

Long ago I learned how to sleep,
In an old apple orchard where the wind swept by, counting
  its money and throwing it away,

---

[8] weald = wold, a piece of open forest land, a woody place.

In a wind-gaunt orchard where the limbs forked out and
listened or never listened at all,
In a passel [9] of trees where the branches trapped the wind
into whistling, " Who, who are you? "
I slept with my head in an elbow on a summer afternoon
and there I took a sleep lesson.
Then I went away saying: I know why they sleep,
I know how they trap the tricky winds.
Long ago I learned how to listen to the singing wind and
how to forget and how to hear the deep whine,
Slapping and lapsing under the day-blue and the night stars:
Who, who are you?

Who can ever forget
listening to the wind go by,
counting its money
and throwing it away?

Carl Sandburg

A VAGABOND SONG

There is something in the autumn that is native to my
blood —
Touch of manner, hint of mood;
And my heart is like a rhyme,
With the yellow and the purple and the crimson keeping
time.

The scarlet of the maple can shake me like a cry
Of bugles going by.
And my lonely spirit thrills
To see the frosty asters like a smoke upon the hills.

There is something in October sets the gypsy blood astir;
We must rise and follow her,
When from every hill of flame
She calls and calls each vagabond by name.

Bliss Carman

[9] passel = a clump or group.

SEA–SONG

O wind from the sea!   O wind from the sea!
    Blow gustily
      Lustily
    Over the sea!
  With thy blast of thunder
     O tear me asunder!
     Annihilate me!
     O scatter my dust,
     My mud, and my rust!
       Mustily,
       Fustily,
       Blind and a-blunder,
So have I lived, but at last I'll be free!
No longer a slave, I'll laugh, I'll rave,
       Rearing,
       Sheering,
  With foam on the wave!
  With the elements blending,
    Life without ending!
      O happy!   O brave!
      O loving and keen!
      O mightily clean!
      Careering,
      Unfearing!
O wind!   O water!   No death!   No grave!

              Irene Rutherford McLeod

THE SEA GYPSY

I am fevered with the sunset,
I am fretful with the bay,
For the wander-thirst is on me
And my soul is in Cathay.

There's a schooner in the offing,
With her topsails shot with fire,
And my heart has gone aboard her
For the Islands of Desire.

I must forth again to-morrow!
With the sunset I must be
Hull down on the trail of rapture
In the wonder of the sea.

Richard Hovey

SEA–FEVER

I must go down to the seas again, to the lonely sea and the
    sky,
And all I ask is a tall ship and a star to steer her by,
And the wheel's kick and the wind's song and the white
    sail's shaking,
And a grey mist on the sea's face and a grey dawn breaking.

I must go down to the seas again, for the call of the running
    tide
Is a wild call and a clear call that may not be denied;
And all I ask is a windy day with the white clouds flying,
And the flung spray and the blown spume, and the sea-
    gulls crying.

I must go down to the seas again to the vagrant gypsy life,
To the gull's way and the whale's way where the wind's like
    a whetted knife;
And all I ask is a merry yarn from a laughing fellow-rover,
And a quiet sleep and a sweet dream when the long trick's [10]
    over.

John Masefield

[10] Trick = in this connection a "trick" is the two-hour spell at the wheel
or on the look-out. In other words, the long watch or vigil.

Write me how many notes there be
In the new robin's ecstasy
  Among astonished boughs;
How many trips the tortoise makes,
How many cups the bee partakes,—
  The debauchee of dews!

                                    — EMILY DICKINSON

THE BULL

See an old unhappy bull,
Sick in soul and body both,
Slouching in the undergrowth
Of the forest beautiful,
Banished from the herd he led,
Bulls and cows a thousand head.

Cranes and gaudy parrots go
Up and down the burning sky;
Tree-top cats purr drowsily
In the dim-day green below;
And troops of monkeys, nutting, some,
All disputing, go and come;
And a dotted serpent curled
Round and round and round a tree,
Yellowing its greenery,
Keeps a watch on all the world,
All the world and this old bull
In the forest beautiful.

Bravely by his fall he came:
One he led, a bull of blood
Newly come to lustihood,

175

Fought and put his prince to shame,
Snuffed and pawed the prostrate head,
Tameless even while it bled.

There they left him, every one,
Left him there without a lick,
Left him for the birds to pick,
Left him there for carrion,
Vilely from their bosom cast
Wisdom, worth and love at last.
When the lion left his lair
And roared his beauty through the hills,
And the vultures pecked their quills
And flew into the middle air,
Then this prince no more to reign
Came to life and lived again.

He snuffed the herd in far retreat,
He saw the blood upon the ground,
And snuffed the burning airs around
Still with beevish odours sweet,
While the blood ran down his head
And his mouth ran slaver red.
Pity him, this fallen chief,
All his splendour, all his strength
All his body's breadth and length
Dwindled down with shame and grief,
Half the bull he was before,
Bones and leather, nothing more.

See him standing dewlap-deep
In the rushes at the lake,
Surly, stupid, half asleep,
Waiting for his heart to break
And the birds to join the flies
Feasting at his bloodshot eyes, —
Standing with his head hung down
In a stupor, dreaming things:

Green savannas, jungles brown,
Battlefields and bellowings,
Bulls undone and lions dead
And vultures flapping overhead.
Dreaming things: of days he spent
With his mother gaunt and lean
In the valley warm and green,
Full of baby wonderment,
Blinking out of silly eyes
At a hundred mysteries. . . .

Dreaming over once again
How he wandered with a throng
Of bulls and cows a thousand strong,
Wandered on from plain to plain,
Up the hill and down the dale,
Always at his mother's tail;
How he lagged behind the herd,
Lagged and tottered, weak of limb
And she turned and ran to him
Blaring at the loathly bird
Stationed always in the skies,
Waiting for the flesh that dies.

Dreaming maybe of a day
When her drained and drying paps
Turned him to the sweets and saps,
Richer fountains by the way,
And she left the bull she bore
And he looked to her no more;
And his little frame grew stout,
And his little legs grew strong,
And the way was not so long;
And his little horns came out
And he played at butting trees
And boulder-stones and tortoises,
Joined a game of knobby skulls

With the youngsters of his year,
All the other little bulls,
Learning both to bruise and bear,
Learning how to stand a shock
Like a little bull of rock.

And the gristles of his youth
Hardened in his comely pow,[1]
And he came to fighting growth,
Beat his bull and won his cow,
And flew his tail and trampled off
Past the tallest, vain enough,
And curved about in splendour full
And curved again and snuffed the airs
As who should say ' Come out who dares! '
And all beheld a bull, a Bull,
And knew that here was surely one
That backed for no bull, fearing none. . . .

And the leader of the herd
Looked and saw, and beat the ground,
And shook the forest with his sound,
Bellowed at the loathly bird
Stationed always in the skies,
Waiting for the flesh that dies.
Dreaming, this old bull forlorn,
Surely dreaming of the hour
When he came to sultan power,
And they owned him master-horn,
Chiefest bull of all among
Bulls and cows a thousand strong.

Not a serpent that survived
Once the terrors of his hoof
Risked a second time reproof,
Came a second time and lived,
Not a serpent in its skin
Came again for discipline;

[1] pow = head.

Not a leopard bright as flame,
Flashing fingerhooks of steel
That a wooden tree might feel,
Met his fury once and came
For a second reprimand,
Not a leopard in the land.

Not a lion of them all,
Not a lion of the hills,
Hero of a thousand kills,
Dared a second fight and fall,
Dared that ram terrific twice,
Paid a second time the price. . . ,

Pity him, this dupe of dream,
Leader of the herd again
Only in his daft old brain,
Once again the bull supreme
And bull enough to bear the part
Only in his tameless heart.

Pity him that he must wake;
Even now the swarm of flies
Blackening his bloodshot eyes
Bursts and blusters round the lake,
Scattered from the feast half-fed,
By great shadows overhead.

And the dreamer turns away
From his visionary herds
And his splendid yesterday,
Turns to meet the loathly birds
Flocking round him from the skies,
Waiting for the flesh that dies.

Ralph Hodgson

THE SNARE [2]

I hear the sullen cry of pain!
    There is a rabbit in a snare:
Now I hear the cry again,
    But I cannot tell from where.

But I cannot tell from where
    He is calling out for aid;
Crying on the frightened air,
    Making everything afraid.

Making everything afraid,
    Wrinkling up his little face,
As he cries again for aid;
    And I cannot find the place!

And I cannot find the place
    Where his paw is in the snare:
Little one! Oh, little one!
    I am searching everywhere.

                    James Stephens

THE BAD KITTENS

You may call, you may call
But the little black cats won't hear you.
The little black cats are maddened
    By the bright green light of the moon;
They are whirling and running and hiding,
They are wild who were once so confiding,
They are crazed when the moon is riding —
    You will not catch the kittens soon.
They care not for saucers of milk,
They think not of pillows of silk;

[2] From *Songs from the Clay* by James Stephens. Reprinted by special arrangement with The Macmillan Company, Publishers.

Your softest, crooningest call
  Is less than the buzzing of flies.
They are seeing more than you see,
They are hearing more than you hear,
And out of the darkness they peer
  With a goblin light in their eyes!

Elizabeth J. Coatsworth

MILK FOR THE CAT

When the tea is brought at five o'clock,
And all the neat curtains are drawn with care,
The little black cat with bright green eyes
Is suddenly purring there.

At first she pretends, having nothing to do,
She has come in merely to blink by the grate,
But, though tea may be late or the milk may be sour,
She is never late.

And presently her agate eyes
Take a soft large milky haze,
And her independent casual glance
Becomes a stiff hard gaze.

Then she stamps her claws or lifts her ears
Or twists her tail and begins to stir,
Till suddenly all her lithe body becomes
One breathing trembling purr.

The children eat and wriggle and laugh;
The two old ladies stroke their silk:
But the cat is grown small and thin with desire,
Transformed to a creeping lust for milk.

The white saucer like some full moon descends
At last from the clouds of the table above;
She sighs and dreams and thrills and glows,
Transfigured with love.

She nestles over the shining rim,
Buries her chin in the creamy sea;
Her tail hangs loose; each drowsy paw
Is doubled under each bending knee.

A long dim ecstasy holds her life;
Her world is an infinite shapeless white,
Till her tongue has curled the last holy drop,
Then she sinks back into the night,

Draws and dips her body to heap
Her sleepy nerves in the great arm-chair,
Lies defeated and buried deep
Three or four hours unconscious there.

Harold Monro

THE HOMECOMING OF THE SHEEP

The sheep are coming home in Greece,
Hark the bells on every hill!
Flock by flock, and fleece by fleece,
Wandering wide a little piece
Thro' the evening red and still.
Stopping where the pathways cease,
Cropping with a hurried will.

Thro' the cotton-bushes low
Merry boys with shouldered crooks
Close them in a single row,
Shout among them as they go
With one bell-ring over the brooks.
Such delight you never know
Reading it from gilded books.

Before the early stars are bright
Cormorants and sea-gulls call,
And the moon comes large and white
Filling with a lovely light

The ferny curtained waterfall.
Then sleep wraps every bell up tight
And the climbing moon grows small.

Francis Ledwidge

THE WORM

Dickie found a broken spade
And said he'd dig himself a well;
And then Charles took a piece of tin,
And I was digging with a shell.

Then Will said he would dig one too.
We shaped them out and made them wide,
And I dug up a piece of clod
That had a little worm inside.

We watched him pucker up himself
And stretch himself to walk away.
He tried to go inside the dirt,
But Dickie made him wait and stay.

His shining skin was soft and wet.
I poked him once to see him squirm.
And then Will said, " I wonder if
He knows that he's a worm."

And then we sat back on our feet
And wondered for a little bit.
And we forgot to dig our wells
Awhile, and tried to answer it.

And while we tried to find it out,
He puckered in a little wad,
And then he stretched himself again
And went back home inside the clod.

Elizabeth Madox Roberts

TO A PHOEBE–BIRD

Under the eaves, out of the wet,
  You nest within my reach;
You never sing for me and yet
  You have a golden speech.

You sit and quirk a rapid tail,
  Wrinkle a ragged crest,
Then pirouette from tree to rail
  And vault from rail to nest.

And when in frequent, dainty fright
  You grayly slip and fade,
And when at hand you re-alight
  Demure and unafraid,

And when you bring your brood its fill
  Of iridescent wings
And green legs dewy in your bill,
  Your silence is what sings.

Not of a feather that enjoys
  To prate or praise or preach,
O phoebe, with so little noise,
  What eloquence you teach!

Witter Bynner

THE DISCOVERER

Mystical, sorrowful, stiff and still,
A sparrow stood on a wintry sill.

The night-wind laden with icy sleet
Ruffled his feathers and stung his feet,

But his right eye peered through a window pane
And visioned the warmth of a June-time lane.

He saw the lights from a fireplace fall
Over the patterns on somebody's wall.

His heart was thrilled by a paper rose —
He had found at last where the summer goes.

Nathalia Crane

PIGEONS JUST AWAKE

As the sun rose
Everything was bathed in gold,
Trees were still and solemn. . . .
Pigeons waded the dew.
Their feet were the color of new June strawberries.
I thought what it must be to fly,
To whirl up into the light,
To know the curved flight of pigeons
Above trees and lawns!
If I could fly
I should not have to leave my mother for long
Nor my dark-eyed sister;
Only a fluttering, a lifting
Up round the elm tree and over,
A cool curving and sliding down the light
Into wet grass.

Hilda Conkling

THE CROWS

The woman who has grown old
And knows desire must die,
Yet turns to love again,
Hears the crows' cry.

She is a stem long hardened,
A weed that no scythe mows.
The heart's laughter will be to her
The crying of the crows

Who slide in the air with the same voice
Over what yields not, and what yields,
Alike in spring, and when there is only bitter
Winter-burning in the fields.

Louise Bogan

DUCKS

I

From troubles of the world
I turn to ducks,
Beautiful comical things
Sleeping or curled,
Their heads beneath white wings
By water cool,
Or finding curious things
To eat in various mucks
Beneath the pool,
Tails uppermost, or waddling
Sailor-like on the shores
Of ponds, or paddling
— Left! right! — with fanlike feet
Which are for steady oars
When they (white galleys) float
Each bird a boat
Rippling at will the sweet
Wide waterway. . . .
When night is fallen *you* creep
Upstairs; but drakes and dillies
Nest with pale water-stars,
Moonbeams and shadow bars,
And water-lilies:
Fearful too much to sleep
Since they've no locks
To click against the teeth
Of weasel and fox.
And warm beneath

Are eggs of cloudy green
Whence hungry rats and lean
Would stealthily suck
New life, but for the mien,
The bold ferocious mien,
Of the mother-duck.

II

Yes, ducks are valiant things
On nests of twigs and straws,
And ducks are soothy things
And lovely on the lake
When that the sunlight draws
Thereon their pictures dim
In colors cool.
And when beneath the pool
They dabble, and when they swim
And make their rippling rings,
O ducks are beautiful things!

But ducks are comical things: —
As comical as you.
Quack!
They waddle round, they do.
They eat all sorts of things,
And then they quack.
By barn and stable and stack
They wander at their will,
But if you go too near
They look at you through black
Small topaz-tinted eyes
And wish you ill.
Triangular and clear
They leave their curious track
In mud at the water's edge,
And there amid the sedge
And slime they gobble and peer
Saying " Quack! quack! "

III

When God had finished the stars and whirl of colored suns
He turned His mind from big things to fashion little ones,
Beautiful tiny things (like daisies) He made, and then
He made the comical ones in case the minds of men
  Should stiffen and become
  Dull, humorless and glum:
And so forgetful of their Maker be
As to take themselves — *quite seriously.*
Caterpillars and cats are lively and excellent puns:
All God's jokes are good — even the practical ones!
And as for the duck, I think God must have smiled a bit
Seeing those bright eyes blink on the day He fashioned it.
And He's probably laughing still at the sound that came out
  of its bill!

F. W. Harvey

REMEMBER ME, GULLS!

This is my hour between the flight and the flight
Of the trumpet gulls manoeuvring in half-light;
Putting their beaks on edge
With colour; making a wedge
Between the livid twilight and the night.

Soon they will quiet their aquiline throats; and soon,
While the sun crumples like a little balloon
On fire, their wings will go slack,
The moon shift almond on black,
And clouds will hook their brooding claws on the moon.

Remember me, gulls; remember me, white birds flying
In narrow circles where the nets are drying!
By water and wind and the hot
Reek of the beach rot,
Remember me, gulls, cutting to the north and crying!

Joseph Auslander

THE BRONCHO THAT WOULD NOT BE BROKEN [3]

A little colt-broncho, loaned to the farm
To be broken in time without fury or harm,
Yet black crows flew past you, shouting alarm,
Calling " Beware," with lugubrious singing . . .
The butterflies there in the bush were romancing,
The smell of the grass caught your soul in a trance,
So why be a-fearing the spurs and the traces,
O broncho that would not be broken of dancing?

You were born with the pride of the lords great and olden
Who danced, through the ages, in corridors golden.
In all the wide farm-place the person most human,
You spoke out so plainly with squealing and capering,
With whinnying, snorting, contorting and prancing,
As you dodged your pursuers, looking askance,
With Greek-footed figures, and Parthenon paces,
O broncho that would not be broken of dancing.

The grasshoppers cheered. " Keep whirling," they said.
The insolent sparrows called from the shed
" If men will not laugh, make them wish they were dead."
But arch were your thoughts, all malice displacing,
Though the horse-killers came, with snake-whips advancing,
You bantered and cantered away your last chance.
And they scourged you, with Hell in their speech and
    their faces,
O broncho that would not be broken of dancing.

" Nobody cares for you," rattled the crows,
As you dragged the whole reaper, next day, down the rows.
The three mules held back, yet you danced on your toes.
You pulled like a racer, and kept the mules chasing.

[3] From *Collected Poems* by Vachel Lindsay. Reprinted by special arrangement with The Macmillan Company, Publishers.

You tangled the harness with bright eyes side-glancing,
While the drunk driver bled you — a pole for a lance —
And the giant mules bit at you — keeping their places.
O broncho that would not be broken of dancing.

In that last afternoon your boyish heart broke.
The hot wind came down like a sledge-hammer stroke.
The blood-sucking flies to a rare feast awoke.
And they searched out your wounds, your death-warrant
    tracing.
And the merciful men, their religion enhancing,
Stopped the red reaper, to give you a chance.
Then you died on the prairie, and scorned all disgraces,
O broncho that would not be broken of dancing.

Vachel Lindsay

Know then thyself, presume not God to scan;
The proper study of mankind is man.

— ALEXANDER POPE

LINCOLN, THE MAN OF THE PEOPLE

When the Norn Mother saw the Whirlwind Hour
Greatening and darkening as it hurried on,
She left the Heaven of Heroes and came down
To make a man to meet the mortal need.
She took the tried clay of the common road —
Clay warm yet with the genial heat of earth,
Dasht through it all a strain of prophecy;
Tempered the heap with thrill of human tears;
Then mixt a laughter with the serious stuff.
Into the shape she breathed a flame to light
That tender, tragic, ever-changing face;
And laid on him a sense of the Mystic Powers,
Moving — all husht — behind the mortal veil.
Here was a man to hold against the world,
A man to match the mountains and the sea.

The color of the ground was in him, the red earth;
The smack and tang of elemental things;
The rectitude and patience of the cliff;
The good-will of the rain that loves all leaves;
The friendly welcome of the wayside well;
The courage of the bird that dares the sea;
The gladness of the wind that shakes the corn;
The pity of the snow that hides all scars;
The secrecy of streams that make their way
Under the mountain to the rifted rock;

The tolerance and equity of light
That gives as freely to the shrinking flower
As to the great oak flaring to the wind —
To the grave's low hill as to the Matterhorn
That shoulders out the sky.   Sprung from the West,
He drank the valorous youth of a new world.
The strength of virgin forests braced his mind,
The hush of spacious prairies stilled his soul.
His words were oaks in acorns; and his thoughts
Were roots that firmly gript the granite truth.

Up from the log cabin to the Capitol,
One fire was on his spirit, one resolve —
To send the keen ax to the root of wrong,
Clearing a free way for the feet of God,
The eyes of conscience testing every stroke,
To make his deed the measure of a man.
He built the rail-pile as he built the State,
Pouring his splendid strength through every blow:
The grip that swung the ax in Illinois
Was on the pen that set a people free.

So came the Captain with the mighty heart;
And when the judgment thunders split the house,
Wrenching the rafters from their ancient rest,
He held the ridgepole up, and spiked again
The rafters of the Home.   He held his place —
Held the long purpose like a growing tree —
Held on through blame and faltered not at praise.
And when he fell in whirlwind, he went down
As when a lordly cedar, green with boughs,
Goes down with a great shout upon the hills,
And leaves a lonesome place against the sky.

Edwin Markham

THE SLEEPER

As Ann came in one summer's day,
   She felt that she must creep,
So silent was the clear cool house,
   It seemed a house of sleep.
And sure, when she pushed open the door,
   Rapt in stillness there,
Her mother sat, with stooping head,
   Asleep upon a chair;
Fast — fast asleep; her two hands laid
   Loose-folded on her knee,
So that her small unconscious face
   Looked half unreal to be:
So calmly lit with sleep's pale light
   Each feature was; so fair
Her forehead — every trouble was
   Smooth'd out beneath her hair.
But though her mind in dream now moved,
   Still seemed her gaze to rest
From out beneath her fast-sealed lids,
   Above her moving breast,
On Ann, as quite, quite still she stood;
   Yet slumber lay so deep
Even her hands upon her lap
   Seemed saturate with sleep.
And as Ann peeped, a cloudlike dread
   Stole over her, and then,
On stealthy, mouselike feet she trod,
   And tiptoed out again.

               Walter de la Mare

SONGS FOR MY MOTHER
Her Hands

My mother's hands are cool and fair,
   They can do anything.
Delicate mercies hide them there
   Like flowers in the spring.

When I was small and could not sleep,
   She used to come to me,
And with my cheek upon her hand
   How sure my rest would be.

For everything she ever touched
   Of beautiful or fine,
Their memories living in her hands
   Would warm that sleep of mine.

Her hands remember how they played
   One time in meadow streams, —
And all the flickering song and shade
   Of water took my dreams.

One time she touched the cloud that kissed
   Brown pastures bleak and far; —
I leaned my cheek into a mist
   And thought I was a star.

All this was very long ago
   And I am grown; but yet
The hand that lured my slumber so
   I never can forget.

For still when drowsiness comes on
   It seems so soft and cool,
Shaped happily beneath my cheek,
   Hollow and beautiful.

Her Words

My mother has the prettiest tricks
  Of words and words and words.
Her talk comes out as smooth and sleek
  As breasts of singing birds.

She shapes her speech all silver fine
  Because she loves it so,
And her own eyes begin to shine
  To hear her stories grow.

And if she goes to make a call
  Or out to take a walk,
We leave our work when she returns
  And run to hear her talk.

We had not dreamed these things were so
  Of sorrow and of mirth.
Her speech is as a thousand eyes
  Through which we see the earth.

God wove a web of loveliness,
  Of clouds and stars and birds,
But made not anything at all
  So beautiful as words.

They shine around our simple earth
  With golden shadowings,
And every common thing they touch
  Is exquisite with wings.

There's nothing poor and nothing small
  But is made fair with them.
They are the hands of living faith
  That touch the garment's hem.

They are as fair as bloom or air,
    They shine like any star,
And I am rich who learned from her
    How beautiful they are.

Anna Hempstead Branch

THE OLD WOMAN

As a white candle
In a holy place,
So is the beauty
Of an aged face.

As the spent radiance
Of the winter sun,
So is a woman
With her travail done.

Her brood gone from her
And her thoughts as still
As the waters
Under a ruined mill.

Joseph Campbell

THE OLD WOMAN OF THE ROADS

O, to have a little house!
To own the hearth and stool and all!
The heaped up sods upon the fire!
The pile of turf again' the wall!

To have a clock with weights and chains,
And pendulum swinging up and down!
A dresser filled with shining delph,[1]
Speckled with white and blue and brown!

---

[1] delph = a kind of pottery, so called because it originated at Delft, Holland.

I could be busy all the day
Cleaning and sweeping hearth and floor,
And fixing on their shelf again
My white and blue and speckled store!

I could be quiet there at night
Beside the fire and by myself,
Sure of a bed, and loth to leave
The ticking clock and shining delph!

Och! but I'm weary of mist and dark,
And roads where there's never a house or bush,
And tired I am of bog and road,
And the crying wind and the lonesome hush!

And I am praying to God on high,
And I am praying Him night and day,
For a little house — a house of my own —
Out of the wind's and the rain's way.

Padraic Colum

WHEN THE YEAR GROWS OLD *

I cannot but remember
   When the year grows old —
October — November —
   How she disliked the cold!

She used to watch the swallows
   Go down across the sky,
And turn from the window
   With a little sharp sigh.

And often when the brown leaves
   Were brittle on the ground,
And the wind in the chimney
   Made a melancholy sound,

* From *Renascence and Other Poems*, published by Harper & Brothers, copyright 1917 by Edna St. Vincent Millay.

She had a look about her
    That I wish I could forget —
The look of a scared thing
    Sitting in a net!

Oh, beautiful at nightfall
    The soft spitting snow!
And beautiful the bare boughs
    Rubbing to and fro!

But the roaring of the fire,
    And the warmth of fur,
And the boiling of the kettle
    Were beautiful to her!

I cannot but remember
    When the year grows old —
October — November —
    How she disliked the cold.

                        Edna St. Vincent Millay

IN SERVICE

Little Nellie Cassidy has got a place in town,
    She wears a fine white apron,
    She wears a new black gown,
An' the quarest little cap at all with straymers hanging
    down.

I met her one fine evening stravagin' [2] down the street,
    A feathered hat upon her head,
    And boots upon her feet,
" Och, Mick," says she, " may God be praised that you and
    I should meet.

            [2] stravagin' = strolling.

" It's lonesome in the city with such a crowd," says she;
  " I'm lost without the bog-land,
  I'm lost without the sea,
An' the harbor an' the fishing-boats that sail out fine and
    free.

" I'd give a golden guinea to stand upon the shore,
  To see the big waves lepping,
  To hear them splash and roar,
To smell the tar and the drying nets, I'd not be asking more.

" To see the small white houses, their faces to the sea,
  The childher in the doorway,
  Or round my mother's knee;
For I'm strange and lonesome missing them, God keep them
    all," says she.

Little Nellie Cassidy earns fourteen pounds and more,
  Waiting on the quality,
  And answering the door —
But her heart is some place far away upon the Wexford
    shore.

Winifred M. Letts

DA GREATA STRONGA MAN

You oughta see my Uncla Joe
  W'en he ees gatta mad.
He ees da strongest man I know
  W'en som' wan treat heem bad.
Hees eye eet flash like blazin' coal,
  An' w'en he ope hees mout'
He growla like you theenk hees soul
  Ees turna eenside out.
He eesa gat so stronga den
  An' swell so big an' fat,
Eet gona taka *seexa* men
  For justa hold hees hat!

You oughta see my Uncla Joe
  W'en he ees mad weeth you.
You bat my life! den you will know
  I eesa speaka true.
He gat so strong eenside of heem
  Eet mak' your hearta freeze,
An' eef he looka at som' cream
  Eet turna eento cheese!
Den you weell run, you bat my life,
  So fast as you can go,
An' throw away your gun or knife.
  Ha! strong man, Uncla Joe.

   .   .   .   .   .

You oughta see my Uncla Joe!
  Ees w'at you call " surprise."
Las' night beeg Irish ponch heem so
  Eet close up bot' hees eyes.
O! my! he eesa looka bad;
  Mus' be ees som'theng wrong,
Baycause w'en Uncla Joe ees mad
  He always been so strong.
I guess dees Irish heet his blow
  So queecka an' so rough
He no geeve time to Uncla Joe
  For gatta mad enough.

                        T. A. Daly

APPLES

Before she went from grieving
  To where all grief is done,
She walked amongst the apple trees
  That grew in Avalon.

I am not good at naming names;
  I am not sure at all,
But that it was in Nineveh:
  The dusk was at the fall.

And through the dwindling of the light,
   And clear unto the town,
Was heard the blunt, rich, huddled sound
   Of apples dropping down.

Her plaintive long hands at her side,
   Her head drooped as of old,
She was that dwindling of the light,
   And the bough growing cold.

Were I to find those apple-trees,
   Half-lit, crabbed, slim with dew,
In Tarshish or in Babylon,
   Would I not find her too?

For was not all her loveliness
   Blown dimly down the air,
The gentle color of her gown,
   The sweet dark of her hair?

Perhaps. But I am sure of this,
   That clear unto the town,
There will be heard that sound again
   Of apples dropping down.

Lizette Woodworth Reese

A LAMENT

I seen her last night
   And nothin' ailed her.
She was singin': and now
   The breath has failed her.

Her hands I held,
   As cold as the clay:
Her warm lips I kissed,
   Agape and gray.

A round black penny
　　On each eye-socket,
And herself
　　In God's pocket.

L. A. G. Strong

WASHERWOMAN'S SONG

Clouds, clouds, clouds in the sky,
The Heavenly washing is hung out to dry!
Billowing, bellying, full in the breeze,
Leaping and tugging as gay as you please.
Look, children, look at 'em! If they was mine,
I'd be in dread that they'd blow off the line.

L. A. G. Strong

A SONG TO ONE

If few are won to read my lays
And offer me a word of praise,
　　If there are only one or two
　　　　To take my rhymes and read them through,
I may not claim the poet's bays.

I care not, when my Fancy plays
Its one sweet note, if it should raise
　　A host of listeners or few —
　　　　If *you* are one.

The homage that my full heart pays
To Womanhood in divers ways,
　　Begins and ends, my love, in you.
　　My lines may halt, but strong and true
My soul shall sing through all its days,
　　　　If you are *won*.

T. A. Daly

TO JAMES WHITCOMB RILEY

Your trail runs to the Westward,
  And mine to my own place;
There is water between our lodges,
  And I have not seen your face.

But since I have read your verses
  'Tis easy to guess the rest,
Because in the hearts of the children
  There is neither East nor West.

Born to a thousand fortunes
  Of good or evil hap,
Once they were kings together,
  Throned in a mother's lap.

Surely they know that secret,
  Yellow, and black, and white,
When they meet as kings together
  In innocent dreams at night,

With a moon they all can play with,
  Grubby, and grimed, and unshod,
Very happy together,
  And very near to God.

Rudyard Kipling

TO A FAT LADY SEEN FROM A TRAIN

O why do you walk through the fields in gloves,
  Missing so much and so much?
O fat white woman whom nobody loves,
Why do you walk through the fields in gloves,
When the grass is soft as the breast of doves
  And shivering sweet to the touch?
O why do you walk through the fields in gloves,
  Missing so much and so much?

Frances Cornford

THE FIDDLER OF DOONEY

When I play on my fiddle in Dooney,
Folk dance like a wave of the sea;
My cousin is priest in Kilvarnet,
My brother in Moharabuiee.

I passed by brother and cousin:
They read in their books of prayer;
I read in my book of songs
I bought at the Sligo fair.

When we come at the end of time,
To Peter sitting in state,
He will smile on the three old spirits,
But call me first through the gate;

For the good are always the merry,
Save by an evil chance,
And the merry love the fiddle
And the merry love to dance:

And when the folk there spy me,
They will all come up to me,
With ' Here is the fiddler of Dooney! '
And dance like a wave of the sea.

William Butler Yeats

A SHROPSHIRE LAD

Oh fair enough are sky and plain,
    But I know fairer far:
Those are as beautiful again
    That in the water are;

The pools and rivers wash so clean
    The trees and clouds and air,
The like on earth was never seen,
    And oh that I were there.

These are the thoughts I often think
  As I stand gazing down
In act upon the cressy brink
  To strip and dive and drown;

But in the golden-sanded brooks
  And azure meres I spy
A silly lad that longs and looks
  And wishes he were I.

A. E. Housman

While he from forth the closet brought a heap
Of candied apple, quince, and plum, and gourd;
With jellies soother than the creamy curd,
And lucent syrops, tinct with cinnamon;
Manna and dates, in argosy transferred
From Fez; and spicèd dainties, every one,
From silken Samarcand to cedared Lebanon.

— JOHN KEATS

WHEN MOONLIGHT FALLS

When moonlight falls on the water
It is like fingers touching the chords of a harp
On a misty day.
When moonlight strikes the water
I cannot get it into my poem:
I only hear the tinkle of ripplings of light.
When I see the water's fingers and the moon's rays
Intertwined,
I think of all the words I love to hear,
And try to find words white enough
For such shining. . . .

Hilda Conkling

PRETTY WORDS

Poets make pets of pretty, docile words:
I love smooth words, like gold-enameled fish
Which circle slowly with a silken swish,
And tender ones, like downy-feathered birds:
Words shy and dappled, deep-eyed deer in herds,
Come to my hand, and playful if I wish,
Or purring softly at a silver dish,

Blue Persian kittens, fed on cream and curds.
I love bright words, words up and singing early;
Words that are luminous in the dark, and sing;
Warm lazy words, white cattle under trees;
I love words opalescent, cool, and pearly,
Like midsummer moths, and honeyed words like bees,
Gilded and sticky, with a little sting.

Elinor Wylie

RHYME FOR A PHONETICIAN

Brave English language, you are strong as trees,
Yet intricate and stately — Thus one sees
Through branches clear-embroidered stars. You please
Our sense as damask roses on the breeze,
And barns that smell of hay, and bread and cheese.
Rustic yet Roman — yours are dignities
Sonorous as the sea's sound. On my knees
1 would give thanks for all your words. Yet these
— Our legacy and our delight — he'd squeeze
And nip and dock and drill, to write with ease
Comershul memoz faw the Pawchoogeeze.[1]

Frances Cornford

THE LITTLE CARVED BOWL

I always wanted
A little carved bowl
With grapes around the edges
And gilt on the whole
And a daffodil garden
And a singing soul;

I wanted gold rings
And a satin dress

---

[1] No, dear reader, this is not a queer foreign language. This is English —
the sort of English that would be written by a believer in phonetic spelling!
Now try the line again, pronouncing the words (out loud) just as they appear.

And a friend who knew
    What no other could guess
And a very great
    Gold happiness. . . .

I never have had
    The satin gown
And no gold happiness
    Ever came down
To be my shelter
    And my shining crown,

Nor a daffodil garden
    Nor a singing soul
Nor ever a friend
    Who knew me whole
But today some one gave me
    A little carved bowl.

Margaret Widdemer

THE BEES' SONG

Thouzandz of thornz there be
On the Rozez where gozez
The Zebra of Zee:
Sleek, striped, and hairy,
The steed of the Fairy
Princess of Zee.

Heavy with blozzomz be
The Rozez that growzez
In the thickets of Zee,
Where grazez the Zebra,
Marked Abracadeebra
Of the Princess of Zee.

And he nozez the poziez
Of the Rozez that growzez
So luvez'm and free;

With an eye, dark and wary,
In search of a Fairy,
Whose Rozez he knowzez
Were not honeyed for he,
But to breathe a sweet incense
To solace the Princess
Of far-away Zee.

Walter de la Mare

SONG

April, April,
Laugh thy girlish laughter;
Then, the moment after,
Weep thy girlish tears,
April, that mine ears
Like a lover greetest,
If I tell thee, sweetest,
All my hopes and fears.
April, April,
Laugh thy golden laughter,
But, the moment after,
Weep thy golden tears!

William Watson

AN ARAB LOVE–SONG

The hunchèd camels of the night [2]
Trouble the bright
And silver waters of the moon,
The Maiden of the Morn will soon
Through Heaven stray and sing,
Star gathering.

Now while the dark about our loves is strewn,
Light of my dark, blood of my heart, O come!
And night will catch her breath up, and be dumb.

[2] Cloud-shapes observed by travellers in the East.

Leave thy father, leave thy mother
And thy brother;
Leave the black tents of thy tribe apart!
Am I not thy father and thy brother,
And thy mother?
And thou — what needest with thy tribe's black tents
Who hast the red pavilion of my heart?

Francis Thompson

But O! that deep romantic chasm which slanted
Down the green hill athwart a cedarn cover!
A savage place! as holy and enchanted
As e'er beneath a waning moon was haunted
By woman wailing for her demon-lover!

— SAMUEL TAYLOR COLERIDGE

OFF THE GROUND

Three jolly Farmers
Once bet a pound
Each dance the others would
Off the ground.
Out of their coats
They slipped right soon,
And neat and nicesome,
Put each his shoon.
One — Two — Three! —
And away they go,
Not too fast,
And not too slow;
Out from the elm-tree's
Noonday shadow,
Into the sun,
And across the meadow.
Past the schoolroom,
With knees well bent
Fingers a-flicking,
They dancing went.
Up sides and over,
And round and round,
They crossed click-clacking,
The Parish bound,

By Tupman's meadow
They did their mile,
Tee-to-tum
On a three-barred stile.
Then straight through Whipham,
Downhill to Week,
Footing it lightsome,
But not too quick,
Up fields to Watchet,
And on through Wye,
Till seven fine churches
They'd seen skip by —
Seven fine churches
And five old mills,
Farms in the valley,
And sheep on the hills;
Old Man's Acre
And Dead Man's Pool
All left behind,
As they danced through Wool.
And Wool gone by,
Like tops that seem
To spin in sleep
They danced in dream:
Withy — Wellover —
Wassop — Wo —
Like an old clock
Their heels did go.
A league and a league
And a league they went,
And not one weary,
And not one spent,
And lo, and behold!
Past Willow-cum-Leigh
Stretched with its waters
The great green sea.
Says Farmer Bates,

' I puffs and I blows,
What's under the water,
Why, no man knows! '
Says Farmer Giles,
' My wind comes weak,
And a good man drowned
Is far to seek.'
But Farmer Turvey,
On twirling toes
Up's with his gaiters,
And in he goes:
Down where the mermaids
Pluck and play
On their twangling harps
In a sea-green day;
Down where the mermaids,
Finned and fair,
Sleek with their combs
Their yellow hair . . . .
Bates and Giles —
On the shingle sat,
Gazing at Turvey's
Floating hat.
But never a ripple
Nor bubble told
Where he was supping
Off plates of gold.
Never an echo
Rilled through the sea
Of the feasting and dancing
And minstrelsy.
They called — called — called:
Came no reply:
Nought but the ripples'
Sandy sigh.
Then glum and silent
They sat instead,

Vacantly brooding
On home and bed,
Till both together
Stood up and said: —
' Us knows not, dreams not,
Where you be,
Turvey, unless
In the deep blue sea;
But axcusing silver —
And it comes most willing —
Here's us two paying
Our forty shilling;
For it's sartin sure, Turvey,
Safe and sound,
You danced us square, Turvey,
Off the ground! '

Walter de la Mare

THE HOUSE ON THE HILL

They are all gone away,
  The House is shut and still,
There is nothing more to say.

Through broken walls and gray
  The winds blow bleak and shrill:
They are all gone away.

Nor is there one to-day
  To speak them good or ill:
There is nothing more to say.

Why is it then we stray
  Around that sunken sill?
They are all gone away.

And our poor fancy-play
  For them is wasted skill:
There is nothing more to say.

There is ruin and decay
  In the House on the Hill:
They are all gone away,
There is nothing more to say.
                    Edwin Arlington Robinson

MOON RIDER

A sky of deepening bronze
Seemed tolling like a bell.
Blue ice filmed shrivelled ponds.
Snow whispering fell.

Trees traced a frieze of black.
One window's spark
Flecked gold upon the farmyard track,
Brightening with the dark.

He cinched the saddle on the colt
That snuffed his hand.
The bar was slid, the bolt
Shot.   The open land

Lay ghostly still from hill to hill.
He sprang.   They were gone.
Like foam below them tossed the snow.
Hoofs beat on.

Blurred in the eyes, like unshed tears,
Stars crackled overhead;
The wind a flickering shears
That snaps a thread.

Swift between drifts the flooding thud
Ran muffled on.
Straight at the moon he rode
In a goblin dawn.

Dark trees to one high house
Closed round him up the drive.
He reined in hush that seemed to rouse
The voice of all alive.

Pebbles that, spattering, ticked the glass
Awoke a crocus stain.
He saw her shadow pass
The blinded pane.

Over the snow-choked portico
The house leaned heavy-beamed.
A footfall light, a footfall low.
The fanlight gleamed.

Cautious, the oak both groaned and spoke.
One golden bud of flame.
Shadows tall thronged from the hall.
Name breathed to name.

In frosted heaven the moon's shell
Filled, overflowed with light,
Welling like ringing of a bell
Through the lingering night.

William Rose Benét

THE BEST GAME THE FAIRIES PLAY

The best game the fairies play,
    The best game of all,
Is sliding down steeples —
    (You know they're very tall).
You fly to the weathercock,
    And when you hear it crow
You fold your wings and clutch your things
    And then let go!

They have a million other games —
   Cloud-catching's one,
And mud-mixing after rain
   Is heaps and heaps of fun;
But when you go and stay with them
   Never mind the rest,
Take my advice — they're very nice,
   But steeple-sliding's best!

Rose Fyleman

THE FAIRY LOUGH [1]

Loughareema! Loughareema
   Lies so high among the heather;
A little lough, a dark lough,
   The weather's black an' deep.
Ould herons go a-fishin' there
   An' sea-gulls all together
Float roun' the one green island
   On the fairy lough asleep.

Loughareema, Loughareema;
   When the sun goes down at seven,
When the hills are dark an' *airy*,
   'Tis a curlew whistles sweet!
Then somethin' rustles all the reeds
   That stand so thick an' even;
A little wave runs up the shore
   An' flees, as if on feet.

Loughareema, Loughareema!
   Stars come out, an' stars are hidin';
The wather whispers on the stones,
   The flutterin' moths are free.
One'st before the mornin' light
   The Horsemen will come ridin'
Roun' an' roun' the fairy lough,
   An' no one there to see.

Moira O'Neill

[1] *Lough:* the old Gaelic name for lake.

FIDDLERS' GREEN

(For Anna, who told me the story of the place " where the souls
do be going that was too bad for Paradise and too charming for
Hell. . . .")

The path that runs to Paradise climbs up a stone-heaped hill,
And strait it is and briar-wound, and you may stumble still.

And you shall know the Elfland Road by tiny bells that
  sound
From where for aye the Faëry Court ride gay with horse
  and hound,

And sweet and tall the lilies grow that you may surely tell
The singing and the sunny road that takes your feet to
  Hell:

But past the ferny Elfland Road, before the Dark Walls
  lean,
There winds a little wayward path that goes to Fiddlers'
  Green.

The souls that dwell in Paradise sing high for happiness,
The souls that walk in Hell they moan for anger and dis-
  tress,

The souls ensnared in Faëryland, until the Judgment Day,
With horse and hound and hawk-bell's sound they fleet the
  time away,

But they who dream on Fiddlers' Green think naught of
  joys or pains,
They only play their fiddles light, as once down earthly
  lanes.

Oh, they were those who loved an hour, and kissed and rode
  away,
Who though they heard their brothers weep could never
  cease to play,

Who gave no gold for any need — who could not stop to
    show
The path to any lost, they loved their own mad music so;

Who were not ever merciful, who were not ever wise,
Whose hearts were all too light for Hell, too hard for Para-
    dise!

(*But when their bows went dancing high above the mocking
    strings
The grave forgot their worldliness, the good forgot their
    wings,*

*And all the world went footing it, the evil and the kind,
Until the fiddlers went their way without a look behind!*)

The winds that blow from Paradise bring sound of feast and
    song,
The winds that blow from Hell are sharp and heavy-weighed
    with wrong,

The Faëry winds bring lilting light, with tinkling bells
    between,
And all the winds of every land blow over Fiddlers' Green:

And when they hear the Elfland bells, a little then they
    grieve
For the fair towers of Faëryland that they may not believe,

And when they hear the weeping wind that wails from out
    of Hell
They laugh because of agonies they have escaped so well,

But when the harps of Paradise strike loud upon their ear
They play their fiddles high and sweet, that they may never
    hear.

Oh, still there play on Fiddlers' Green a many that we
    know —
We fare to Heaven or Hell, who loved their mocking music
    so,

And as we mount the stony hill or run the lilied way
Still from their little wayward path the mocking echoes
  play . . . .

(*They were not ever merciful; they were not ever wise;
Their hearts were all too light for Hell, too hard for Paradise. . . .*)

Oh, even from the gates of Heaven the blessed souls may
  lean
To hear the careless violins lilt up from Fiddlers' Green!

Margaret Widdemer

STARS [2]

Alone in the night
  On a dark hill
With pines around me
  Spicy and still,

And a heaven full of stars
  Over my head,
White and topaz
  And misty red;

Myriads with beating
  Hearts of fire
That aeons
  Cannot vex or tire;

Up the dome of heaven
  Like a great hill,
I watch them marching
  Stately and still,

And I know that I
  Am honored to be
Witness
  Of so much majesty.

Sara Teasdale

[2] From *Flame and Shadow* by Sara Teasdale. Reprinted by special arrangement with The Macmillan Company, Publishers.

TRIOLET

The night is full of the crying
Of dreams that will not die, —
Deathless and time defying, —
The night is full of the crying
Of restless phantoms flying
Mysteriously by.
The night is full of the crying
Of dreams that will not die.

A. K. Laing

FOG

What grave has cracked and let this frail thing out,
To press its poor face to the window-pane;
Or, head hid in frayed cloak, to drift about
The mallow bush, then out to the wet lane?
Long-closeted scents across the drippings break,
Of violet petunias blowing there,
A shred of mint, mixed with whatever ache
Old springs have left behind wedged tight in air.
Small, agèd things peer in, ready to slip
Into the chairs, and watch and stare apace;
The house has loosened from its grasp of yore
Dark-horded tales.   Were I, finger on lip,
To climb the stair, might I not find the place
Turned all to huddled shape, white on the floor?

Lizette Woodworth Reese

EVENING

The light passes
from ridge to ridge,
from flower to flower —
the hypaticas, wide-spread
under the light
grow faint —

the petals reach inward,
the blue tips bend
toward the bluer heart
and the flowers are lost.

The cornel-buds are still white,
but shadows dart
from the cornel-roots —
black creeps from root to root,
each leaf
cuts another leaf on the grass,
shadow seeks shadow,
then both leaf
and leaf-shadow are lost.

" H. D."

LULLABY FOR A MAN–CHILD

The mountains waver through my tears,
Hush, my son —
The trees are bending at the knees
Like women broken by the years.
But you, my child, need have no fears;
Only for Woman, love has spears.
Sleep, my son.

So cuddle closer to my heart.
Dream, my son —
'Tis strange to think that you find peace
Here, where all stormy passions start.
But you need fear no ache or smart —
The pain is always woman's part.
Sleep, my son.

Jean Starr Untermeyer

BOY AND TADPOLES

I

He brought them from the muddy creek
  And clapped them in this glassy sphere;
He studies them but does not speak
  While they flash by and disappear.
They curve and veer, they swerve and roll,
  A world of brown and yellow gleams —
Six tadpoles in a green glass bowl. . . .
  He watches them — and dreams:

Black water and a burnished moon.
What ship is that in the dark lagoon?
Over an oily sea she slips
And drips a phosphorescent spray.
One hears the rattle of dice at play
The cheers and clatter of drunken quips
And thick lips roaring a ribald tune.
Her sides are gashed and pitted and scarred
And marred with slashes of brilliant rust. . . .
Is it blood that glows like an evil crust?
Or mud that has grown like a stone, fixed hard
On this ill-starred vessel of loot and lust?

What's that? That spot on the faint horizon?
They glue their eyes on the tossing dot.
It crosses the moon like a curious blot
While furious cries of " Blast 'em! " and " Pizen! "
Reveal that the missing prize has been sought for
And soon will be caught, for the little speck,
Towering in size, turns round the neck
Of forbidden land with its hidden ship;
Pauses, inquires — and fires a shot!
Crash! There's the clash of cutlass and sword.
Gun barrels flash on the swarming deck.
The storming-party surges aboard.

A hot wind scourges; the bullets whip
The figures that stumble in blood that is poured
In a tumbling flood through the crumbling night
And stains the white dawn with a hideous light.

Ripples of dappled crimson and brown
Show where the sloops have grappled and split.
Here's where *The Royal Ben* went down;
And there, ten yards to the right of it,
The Black Avenger, full to the guards,
Riding the track of a lone disgrace,
Sank in her own dank hiding-place.
Nothing's afloat but the broken shards,
A boat and an oaken beam or two. . . .
What of the captain?   What of the crew?
Go, ask the sharks in the dark and bloody
Depths where the clean green tides turn muddy.
Ask of those bloated bellies that veer
In the muddy welter that shelters them all.
Ask, as they plash their watery wall,
Before they flash and disappear,
And dwindle . . . and shrink . . . and sink to their
      hole . . .
And change to . . . little things . . . with gleams,
Describing rings as they roll . . . and pass. . . .
Six tadpoles in a green glass bowl —
He watches them and dreams. . . .

II

A sea of lapis lazuli,
With casual sunbeams lacing gold
On light skiffs facing the west, on old
Bright cliffs that rise from some mythical story,
On clouds that rest on the promontory,
On waves that reach white arms to the beach.
Sparkle and shimmer . . . glimmer and shine. . . .
The sea grows dimmer . . . and darkens . . . like wine.

Who is that swimmer, untiring, returning,
Churning the brine?
Is it Leander . . . that daring boy?
Those skiffs . . . Agamemnon's? That cliff . . . is it
    Troy?
A glow of sea-faring, home-yearning faces
Flares like a torch through these burning spaces.
The sea is turning a livelier hue.
Pools of the sun are gold oases
On a sweeping plain of purple and blue.
And — leap and curve — and swerve and flicker —
And — dip and swirl — with a flip of the tail
The dolphins, coming faster, thicker,
Dive through the alabaster foam.
Under a sapphire dome they sail
And scale the breakers that drive them home.

But some more stately and corpulent fishes
Move sedately, as though suspicious
Of these young friskers; their weedy whiskers
Lie in a wry disapprobation
Of such spry methods of navigation.
They wag their heads in a solemn gesture —
And still the column moves, a nation
Of dapper fins and swishing flappers.

But what is advancing in radiant vesture?
A mock sun dancing, it floats along!
Notes of a song: low, gradient cries
Rise from the image — or is it a god
Come to revisit the haunts of his youth.
Fable or truth — can the boy trust his eyes? —
There, with bright hair, like a tossing fire
Crossing the sunset, a Shape with a lyre
Calls to the tides . . . where no being has trod!
He guides his strange courser with never a rein;
And spurring the jeweled sides of a slender
Dolphin that glides on this rollicking lane,

Apollo rides in his antique splendor!
The sea has become a dazzling rout: —
Sea-urchins hum and the great tides shout.
Star-fish sing in their shining courses.
Sea-horses whinny and gild their manes.
Thrilled by these strains to its finny sources,
Ocean strikes off its ancient chains;
And, from its rivers and hurricanes,
Strains and delivers its cherished dead.
Perished adventurers, sailors and mariners,
Clean-shaven natives and thick-bearded foreigners —
Up from the graves with a mountainous tread,
Roll out the staves of their chanteys and calls.

Evening falls . . . but the revel continues.
An ivory moon crawls down and whitens
The backs of Tritons and bathes their sinews.
Here in this amorous, glamorous weather,
Mermaids and pirates whisper together. . . .

And, during it all, the dolphins are leaping,
Sweeping their silver-tipped tails in a sway
Of rhythms so gay that they play without sleeping;
Dancing and dipping, glancing and flipping
Sparks from the arcs they describe in the spray.
Mirth that is bounded by nothing but clear
Earth, sea and sky in a high, hollow sphere.
Spirit-surrounded, with tingling elation,
The green shuttles fly and a subtle persuasion,
A magic, half-Asian, invites him away. . . .
As over his scarce lifted eyelids there streams
A dim, shifting blur of disaster and drifting,
Of blood flowing faster, of livelier measures . . .
Of treasures . . . and time . . . and secret veils lifting
And heroes . . . and tadpoles . . . and dreams.

Louis Untermeyer

There, in the night, where none can spy,
All in my hunter's camp I lie,
And play at books that I have read
Till it is time to go to bed.

These are the hills, these are the woods,
These are my starry solitudes;
And there the river by whose brink
The roaring lions come to drink.

— ROBERT LOUIS STEVENSON

MANDALAY

By the old Moulmein Pagoda, lookin' eastward to the sea,
There's a Burma girl a-settin', an' I know she thinks o' me:
For the wind is in the palm-trees, an' the temple-bells they
    say:
" Come you back, you British soldier; come you back to
    Mandalay!
  Come you back to Mandalay,
  Where the old Flotilla lay:
  Can't you 'ear their paddles chunkin' from Rangoon to
    Mandalay?
  On the road to Mandalay,
  Where the flyin'-fishes play,
  An' the dawn comes up like thunder outer China 'crost
    the Bay!

'Er petticut was yaller an' 'er little cap was green,
An' 'er name was Supi-yaw-lat — jes' the same as Thee-
  baw's Queen,
An' I seed her fust a-smokin' of a whackin' white cheroot,
An' a-wastin' Christian kisses on an 'eathen idol's foot:

Bloomin' idol made o' mud —
Wot they called the Great Gawd Budd —
Plucky lot she cared for idols when I kissed 'er where
she stud!
On the road to Mandalay —

When the mist was on the rice-fields an' the sun was drop-
pin' slow,
She'd git 'er little banjo an' she'd sing " *Kulla-lo-lo!* "
With 'er arm upon my shoulder an' her cheek agin my cheek
We useter watch the steamers an' the *hathis* [1] pilin' teak.
Elephints a-pilin' teak,
In the sludgy, squdgy creek,
Where the silence 'ung that 'eavy you was 'arf afraid to
speak!
On the road to Mandalay —

But that's all shove be'ind me — long ago an' fur away,
An' there ain't no 'buses runnin' from the Bank to Man-
dalay;
An' I'm learnin' 'ere in London what the ten-year sodger [2]
tells:
" If you've 'eard the East a-callin', why, you won't 'eed
nothin' else."
No! you won't 'eed nothin' else
But them spicy garlic smells
An' the sunshine an' the palm-trees an' the tinkly temple-
bells!
On the road to Mandalay —

I am sick o' wastin' leather on these gritty pavin' stones,
An' the blasted Henglish drizzle wakes the fever in my
bones;
Tho' I walks with fifty 'ousemaids outer Chelsea to the
Strand,

[1] *hathis* = elephants (see *The Jungle Book*).
[2] *sodger* = Tommy Atkins' way of pronouncing "soldier."

An' they talks a lot o' lovin', but wot do they understand?
  Beefy face an' grubby 'and —
  Law! wot *do* they understand?
  I've a neater, sweeter maiden in a cleaner, greener land!
  On the road to Mandalay —

Ship me somewheres east of Suez where the best is like the
      worst,
Where there aren't no Ten Commandments, an' a man can
      raise a thirst;
For the temple-bells are callin', an' it's there that I would
      be —
By the old Moulmein Pagoda, looking lazy at the sea —
  On the road to Mandalay,
  Where the old Flotilla lay,
  With our sick beneath the awnings when we went to
      Mandalay!
  Oh, the road to Mandalay,
  Where the flyin'-fishes play,
  An' the dawn comes up like thunder outer China 'crost
      the Bay!

                                        Rudyard Kipling

" FUZZY–WUZZY "
(*Soudan Expeditionary Force*)

We've fought with many men acrost the seas,
    An' some of 'em was brave an' some was not:
The Paythan an' the Zulu an' Burmese;
    But the Fuzzy was the finest o' the lot.
We never got a ha'porth's [3] change of 'im:
    'E squatted in the scrub an' 'ocked our 'orses,
'E cut our sentries up at Sua*kim*,
    An' 'e played the cat an' banjo [4] with our forces.

---

[3] *ha'porth's* = half-penny's worth. In other words, the British soldier
humorously admits he rarely got the better of the native, crudely armed troops
of the Soudan.
[4] *played the cat and banjo* = a piece of Tommy Atkins' slang equivalent to
"played the devil."

So 'ere's *to* you, Fuzzy-Wuzzy, at your 'ome in the
    Sowdan;
You're a pore benighted 'eathen but a first-class fightin'
    man;
We give you your certifikit, an' if you want it signed
We'll come an' 'ave a romp with you whenever you're
    inclined.

We took our chanst among the Kyber 'ills,
    The Boers knocked us silly at a mile,
The Burman guv us Irriwaddy chills,
    An' a Zulu *impi* dished us up in style:
But all we ever got from such as they
    Was pop [5] to what the Fuzzy made us swaller;
We 'eld our bloomin' own, the papers say,
    But man for man the Fuzzy knocked us 'oller.

Then 'ere's *to* you, Fuzzy-Wuzzy, an' the missis and
    the kid;
Our orders was to break you, an' of course we went
    an' did.
We sloshed you with Martinis,[6] an' it wasn't 'ardly
    fair;
But for all the odds agin you, Fuzzy-Wuzz, you bruk
    the square.

'E 'asn't got no papers of 'is own,
    'E 'asn't got no medals nor rewards,
So we must certify the skill 'e's shown
    In usin' of 'is long two-'anded swords:
When 'e's 'oppin' in an' out among the bush
    With 'is coffin-'eaded shield an' shovel-spear,
A 'appy day with Fuzzy on the rush
    Will last a 'ealthy Tommy for a year!

[5] *was pop* = was as easy as drinking soda-water.
[6] *Martinis* = the rapid-firing rifles used by the British infantry

So 'ere's *to* you, Fuzzy-Wuzzy, an' your friends which
    is no more,
If we 'adn't lost some messmates we would 'elp you to
    deplore;
But give an' take's the gospel, an' we'll call the bargain
    fair,
For if you 'ave lost more than us, you crumpled up
    the square!

'E rushes at the smoke when we let drive,
  An', before we know, 'e's 'ackin' at our 'ead;
'E's all 'ot sand an' ginger when alive,
  An' 'e's generally shammin' when 'e's dead.
'E's a daisy, 'e's a ducky, 'e's a lamb!
  'E's a injia-rubber idiot on the spree,
'E's the on'y thing that doesn't care a damn
  For a Regiment o' British Infantree.

    So 'ere's *to* you, Fuzzy-Wuzzy, at your 'ome in the
        Sowdan;
    You're a pore benighted 'eathen but a first-class fightin'
        man;
    An' 'ere's *to* you, Fuzzy-Wuzzy, with your 'ayrick [7]
        'ead of 'air —
    You big black boundin' beggar — for you bruk a
        British square.

                        Rudyard Kipling

THE BALLAD OF THE HARP–WEAVER [8]

    " Son," said my mother,
      When I was knee-high,
    " You've need of clothes to cover you,
      And not a rag have I.

---

[7] *'ayrick* = hayrick-shaped.
[8] From *The Harp-Weaver and Other Poems*, published by Harper & Brothers.
Copyright 1920, 1921, 1922, 1923 by Edna St. Vincent Millay.

" There's nothing in the house
   To make a boy breeches,
No shears to cut a cloth with
   Nor thread to take stitches.

" There's nothing in the house
   But a loaf-end of rye,
And a harp with a woman's head
   Nobody will buy,"
     And she began to cry.

That was in the early fall.
   When came the late fall,
" Son," she said, " the sight of you
   Makes your mother's blood crawl, —

" Little skinny shoulder-blades
   Sticking through your clothes!
And where you'll get a jacket from
   God above knows.

" It's lucky for me, lad,
   Your daddy's in the ground,
And can't see the way I let
   His son go around! "
     And she made a queer sound.

That was in the late fall.
   When the winter came,
I'd not a pair of breeches
   Nor a shirt to my name.

I couldn't go to school,
   Or out of doors to play.
And all the other little boys
   Passed our way.

" Son," said my mother,
  " Come, climb into my lap,
And I'll chafe your little bones
  While you take a nap."

And, oh, but we were silly
  For half an hour or more,
Me with my long legs
  Dragging on the floor,

A-rock-rock-rocking
  To a mother-goose rhyme!
Oh, but we were happy
  For a half an hour's time!

But there was I, a great boy,
  And what would folks say
To hear my mother singing me
  To sleep all day,
    In such a daft way?

Men say the winter
  Was bad that year;
Fuel was scarce,
  And food was dear.

A wind with a wolf's head
  Howled about our door,
And we burned up the chairs
  And sat upon the floor.

All that was left us
  Was a chair we couldn't break,
And the harp with a woman's head
  Nobody would take,
    For song or pity's sake.

The night before Christmas
　　I cried with the cold,
I cried myself to sleep
　　Like a two-year-old.

And in the deep night
　　I felt my mother rise,
And stare down upon me
　　With love in her eyes.

I saw my mother sitting
　　On the one good chair,
A light falling on her
　　From I couldn't tell where,

Looking nineteen,
　　And not a day older,
And the harp with a woman's head
　　Leaned against her shoulder.

Her thin fingers, moving
　　In the thin, tall strings,
Were weav-weav-weaving
　　Wonderful things.

Many bright threads,
　　From where I couldn't see,
Were running through the harp-strings
　　Rapidly,

And gold threads whistling
　　Through my mother's hand,
I saw the web grow,
　　And the pattern expand.

She wove a child's jacket,
　　And when it was done
She laid it on the floor
　　And wove another one.

She wove a red cloak
  So regal to see,
" She's made it for a king's son,"
  I said, " and not for me."
  But I knew it was for me.

She wove a pair of breeches
  Quicker than that!
She wove a pair of boots
  And a little cocked hat.

She wove a pair of mittens,
  She wove a little blouse,
She wove all night
  In the still, cold house.

She sang as she worked,
  And the harp-strings spoke;
Her voice never faltered,
  And the thread never broke.
  And when I awoke, —

There sat my mother
  With the harp against her shoulder,
Looking nineteen
  And not a day older,

A smile about her lips,
  And a light about her head,
And her hands in the harp-strings
  Frozen dead.

And piled up beside her
  And toppling to the skies,
Were the clothes of a king's son,
  Just my size.

            Edna St. Vincent Millay

THE BALLAD OF THE BATTLE OF GIBEON

Five kings rule o'er the Amorite,
Mighty as fear and old as night;
Swarthed with unguent and gold and jewel,
Waxed they merry and fat and cruel.
Zedek of Salem, a terror and glory,
Whose face was hid while his robes were gory;
And Hoham of Hebron, whose loathly face is
Heavy and dark o'er the ruin of races;
And Priam of Jarmuth, drunk with strange wine,
Who dreamed he had fashioned all stars that shine;
And Debir of Eglon wild, without pity,
Who raged like a plague in the midst of his city;
And Japhia of Lachish, a fire that flameth,
Who did in the daylight what no man nameth.

These five kings said one to another,
' King unto king o'er the world is brother,
Seeing that now, for a sign and a wonder,
A red eclipse and a tongue of thunder,
A shape and a finger of desolation,
Is come against us a kingless nation.
Gibeon hath failed us: it were not good
That a man remember where Gibeon stood.'
Then Gibeon sent to our captain, crying,
' Son of Nun, let a shaft be flying,
For unclean birds are gathering greedily;
Slack not thy hand, but come thou speedily.
Yea, we are lost save thou maintain'st us,
For the kings of the mountains are gathered against us.'

Then to our people spake the Deliverer,
' Gibeon is high, yet a host may shiver her;
Gibeon hath sent to me crying for pity,
For the lords of the cities encompass the city

With chariot and banner and bowman and lancer,
And I swear by the living God I will answer.
Gird you, O Israel, quiver and javelin,
Shield and sword for the road we travel in;
Verily, as I have promised, pay I
Life unto Gibeon, death unto Ai.'

Sudden and still as a bolt shot right
Up on the city we went by night.
Never a bird of the air could say,
' This was the children of Israel's way.'
Only the hosts sprang up from sleeping,
Saw from the heights a dark stream sweeping;
Sprang up as straight as a great shout stung them,
And heard the Deliverer's war-cry among them,
Heard under cupola, turret, and steeple
The awful cry of the kingless people.
Started the weak of them, shouted the strong of them,
Crashed we a thunderbolt into the throng of them,
Blindly with heads bent, and shields forced before us,
We heard the dense roar of the strife closing o'er us.
And drunk with the crash of the song that it sung them,
We drove the great spear-blade in God's name among them.

Redder and redder the sword-flash fell,
Our eyes and our nostrils were hotter than hell;
Till full all the crest of the spear-surge shocking us,
Hoham of Hebron cried out mocking us,
' Nay, what need of the war-sword's plying,
Out of the desert the dust comes flying,
A little red dust, if the wind be blowing —
Who shall reck of its coming or going? '
Back the Deliverer spake as a clarion,
' Mock at thy slaves, thou eater of carrion!
Laughest thou at us, in thy kingly clowning,
We, that laughed upon Rameses frowning,
We that stood up, proud, unpardoned,
When his face was dark and his heart was hardened?

Pharaoh we knew and his steeds, not faster
Than the word of the Lord in thine ear, O master.'
Sheer through the turban his wantons wove him,
Clean to the skull the Deliverer clove him;
And the two hosts reeled at the sign appalling,
As the great king fell like a great house falling.

Loudly we shouted, and living and dying,
Bore them all backward with strength and strong crying;
The war-swords and axes were clashing and groaning,
The fallen were fighting and foaming and moaning,
The war-spears were breaking, the war-horns were braying,
Ere the hands of the slayers were sated with slaying.
And deep in the grasses grown gory and sodden,
The treaders of all men were trampled and trodden;
And over them, routed and reeled like cattle,
High over the turn of the tide of the battle,
High over noises that deafen and cover us,
Rang the Deliverer's voice out over us.

' Stand thou still, thou sun upon Gibeon,
Stand thou, moon, in the valley of Ajalon!
Shout thou, people, a cry like thunder,
For the kings of the earth are broken asunder.
Now we have said as the thunder says it,
Something is stronger than strength and slays it.
Now we have written for all time later,
Five kings are great, yet a law is greater.
Stare, O sun! in thine own great glory,
This is the turn of the whole world's story.
Stand thou still, thou sun upon Gibeon,
Stand thou, moon, in the valley of Ajalon!

' Smite! amid spear-blades blazing and breaking,
More than we know of is rising and making.
Stab with the javelin, crash with the car!
Cry! for we know not the thing that we are.

Stand, O sun! that in horrible patience
Smiled on the smoke and the slaughter of nations.
Stand thou still, thou sun upon Gibeon,
Stand thou, moon in the valley of Ajalon! '

After the battle was broken and spent
Up to the hill the Deliverer went,
Flung up his arms to the storm-clouds flying,
And cried unto Israel, mightily crying,
' Come up, O warriors! come up, O brothers!
Tribesmen and herdsmen, maidens and mothers;
The bondsman's son and the bondsman's daughter,
The hewer of wood and the drawer of water,
He that carries and he that brings,
And set your foot on the neck of kings.'

This is the story of Gibeon fight —
Where we smote the lords of the Amorite;
Where the banners of princes with slaughter were sodden,
And the beards of seers in the rank grass trodden;
Where the trees were wrecked by the wreck of cars,
And the reek of the red field blotted the stars;
Where the dead heads dropped from the swords that sever,
Because His mercy endureth for ever.

G. K. Chesterton

THE TRUE STORY OF SKIPPER IRESON [9]

Here's Flood Ireson, for his hard heart
Tarr'd and feather'd and carried in a cart
By the women of Marblehead!

—Old Song.

I

Out of the fog and the gloom,
  Chased by the lift of the sea,
Dripping with spindrift and spume
  Races the *Betty*, free.

---

[9] This is a modern sequel to the poem by Whittier on page 73.

Hold-full of cod to the planks,
   Staggering under her spread —
Never such luck from the banks
   Sailed into Marblehead!

Full — keep her full!   Drown her rail —
   Lee-decks [10] awash to the hatch!
While the rest ride out the gale,
   Flood Ireson's home with his catch!
Cape Cod abeam to the south'ard —
   Up sprang the skipper on deck:
What was that hail the wind smothered?
   " Wreck, O — to port, there — a wreck! "

Logged, and awash in the sea,
   Ready to sink by the head —
" Looks like the *Active* to me —
   Stand by those head sheets! " he said;
" Keep your helm up all you can —
   We'll round-to and bring her to weather [11]
Keep her away, I said, man!
   Are you all mad there, together?

" God, men! — " He stopped on the word,
   Sullen his crew stood, and grim;
Never a man of them stirred,
   Save as if guarding from him
Halyard and sheet; so he stood,
   One man against the whole ship —
Skipper?   Ay —what was the good?
   Greed was the captain this trip!

Order, when none would obey?
   Threaten?   'Twas idle, he knew;
Reason?   Ay — argue and pray
   And plead with a mutinied crew!

[10] lee-decks = the protected decks, away from the wind.
[11] to weather = toward the wind.

" Look at her signals! " he said: —
    " Stand by her!   Shall it go down
That seamen of old Marblehead
    Left sinking shipmates to drown? "

" Ay! " growled the mate: — " and by God,
    What if a story were told
How the year's best catch of cod
    Rotted and spoiled in our hold?
Risk such a catch as we've got?
    No! . . .   Let them chance it! " said he: —
" Sink or swim . . . that is the lot
    Of all men who follow the sea! "

Heartsick, Flood Ireson sailed past,
    Helpless to answer their hail.
Deaf as the shriek of the blast,
    Blind as the scud of the gale,
Lee-decks awash to the hatch,
    Tearing her way through the foam —
Blood of men's lives on her catch,
    On drove the *Betty* for home.

II

The day was cool; white-crested ripples sung
    Along the beach, and all the sky was clear
When, safe into the quiet harbor, swung
    The *Betty*, gliding smoothly to her pier.

First of the fleet, and welcome as the day —
    A little fortune in her close-filled hold —
Why did her crew, then, seem to turn away
    From friendly greetings?   Ireson, too, of old
Kindly of heart, whose brave words often cheered
    The poor home-comings of an empty trip —
Why was it he himself had not appeared,
    But sent his crew ashore, and kept his ship?

Then, bit by bit, was forged a black report;
    From mouth to mouth the cruel story spread,
And murmurs rose — till, sailing into port
    Like some accuser risen from the dead,

The rescued skipper of the *Active* came,
    And told the angry gossips of the town
How skipper Ireson, to their lasting shame,
    Heedless of signals, left him to go down.

" Heedless of love of man or laws of God,
    Or all the brave old honor of the sea,
He sold us, shipmates, for a mess of cod —
    And Marblehead shall bear the shame! " said he.

" He left us — and before the *Swallow* came
    Four of my men were washed away. The dead
Shall haunt your cape, to cry Flood Ireson shame —
    The whole world know the shame of Marblehead! "

Then strong men, cursing, swore to purge the town
    Of such dishonor; smarting with disgrace,
They dragged Flood Ireson, unresisting, down
    And stripped him in the public market-place.

The rest you know — the tar-and-feather coat,
    The shameful ride they gave him, dragged with jeers
To Salem village, in a fishing-boat —
    The cruel, lying song that lived for years.

And all he bore, thinking it best the shame
    Should cling to one man, though that man were he
If that would save the honorable name
    Of Marblehead, and of her sons at sea.

III

So Ireson won the day, and no one hears
    His crew's disgrace. Their very names are lost,
While he has borne the blame through all these years
    And paid the cost.

All they are gone who wronged him — some asleep
   In quiet graveyards, others roving free
Till God shall call by name from out the deep
   Those lost at sea.

For that was all a hundred years ago;
   Long is Flood Ireson's rest among the dead;
But still the fishing-schooners come and go
   At Marblehead.

And those who sailed them have been true and brave —
   Heroes of surf and rescue, storm and wreck,
Gone, unafraid, to death on shore and wave
   And battle-deck.

Then let the blood and seas blot out the wrong
   Done long ago; we will not judge the dead,
But lay our laurel wreath where thorns pressed long
   On Ireson's head.

Charles Buxton Going

THE HIGHWAYMAN

Part One

The wind was a torrent of darkness among the gusty trees,
The moon was a ghostly galleon tossed upon cloudy seas,
The road was a ribbon of moonlight over the purple moor,
And the highwayman came riding —
   Riding — riding —
The highwayman came riding, up to the old inn-door.

He'd a French cocked-hat on his forehead, a bunch of lace
   at his chin,
A coat of the claret velvet, and breeches of brown doe-
   skin;

They fitted with never a wrinkle: his boots were up to the
    thigh!
And he rode with a jeweled twinkle,
  His pistol butts a-twinkle,
His rapier hilt a-twinkle, under the jeweled sky.

Over the cobbles he clattered and clashed in the dark inn-
    yard,
And he tapped with his whip on the shutters, but all was
    locked and barred;
He whistled a tune to the window, and who should be wait-
    ing there
But the landlord's black-eyed daughter,
  Bess, the landlord's daughter,
Plaiting a dark red love-knot into her long black hair.

And dark in the dark old inn-yard a stable-wicket creaked
Where Tim the ostler [12] listened; his face was white and
    peaked;
His eyes were hollows of madness, his hair like mouldy hay,
But he loved the landlord's daughter,
  The landlord's red-lipped daughter,
Dumb as a dog he listened, and he heard the robber say —

"One kiss, my bonny sweetheart, I'm after a prize to-
    night,
But I shall be back with the yellow gold before the morning
    light;
Yet, if they press me sharply, and harry me through the
    day,
Then look for me by moonlight,
  Watch for me by moonlight,
I'll come to thee by moonlight, though hell should bar the
    way."

[12] ostler = the groom, the man who looks after the horses.

He rose upright in the stirrups; he scarce could reach her
    hand,
But she loosened her hair i' the casement! His face burnt
    like a brand
As the black cascade of perfume came tumbling over his
    breast;
And he kissed its waves in the moonlight,
  (Oh, sweet black waves in the moonlight!)
Then he tugged at his rein in the moonlight, and galloped
    away to the West.

Part Two

He did not come in the dawning; he did not come at noon;
And out o' the tawny sunset, before the rise o' the moon,
When the road was a gipsy's ribbon, looping the purple
    moor,
A red-coat troop came marching —
  Marching — marching —
King George's men came marching, up to the old inn-door.

They said no word to the landlord, they drank his ale in-
    stead,
But they gagged his daughter and bound her to the foot of
    her narrow bed;
Two of them knelt at her casement, with muskets at their
    side!
There was death at every window;
  And hell at one dark window;
For Bess could see, through her casement, the road that *he*
    would ride.

They had tied her up to attention, with many a sniggering
    jest;
They had bound a musket beside her, with the barrel be-
    neath her breast!

" Now keep good watch! " and they kissed her.
  She heard the dead man say —
Look for me by moonlight;
  Watch for me by moonlight;
I'll come to thee by moonlight, though hell should bar the
    way!

She twisted her hands behind her; but all the knots held
    good!
She writhed her hands till her fingers were wet with sweat
    or blood!
They stretched and strained in the darkness, and the hours
    crawled by like years,
Till, now, on the stroke of midnight,
  Cold, on the stroke of midnight,
The tip of one finger touched it! The trigger at least was
    hers!

The tip of one finger touched it; she strove no more for the
    rest!
Up, she stood up to attention, with the barrel beneath her
    breast,
She would not risk their hearing; she would not strive
    again;
For the road lay bare in the moonlight;
  Blank and bare in the moonlight;
And the blood of her veins in the moonlight throbbed to
    her love's refrain.

Tlot-tlot; tlot-tlot! Had they heard it? The horse-hoofs
    ringing clear;
Tlot-tlot, tlot-tlot, in the distance? Were they deaf that
    they did not hear?
Down the ribbon of moonlight, over the brow of the hill,
The highwayman came riding,
  Riding, riding!
The red-coats looked to their priming! She stood up,
    straight and still!

Tlot-tlot, in the frosty silence! *Tlot-tlot*, in the echoing
    night!
Nearer he came and nearer! Her face was like a light!
Her eyes grew wide for a moment; she drew one last deep
    breath,
Then her finger moved in the moonlight,
  Her musket shattered the moonlight,
Shattered her breast in the moonlight and warned him —
    with her death.

He turned; he spurred to the West; he did not know who
    stood
Bowed, with her head o'er the musket, drenched with her
    own red blood!
Not till the dawn he heard it, his face grew grey to hear
How Bess, the landlord's daughter,
  The landlord's black-eyed daughter,
Had watched for her love in the moonlight, and died in the
    darkness there.

Back, he spurred like a madman, shrieking a curse to the
    sky,
With the white road smoking behind him and his rapier
    brandished high!
Blood-red were his spurs i' the golden noon: wine-red was his
    velvet coat,
When they shot him down on the highway,
  Down like a dog in the highway,
And he lay in his blood on the highway, with the bunch of
    lace at his throat.

      *   *   *   *   *   *

And still of a winter's night, they say, when the wind is in
    the trees,
When the moon is a ghostly galleon tossed upon cloudy
    seas,

When the road is a ribbon of moonlight over the purple
    moor,
A highwayman comes riding —
    Riding — riding —
A highwayman comes riding, up to the old inn-door.

Over the cobbles he clatters and clangs in the dark inn-
    yard;
He taps with his whip on the shutters, but all is locked and
    barred;
He whistles a tune to the window, and who should be wait-
    ing there
But the landlord's black-eyed daughter,
    Bess, the landlord's daughter,
Plaiting a dark red love-knot into her long black hair.

Alfred Noyes

THE SWINGING STAIR

From the flotsam of a city street we built the Swinging
    Stair,
And latitude, or longitude, the least of all our care.

A tilting board — an orange crate — the sparrows screamed
    with glee,
As we swung to port and starboard like a lugger on the sea.

We cruised without a compass, but with merchandise of
    worth,
To barter pins and needles at the portals of the Earth.

The helmsman was my hero brave, his hair as red could be;
Perhaps he *was* the janitor's boy, but he belonged to me!

He was mine because I made him master of the Swinging
    Stair,
And because I liked the color of his very auburn hair.

The surf upon the sandbars called the price of sugar
    cane:
It was mounting every moment down upon the Spanish
    Main.

The trades were in the topsails, in the scuppers raced the
    foam,
But never did we get beyond the gateway of our home.

We have notions that the motions of a lugger 'neath a
    tree
Do not exactly tally with the leagues she makes at sea;

Yet the glory of the ocean lies in no far distant goal,
But reflections in the water, and the port to starboard roll.

Nathalia Crane

AN ANTE–BELLUM SERMON

We is gathered hyeah, my brothahs,
    In dis howlin' wildaness,
Fu' to speak some words of comfo't
    To each othah in distress.
An' we chooses fu' ouah subjic'
    Dis — we'll 'splain it by an' by:
" An' de Lawd said, ' Moses, Moses,'
    An' de man said, ' Hyeah am I.' "

Now ole Pher'oh, down in Egypt,
    Was de wuss man evah bo'n,
An' he had de Hebrew chillun
    Down dah wukin' in his co'n;
'Twell de Lawd got tiahed o' his foolin',
    An' sez He: " I'll let him know —
Look hyeah, Moses, go tell Pher'oh
    Fu' to let dem chillun go.

" An' ef he refuse to do it,
    I will make him rue de houah,
Fu' I'll empty down on Egypt
    All de vials of my powah."
Yes, He did — an' Pher'oh's ahmy
    Wasn't wuth a ha'f a dime;
Fu' de Lawd will he'p his chillun,
    You kin trust Him evah time.

An' yo' enemies may 'sail you
    In de back an' in de front;
But de Lawd is all aroun' you,
    Fu' to ba' de battle's brunt.
Dey kin fo'ge yo' chains an' shackles
    F'om de mountains to de sea;
But de Lawd will sen' some Moses
    Fu' to set His chillun free.

An' de lan' shall hyeah his thundah,
    Lak a blas' f'om Gab'el's ho'n,
Fu' de Lawd of hosts is mighty
    When He girds His ahmor on.
But fu' feah some one mistakes me,
    I will pause right hyeah to say,
Dat I'm still a-preaching ancient,
    I ain't talkin' 'bout to-day.

But I tell you, fellah Christiuns,
    Things'll happen mighty strange;
Now, de Lawd done dis fu' Isrul,
    An' His ways don't nevah change.
An' de love He showed to Isrul
    Wasn't all on Isrul spent;
Now don't run an' tell yo' mastahs
    Dat I'se preachin' discontent.

'Cause I isn't; I'se a-judgin'
  Bible people by deir ac's;
I'se a-givin' you de Scriptuah,
  I'se a-handin' you de fac's.
Cose ole Pher'oh b'lieved in slav'ry,
  But de Lawd He let him see,
Dat de people He put bref in, —
  Evah mothah's son was free.

An' dahs othahs thinks lak Pher'oh,
  But dey calls de Scriptuah liar,
Fu' de Bible says " a servant
  Is a-worthy of his hire."
An' you cain't git roun' nor thoo dat,
  An' you cain't git ovah it,
Fu' whatevah place you git in,
  Dis hyeah Bible too'll fit.

So you see de Lawd's intention,
  Evah sence de worl' began,
Was dat His almighty freedom
  Should belong to evah man,
But I think it would be bettah,
  Ef I'd pause agin to say,
Dat I'm talkin' 'bout ouah freedom
  In a *Bibleistic* way.

But de Moses is a-comin',
  An' he's comin', suah and fas'
We kin hyeah his feet a-trompin',
  We kin hyeah his trumpit blas'.
But I want to wa'n you people,
  Don't you talk too mightily
An' don't you git to braggin'
  'Bout dese things — you wait an' see.

But when Moses wif his powah
    Comes an' sets us chillun free,
We will praise de gracious Mastah
    Dat has gin us liberty;
An' we'll shout ouah halleluyahs,
    On dat mighty reck'nin' day,
When we'se reco'nised ez citiz'—
    Huh uh!   Chillun, let us pray!

Paul Laurence Dunbar

DA LEETLA BOY

Da spreeng ees com'; but O! da joy
    Eet ees too late!
He was so cold, my leetla boy,
    He no could wait.

I no can count how many week,
How many day, dat he ees seeck;
How many night I seet an' hold
Da leetla hand dat was so cold.
He was so patience, O! so sweet!
Eet hurt my throat for theenk of eet;
An' all he evra ask ees w'en
Ees gona com' da spreeng agen.
Wan day, wan brighta sunny day,
He see, across da alleyway,
Da leetla girl dat's livin' dere
Ees raise her window for da air,
An' put outside a leetla pot
Of — w'at-you-call? — forgat-me-not.
So smalla flower, so leetla theeng!
But steell eet mak' hees hearta sing:
" O! now, at las', ees com' da spreeng!
Da leetla plant ees glad for know
Da sun ees com' for mak' eet grow.

So, too, I am grow warm and strong."
So, lika dat he seeng hees song.
But, ah! da night com' down an' den
Da weenter ees sneak back agen,
An' een da alley all da night
Ees fall da snow, so cold, so white,
An' cover up da leetla pot
Of — w'at-you-call? — forgat-me-not.
All night da leetla hand I hold
Ees grow so cold, so cold, so cold!

Da spreeng ees com'; but O! da joy
  Eet ees too late!
He was so cold, my leetla boy,
  He no could wait.

T. A. Daly

DUTCHMAN'S BREECHES

(Just after the starry flowers of the hepatica have appeared among the dead leaves, yet before the violets have come, the wooded spaces on and near the Island of Manhattan are beautified with innumerable clusters of quaint little white-and-yellow blossoms known to the schoolmen as *Dicentra cucullaria*; but the children, ever quick to recognize true resemblances, call them " Dutchman's breeches." That this name is not due to a mere chance resemblance is shown by this tale of the founding of a great city which will be found, in part, confirmed in the chronicles of the immortal Diedrich Knickerbocker.)

'Twas in the month when lilacs bloom,
When apple-blossoms breathe perfume
To call the bees; when bluebirds throng,
When bobolink regains his song;
When clear and cloudless, archly smile
The dear blue skies that love our isle.

Across a dimpling, dancing bay
That laved its bows with golden spray,

Full-sailed, a little squadron bore
To Mannahatta's virgin shore
A city's founders — Kips, Van Dorns,
Van Tienhovens, Schermerhorns,
Van Dams, Van Wycks, Van Dycks, Van Pelts,
And Onderdoncks and Roosevelts.

Right glad they leaped ashore — when lo!
With threatening spear, and supple bow
In menace bent, a stately band
Of woodland chieftains barred the strand.
" In peace return! " a sachem old
Began; " This bowered isle we hold
As sacred — ever blessed anew
By footprints of the Manitou; [13]
Nor may we yield, for blood or spoil,
Our birthright in its hallowed soil."

Rejoined that man of subtle wit
The wily Peter Minuit,
" Hail, noble chiefs!   Your island's fame
Hath reached the land from whence we came,
Wide leagues away.   But little space
We crave — a meager resting-place.
Behold these keen-edged knives; this store
Of well-barbed hooks and beads galore;
These blankets and this fragrant cask!
For all, a poor exchange we ask;
A scanty plot of countryside
A Dutchman's breeches serve to hide! "

The chief assented with a smile —
(Alas! unskilled in Paleface guile!)
Then, loyal to his leader's look,
Advanced the sturdy Gert Ten Broeck —
Through Holland noted far and near
For amplitude of nether gear —

[13] Manitou = the Indian god.

And spread, amid a hush profound,
His mighty garment on the ground!

Perhaps the wonder came to pass
By grace of good Saint Nicholas;
Perhaps a marvelous array
The Dutchman wore — I cannot say;
But, while the Red Men stared, dismayed,
Ten Broeck, in silence, stripped and laid
His mystic garments, row on row,
Until to Spuyten Duyvil's flow
A cloud of knickerbockers quite
Obscured the soil from mortal sight!
And thus our cherished dwelling-place
Was ransomed from the savage race.

For proof you ask!   Ah, skeptic few!
Will Nature's word suffice for you?
Attend!   When flower-laden May
Is ushered in by Moving Day,
And all our folk, with van and stage,
Renew the ancient pilgrimage —
Where still, unchained by steel and stone,
The Gentle Goddess holds her own,
Appear on clustered stems a clan
Of dancing blossoms, known to man
As " Dutchman's Breeches " — in the style
Of Sixteen-Twenty.   Thus our isle
Again displays in every nook
The garments of the great Ten Broeck!

Arthur Guiterman

WIND AND WINDOW–FLOWER

Lovers, forget your love,
    And list to the love of these,
She a window-flower,
    And he a winter breeze.

When the frosty window veil
    Was melted down at noon,
And the cagèd yellow bird
    Hung over her in tune,

He marked her through the pane,
    He could not help but mark,
And only passed her by,
    To come again at dark.

He was a winter wind,
    Concerned with ice and snow,
Dead weeds and unmated birds,
    And little of love could know.

But he sighed upon the sill,
    He gave the sash a shake,
As witness all within
    Who lay that night awake.

Perchance he half prevailed
    To win her for the flight
From the firelit looking-glass
    And warm stove-window light.

But the flower leaned aside
    And thought of naught to say,
And morning found the breeze
    A hundred miles away.

Robert Frost

THE BOMBARDMENT

Slowly, without force, the rain drops into the city. It stops a moment on the carved head of Saint John, then slides on again, slipping and trickling over his stone cloak. It splashes from the lead conduit of a gargoyle, and falls from it in turmoil on the stones in the Cathedral square. Where are the people, and why does the fretted steeple seep about in the sky? Boom! The sound swings against the rain. Boom, again! After it, only water rushing in the gutters, and the turmoil from the spout of the gargoyle. Silence. Ripples and mutters. Boom!

The room is damp, but warm. Little flashes swarm about from the firelight. The lustres of the chandelier are bright, and clusters of rubies leap in the bohemian glasses on the *étagère*. Her hands are restless, but the white masses of her hair are quite still. Boom! Will it never cease to torture, this iteration! Boom! The vibration shatters a glass on the *étagère*. It lies there, formless and glowing, with all its crimson gleams shot out of pattern, spilled, flowing red, blood-red. A thin bell-note pricks through the silence. A door creaks. The old lady speaks: " Victor, clear away that broken glass." " Alas! Madam, the bohemian glass! " " Yes, Victor, one hundred years ago my father brought it — " Boom! The room shakes, the servitor quakes. Another goblet shivers and breaks. Boom!

It rustles at the window-pane, the smooth, streaming rain, and he is shut within its clash and murmur. Inside is his candle, his table, his ink, his pen, and his dreams. He is thinking, and the walls are pierced with beams of sunshine, slipping through young green. A fountain tosses itself up at the blue sky, and through the spattered water in the basin he can see copper carp, lazily floating among cold leaves. A wind-harp in a cedar-tree grieves and whispers, and words blow into his brain, bubbled, iridescent, shooting up like flowers of fire, higher and higher. Boom! The flame-flowers snap on their slender stems. The fountain rears up in long broken spears of dishevelled water and flattens into the earth. Boom! And there is only the room, the table, the candle, and the sliding rain. Again, Boom! — Boom! Boom! He stuffs his fingers into his ears. He sees corpses, and cries out in fright. Boom! It is night, and they are shelling the city! Boom! Boom!

A child wakes and is afraid, and weeps in the darkness. What has made the bed shake? " Mother, where are you? I am awake." " Hush, my Darling, I am here." " But, Mother, something so queer happened, the room shook." Boom! " Oh! What is it? What is the matter? " Boom! " Where is Father? I am so afraid." Boom! The child sobs and shrieks. The house trembles and creaks. Boom!

Retorts, globes, tubes, and phials lie shattered. All his trials oozing across the floor. The life that was his choosing, lonely, urgent, goaded by a hope, all gone. A weary man in a ruined laboratory, that is his story. Boom! Gloom and ignorance, and the jig of drunken brutes.

Diseases like snakes crawling over the earth, leaving trails of slime. Wails from people burying their dead. Through the window, he can see the rocking steeple. A ball of fire falls on the lead of the roof, and the sky tears apart on a spike of flame. Up the spire, behind the lacings of stone, zigzagging in and out of the carved tracings, squirms the fire. It spouts like yellow wheat from the gargoyles, coils round the head of Saint John, and aureoles him in light. It leaps into the night and hisses against the rain. The Cathedral is a burning stain on the white, wet night.

Boom! The Cathedral is a torch, and the houses next to it begin to scorch. Boom! The bohemian glass on the *étagère* is no longer there. Boom! A stalk of flame sways against the red damask curtains. The old lady cannot walk. She watches the creeping stalk and counts. Boom! — Boom! — Boom!

The poet rushes into the street, and the rain wraps him in a sheet of silver. But it is threaded with gold and powdered with scarlet beads. The city burns. Quivering, spearing, thrusting, lapping, streaming, run the flames. Over roofs, and walls, and shops, and stalls. Smearing its gold on the sky, the fire dances, lances itself through the doors, and lisps and chuckles along the floors.

The child wakes again and screams at the yellow petalled flower flickering at the window. The little red lips of flame creep along the ceiling beams.

The old man sits among his broken experiments and looks at the burning Cathedral. Now the streets are swarming with people. They seek shelter and crowd into the cellars. They shout and call, and over all, slowly and without force, the rain drops into the city. Boom! And the steeple crashes down among the people. Boom! Boom, again! The water rushes along the gutters. The fire roars and mutters. Boom!

Amy Lowell

THE MOUNTAIN WHIPPOORWILL

(*Or, How Hill-Billy Jim Won the Great Fiddlers' Prize*)

(*A Georgia Romance*)

Up in the mountains, it's lonesome all the time,
(Sof' win' slewin' thu' the sweet-potato vine.)

Up in the mountains, it's lonesome for a child,
(Whippoorwills a-callin' when the sap runs wild.)

Up in the mountains, mountains in the fog,
Everythin's as lazy as an old houn' dog.

Born in the mountains, never raised a pet,
Don't want nuthin' an' never got it yet.

Born in the mountains, lonesome-born,
Raised runnin' ragged thu' the cockleburrs and corn.

Never knew my pappy, mebbe never should.
Think he was a fiddle made of mountain laurel-wood.

Never had a mammy to teach me pretty-please.
Think she was a whippoorwill, a-skitin' thu' the trees.

Never had a brother ner a whole pair of pants,
But when I start to fiddle, why, yuh got to start to dance!

Listen to my fiddle — Kingdom Come — Kingdom Come!
Hear the frogs a-chunkin' " Jug o' rum, Jug o' rum! "
Hear that mountain whippoorwill be lonesome in the air,
An' I'll tell yuh how I travelled to the Essex County Fair.

Essex County has a mighty pretty fair,
All the smarty fiddlers from the South come there.

Elbows flyin' as they rosin up the bow
For the First Prize Contest in the Georgia Fiddlers' Show.

Old Dan Wheeling, with his whiskers in his ears,
King-pin fiddler for nearly twenty years.

Big Tom Sargent, with his blue wall-eye,
An' Little Jimmy Weezer that can make a fiddle cry.

All sittin' roun', spittin' high an' struttin' proud,
(Listen, little whippoorwill, yuh better bug yore eyes!)
Tun-a-tun-a-tunin' while the jedges told the crowd
Them that got the mostest claps 'd win the bestest prize.

Everybody waitin' for the first tweedle-dee,
When in comes a-stumblin' — hill-billy [14] me!

---

[14] A "hill-billy" is a Southern term meaning a poor, country fellow (usually one from some little hill-village), a "rube," a "hayseed."

Bowed right pretty to the jedges an' the rest,
Took a silver dollar from a hole inside my vest,

Plunked it on the table an' said, " There's my callin' card! "
" An' anyone that licks me — well, he's got to fiddle hard! "

Old Dan Wheeling, he was laughin' fit to holler,
Little Jimmy Weezer said, " There's one dead dollar! "

Big Tom Sargent had a yaller-toothy grin,
But I tucked my little whippoorwill spang underneath my
    chin,
An' petted it an' tuned it till the jedges said, " Begin! "

Big Tom Sargent was the first in line;
He could fiddle all the bugs off a sweet-potato vine.

He could fiddle down a possum from a mile-high tree,
He could fiddle up a whale from the bottom of the sea.

Yuh could hear hands spankin' till they spanked each
    other raw,
When he finished variations on " Turkey in the Straw."

Little Jimmy Weezer was the next to play;
He could fiddle all night, he could fiddle all day.

He could fiddle chills, he could fiddle fever,
He could make a fiddle rustle like a lowland river.

He could make a fiddle croon like a lovin' woman.
An' they clapped like thunder when he'd finished strum-
    min'.

Then came the ruck of the bob-tailed fiddlers,
The let's-go-easies, the fair-to-middlers.

They got their claps an' they lost their bicker,
An' they all settled back for some more corn-licker.

An' the crowd was tired of their no-count squealing,
When out in the center steps Old Dan Wheeling.

He fiddled high and he fiddled low,
(Listen, little whippoorwill, yuh got to spread yore wings!)
He fiddled and fiddled with a cherrywood bow,
(Old Dan Wheeling's got bee-honey in his strings).

He fiddled the wind by the lonesome moon,
He fiddled a most almighty tune.

He started fiddling like a ghost.
He ended fiddling like a host.

He fiddled north and he fiddled south,
He fiddled the heart right out of yore mouth.

He fiddled here an' he fiddled there.
He fiddled salvation everywhere.

When he was finished, the crowd cut loose,
(Whippoorwill, they's rain on yore breast.)
An' I sat there wonderin' " What's the use? "
(Whippoorwill, fly home to yore nest.)

But I stood up pert an' I took my bow,
An' my fiddle went to my shoulder, so.

An' — they wasn't no crowd to get me fazed —
But I was alone where I was raised.

Up in the mountains, so still it makes yuh skeered.
Where God lies sleepin' in his big white beard.

An' I heard the sound of the squirrel in the pine,
An' I heard the earth a-breathin' thu' the long night-time.

They've fiddled the rose, and they've fiddled the thorn,
But they haven't fiddled the mountain-corn.

They've fiddled sinful an' fiddled moral,
But they haven't fiddled the breshwood-laurel.

They've fiddled loud, and they've fiddled still,
But they haven't fiddled the whippoorwill.

I started off with a *dump-diddle-dump,*
(*Oh, hell's broke loose in Georgia!*)
Skunk-cabbage growin' by the bee-gum stump.
(*Whippoorwill, yo're singing' now!*)

My mother was a whippoorwill pert,
My father, he was lazy,
But I'm hell broke loose in a new store shirt
To fiddle all Georgia crazy.
Swing yore partners — up an' down the middle!
Sashay now — oh, listen to that fiddle!
Flapjacks flippin' on a red-hot griddle,
An' hell's broke loose,
Hell's broke loose,
Fire on the mountains — snakes in the grass.
Satan's here a-bilin' — oh, Lordy, let him pass!
Go down Moses, set my people free;
Pop goes the weasel thu' the old Red Sea!
Jonah sittin' on a hickory-bough,
Up jumps a whale — an' where's yore prophet now?
Rabbit in the pea-patch, possum in the pot,
Try an' stop my fiddle, now my fiddle's gettin' hot!
Whippoorwill, singin' thu' the mountain hush,
Whippoorwill, shoutin' from the burnin' bush,

Whippoorwill, cryin' in the stable-door,
Sing tonight as yuh never sang before!
Hell's broke loose like a stompin' mountain-shoat,
Sing till yuh bust the gold in yore throat!
Hell's broke loose for forty miles aroun'
Bound to stop yore music if yuh don't sing it down.
Sing on the mountains, little whippoorwill,
Sing to the valleys, an' slap 'em with a hill,
For I'm struttin' high as an eagle's quill,
An' hell's broke loose,
Hell's broke loose,
Hell's broke loose in Georgia!

They wasn't a sound when I stopped bowin',
(*Whippoorwill, yuh can sing no more.*)
But, somewhere or other, the dawn was growin',
(*Oh, mountain whippoorwill!*)

An' I thought, "I've fiddled all night an' lost,
Yo're a good hill-billy, but yuh've been bossed."

So I went to congratulate old man Dan,
— But he put his fiddle into my han' —
An' then the noise of the crowd began!

                                        Stephen Vincent Benét

"THE SPIRIT, SIR, IS ONE OF MOCKERY"

There was a man of our town,
And he was wondrous wise,
He jumped into a bramble bush,
And scratched out both his eyes;
But when he saw his eyes were out,
With all his might and main,
He jumped into another bush,
And scratched 'em in again.

— MOTHER GOOSE

THE BALLAD OF JACK AND JILL

(*After Rudyard Kipling*)

Here is the tale — and you must make the most of it!
Here is the rhyme — ah, listen and attend!
Backwards — forwards — read it all and boast of it
If you are anything the wiser at the end!

Now Jack looked up — it was time to sup, and the bucket was yet to fill,
And Jack looked around for a space and frowned, then beckoned his sister Jill,
And twice he pulled his sister's hair, and thrice he smote her side:
" Ha' done, ha' done with your impudent fun — ha' done with your games! " she cried;
" You have made mud-pies of a marvellous size — finger and face are black,
You have trodden the Way of the Mire and Clay — now up and wash you, Jack!

Or else, or ever we reach our home, there waiteth an angry
dame —
Well you know the weight of her blow — the supperless
open shame!
Wash, if you will, on yonder hill — wash, if you will, at
the spring, —
Or keep your dirt, to your certain hurt, and an imminent
walloping!"

"You must wash — you must scrub — you must scrape!"
growled Jack, "you must traffic with cans and
pails,
Nor keep the spoil of the good brown soil in the rim of
your finger-nails!
The morning path you must tread to your bath — you must
wash ere the night descends.
And all for the cause of conventional laws and the soap-
maker's dividends!
But if 'tis sooth that our meals in truth depend on our
washing, Jill,
By the sacred right of our appetite — haste — haste to the
top of the hill!"

They have trodden the Way of the Mire and Clay, they
have toiled and travelled far.
They have climbed to the brow of the hill-top now, where
the bubbling fountains are.
They have taken the bucket and filled it up — yea, filled it
up to the brim;
But Jack he sneered at his sister Jill, and Jill she jeered at
him:
"What, blown already!" Jack cried out (and his was a
biting mirth!)
"You boast indeed of your wonderful speed — but what is
the boasting worth?

Now, if you can run as the antelope runs, and if you can
turn like a hare,
Come, race me, Jill, to the foot of the hill — and prove your
boasting fair! "

" Race? what is a race " (and a mocking face had Jill
as she spake the word)
" Unless for a prize the runner tries?   The truth indeed ye
heard,
For I can run as the antelope runs, and I can turn like a
hare: —
The first one down wins half-a-crown — and I will race you
there! "
" Yea, if for the lesson that you will learn (the lesson of
humbled pride)
The price you fix at two-and-six, it shall not be denied:
Come, take your stand at my right hand, for here is the
mark we toe:
Now, are you ready, and are you steady?   Gird up your
petticoats!   Go! "

And Jill she ran like a winging bolt, a bolt from the bow
released,
But Jack like a stream of the lightning gleam, with its path-
way duly greased;
He ran down hill in front of Jill like a summer-lightning
flash —
Till he suddenly tripped on a stone, or slipped, and fell to
the earth with a crash.
Then straight did rise on his wondering eyes the constella-
tions fair,
Arcturus and the Pleiades, the Greater and Lesser Bear,
The swirling rain of a comet's train he saw, as he swiftly
fell —
And Jill came tumbling after him with a loud triumphant
yell:

" You have won, you have won, the race is done!   And as
for the wager laid —
You have fallen down with a broken crown — the half-
crown debt is paid! "
They have taken Jack to the room at the back where the
family medicines are,
And he lies in bed with a broken head in a halo of vinegar;
While, in that Jill had laughed her fill as her brother fell
to earth,
She hath felt the sting of a walloping — she hath paid the
price of her mirth!

Here is the tale — and now you have the whole of it,
Here is the story — well and wisely planned,
Beauty — Duty — these make up the soul of it —
But, ah, my little readers, will you mark and under-
stand?   Anthony C. Deane

THE HARMONIOUS HEEDLESSNESS OF
LITTLE BOY BLUE

Composing scales beside the rails
    That flanked a field of corn,
A farmer's boy with vicious joy
    Performed upon a horn:
The vagrant airs, the fragrant airs
    Around the field that strayed,
Took flight before the flagrant airs
    That noisome urchin played.

He played with care " The Maiden's Prayer ";
    He played " God Save the Queen,"
" Die Wacht am Rhein," and " Auld Lang Syne,"
    And " Wearing of the Green ":
With futile toots, and brutal toots,
    And shrill chromatic scales,
And utterly inutile toots,
    And agonizing wails.

The while he played, around him strayed,
   And calmly chewed the cud,
Some thirty-nine assorted kine,
   All ankle-deep in mud:
They stamped about and tramped about
   That mud, till all the troupe
Made noises, as they ramped about,
   Like school-boys eating soup.

Till, growing bored, with one accord
   They broke the fence forlorn:
The field was doomed. The cows consumed
   Two-thirds of all the corn,
And viciously, maliciously,
   Went prancing o'er the loam.
That landscape expeditiously
   Resembled harvest-home.

" Most idle ass of all your class,"
   The farmer said with scorn:
" Just see, my son, what you have done!
   The cows are in the corn! "
" Oh drat," he said, " the brat! " he said.
   The cowherd seemed to rouse.
" My friend, it's worse than that," he said.
   " The corn is in the cows."

THE MORAL lies before our eyes.
   When tending kine and corn,
Don't spend your noons in tooting tunes
   Upon a blatant horn:
Or scaling, and assailing, and
   With energy immense,
Your cows will take a railing, and
   The farmer take offence.

Guy Wetmore Carryl

THE GASTRONOMIC GUILE OF SIMPLE SIMON

Conveniently near to where
    Young Simple Simon dwelt
There was to be a county fair,
    And Simple Simon felt
That to the fair he ought to go
In all his Sunday clothes, and so,
Determined to behold the show,
    He put them on and went.
(One-half his clothes was borrowed and the other half was
    lent.)

He heard afar the cheerful sound
    Of horns that people blew,
Saw wooden horses swing around
    A circle, two and two,
Beheld balloons arise, and if
He scented with a gentle sniff
The smells of pies, what is the dif-
    Ference to me or you?
(You cannot say my verse is false, because I know it's
    true.)

So when he saw upon the road,
    Some fifty feet away,
A pieman, Simple Simon strode
    Toward him, shouting: " Hey!
What kinds? " as lordly as a prince.
The pieman said: " I've pumpkin, quince,
Blueberry, lemon, peach, and mince."
    And, showing his array,
He added: " Won't you try one, sir?   They're very nice
    today."

Now Simon's taste was most profuse,
    And so, by way of start,
He ate two cakes, a Charlotte Russe,
    Six buns, the better part
Of one big gingerbread, a pair
Of lady-fingers, an eclair,
And ten assorted pies, and there,
    His hand upon his heart,
He paused to choose between an apple dumpling and a
    tart.

Observing that upon his tray
    His goods were growing few,
The pieman cried: " I beg to say
    That patrons such as you
One does not meet in many a moon.
Pray, won't you try this macaroon? "
But soon suspicious, changed his tune,
    Continuing: " What is due
I beg respectfully to add's a dollar twenty-two."

Then Simple Simon put a curb
    Upon his appetite,
And turning with an air superb
    He suddenly took flight,
While o'er his shoulder this absurd
And really most offensive word
The trusting pieman shortly heard
    To soothe his bitter plight:
" Perhaps I should have said before your wares are out
    of sight."

THE MORAL is a simple one,
    But still of consequence.
We've seen that Simon's sense of fun
    Was almost *too* intense:

Though blaming his deceitful guise,
We with the pieman sympathize,
The latter we must criticize
    Because he was so dense:
He might have known from what he ate that Simon had no
    cents.

Guy Wetmore Carryl

MATILDA,

Who Told Lies, and was Burned to Death

Matilda told such Dreadful Lies,
It made one Gasp and Stretch one's Eyes;
Her Aunt, who, from her Earliest Youth,
Had kept a Strict Regard for Truth,
Attempted to believe Matilda:
The effort very nearly killed her,
And would have done so, had not She
Discovered this Infirmity.
For once, towards the Close of Day,
Matilda, growing tired of play,
And finding she was left alone,
Went tiptoe to the Telephone
And summoned the Immediate Aid
Of London's Noble Fire-Brigade.
Within an hour the Gallant Band
Were pouring in on every hand,
From Putney, Hackney Downs, and Bow
With Courage high and Hearts a-glow
They galloped, roaring through the Town,
" Matilda's House is Burning Down! "
Inspired by British Cheers and Loud
Proceeding from the Frenzied Crowd,
They ran their Ladders through a Score
Of windows on the Ball Room Floor;

And took Peculiar Pains to Souse
The Pictures up and down the House,
Until Matilda's Aunt succeeded
In showing them they were not needed;
And even then she had to Pay
To get the Men to go Away!

.   .   .   .   .   .

It happened that a few Weeks later
Her Aunt was off to the Theatre
To see that Interesting Play
The Second Mrs. Tanqueray.
She had refused to take her Niece
To hear this Entertaining Piece:
(A Deprivation Just and Wise
To punish her for Telling Lies.)
That Night a Fire *did* break out —
You should have heard Matilda Shout!
You should have heard her Scream and Bawl,
And throw the window up and call
To People passing in the Street —
(The rapidly increasing Heat
Encouraging her to obtain
Their confidence) — but all In Vain!
For every time She shouted " Fire! "
They only answered " Little Liar! "
And therefore when her Aunt returned,
Matilda, and the House, were Burned.

Hilaire Belloc

GEORGE,

*Who played with a Dangerous Toy, and suffered a
Catastrophe of Considerable Dimensions*

When George's Grandmamma was told
That George had been as Good as Gold,
She Promised in the Afternoon
To buy him an *Immense* Balloon.

And so she did; but when It came,
It got into the candle flame,
And being of a dangerous sort
Exploded with a Loud Report!
The Lights went out! The Windows broke!
The Room was filled with Reeking Smoke.
And in the darkness Shrieks and Yells
Were mingled with Electric Bells,
And falling Masonry and Groans,
And crunching, as of broken bones,
And dreadful Shrieks, when, worst of all,
The House itself began to fall!
It tottered, shuddering to and fro,
Then crashed into the street below —
Which happened to be Saville Row.

. . . . . .

When Help arrived, among the Dead
Were Cousin Mary, Little Fred,
The Footmen (both of them), the Groom,
The Man that cleaned the Billiard-Room,
The Chaplain, and the Still-Room Maid.
And I am dreadfully afraid
That Monsieur Champignon, the Chef,
Will now be permanently deaf —
And both his Aides are much the same;
While George, who was in part to blame,
Received, you will regret to hear,
A nasty lump behind the ear.

MORAL

The Moral is that little Boys
Should not be given Dangerous Toys.

Hilaire Belloc

THE TIRED MAN

I am a quiet gentleman,
And I would sit and dream;
But my wife is on the hillside,
Wild as a hill-stream.

I am a quiet gentleman,
And I would sit and think;
But my wife is walking the whirlwind
Through a night as black as ink.

O, give me a woman of my race
As well controlled as I,
And let us sit by the fire,
Patient till we die!

Anna Wickham

THE LILAC

Who thought of the lilac?
" I," dew said,
" I made up the lilac
out of my head."

" She made up the lilac!
Pooh! " trilled a linnet,
and each dew-note had a
lilac in it.

Humbert Wolfe

DOES IT MATTER?

Does it matter? — losing your leg? . . .
For people will always be kind,
And you need not show that you mind
When the others come in after hunting
To gobble their muffins and egg.

Does it matter? — losing your sight? . . .
There's such splendid work for the blind;
And people will always be kind,
As you sit on the terrace remembering
And turning your face to the light.

Do they matter? — those dreams from the pit? . . .
You can drink and forget and be glad,
And people won't say that you're mad;
For they'll know that you've fought for your country,
And no one will worry a bit.

Siegfried Sassoon

ENCOURAGEMENT

Who dat knockin' at de do'?
Why, Ike Johnson, — yes, fu' sho!
Come in, Ike. I's mighty glad
You come down. I t'ought you's mad
At me 'bout de othah night,
An' was stayin' 'way fu' spite.
Say, now, was you mad fu' true
W'en I kin' o' laughed at you?
Speak up, Ike, an' 'spress yo'se'f.

'Tain't no use a-lookin' sad,
An' a-mekin' out you's mad;
Ef you's gwine to be so glum,
Wondah why you evah come.
I don't lak nobody 'roun'
Dat jes' shet dey mouf an' frown, —
Oh, now, man, don't act a dunce!
Cain't you talk? I tol' you once,
Speak up, Ike, an' 'spress yo'se'f.

Wha'd you come hyeah fu' tonight?
Body'd t'ink yo' haid ain't right.
I's done all dat I kin do, —
Dressed perticuler, jes' fu' you;
Reckon I'd a' bettah wo'
My ol' ragged calico.
Aftah all de pains I's took,
Cain't you tell me how I look?
   Speak up, Ike, an' 'spress yo'se'f.

Bless my soul! I 'most fu'got
Tellin' you 'bout Tildy Scott.
Don't you know, come Thu'sday night,
She gwine ma'y Lucius White?
Miss Lize say I allus wuh
Heap sight laklier 'n huh;
An' she'll git me somepin new,
Ef I wants to ma'y too.
   Speak up, Ike, an' 'spress yo'se'f.

I could ma'y in a week,
Ef de man I wants 'ud speak.
Tildy's presents'll be fine,
But dey wouldn't ekal mine.
Him whut gits me fu' a wife
'Ll be proud, you bet yo' life.
I's had offers; some ain't quit;
But I hasn't ma'ied yit!
   Speak up, Ike, an' 'spress yo'se'f.

Ike, I loves you, — yes, I does;
You's my choice, and allus was.
Laffin' at you ain't no harm. —
Go 'way, dahky, whah's yo' arm?
Hug me closer — dah, dat's right!
Wasn't you a awful sight,

Havin' me to baig you so?
Now ax whut you want to know, —
Speak up, Ike, an' 'spress yo'se'f!

Paul Laurence Dunbar

THEN AND NOW

Oh, when I was in love with you,
    Then I was clean and brave,
And miles around the wonder grew
    How well did I behave.

And now the fancy passes by,
    And nothing will remain,
And miles around they'll say that I
    Am quite myself again.

A. E. Housman

SAD SEPTEMBER SENTIMENTS

One of the days when one's a martyr
    To circumstance today is mine;
I've broke a shoe-lace and a garter,
    A cuff-link and a date to dine.
Against the pane the raindrops patter,
    And all the birds have ceased to sing;
There's something horribly the matter
        With everything!

The autumn winds are sadly sighing,
    The wet turf smells like churchyard mold!
The teardrops start, for Summer's dying,
    And I'm afraid I've taken cold.
My heart is stirred with apprehension,
    And sleeping sorrows start awake,
And that old tooth that needs attention
        Begins to ache!

The eaves in dreary anguish dripping,
    Weep, too, like sympathetic souls —
Alas!   Five mornings without skipping,
    I've found my socks all full of holes;
I suffer dumbly — not abusive
    Am I, though all the house goes wrong;
Such lapses, though, are not conducive
        To lyric song.

Though fast were drawn each shade and curtain,
    And fires were lit, the gloom to hide,
Still would my weary heart be certain
    That rain was weighing there outside;
Bleak land, with leaden clouds above it —
    Cold sodden nights and drizzling morns;
My sobbing soul would tell me of it —
        Also my corns!

Enough!   Perhaps I should remember
    That e'en the worst of luck must mend;
A few more days, and then September
    With all its bitterness will end.
I'm not yet blind — I still am goutless —
    I still can grind my daily verse.
Now comes October (which will doubtless
        Be even worse!)

                                        Edwin Meade Robinson

THE CREMATION OF SAM McGEE [1]

There are strange things done in the midnight sun
    By the men who moil for gold;
The Arctic trails have their secret tales
    That would make your blood run cold;

[1] From *The Spell of the Yukon and Other Verses* by Robert W. Service.
Copyright by Barse & Hopkins, New York.

> *The Northern Lights have seen queer sights,*
>   *But the queerest they ever did see*
> *Was that night on the marge of Lake Lebarge*
>   *I cremated Sam McGee.*

Now Sam McGee was from Tennessee, where the cotton
    blooms and blows,
Why he left his home in the South to roam 'round the Pole,
    God only knows.
He was always cold, but the land of gold seemed to hold
    him like a spell;
Though he'd often say in his homely way that " he'd sooner
    live in hell."

On Christmas Day we were mushing our way over the
    Dawson Trail.
Talk of your cold! through the parka's fold it stabbed like
    a driven nail.
If our eyes we'd close, then the lashes froze till sometimes
    we couldn't see;
It wasn't much fun, but the only one to whimper was Sam
    McGee.

And that very night, as we lay packed tight in our robes
    beneath the snow,
And the dogs were fed, and the stars o'erhead were dancing
    heel and toe,
He turned to me, and " Cap," says he, " I'll cash in this
    trip, I guess;
And if I do, I'm asking that you won't refuse my last re-
    quest."

Well, he seemed so low that I couldn't say no; then he says
    with a sort of moan:
"It's the cursed cold, and it's got right hold till I'm chilled
    clean through to the bone.

Yet 'tain't being dead — it's my awful dread of the icy
    grave that pains;
So I want you to swear that, foul or fair, you'll cremate
    my last remains."

A pal's last need is a thing to heed, so I swore I would not
    fail;
And we started on at the streak of dawn; but God! he
    looked ghastly pale.
He crouched on the sleigh, and he raved all day of his
    home in Tennessee;
And before nightfall a corpse was all that was left of Sam
    McGee.

There wasn't a breath in that land of death, and I hurried,
    horror-driven,
With a corpse half hid that I couldn't get rid, because of a
    promise I'd given;
It was lashed to the sleigh, and it seemed to say: " You may
    tax your brawn and brains,
But you promised true, and it's up to you to cremate those
    last remains."

Now a promise made is a debt unpaid, and the trail has its
    own stern code.
In the days to come, though my lips were dumb, in my
    heart how I cursed that load.
In the long, long night, by the lone firelight, while the
    huskies, round in a ring,
Howled out their woes to the homeless snows — O God!
    how I loathed the thing.

And every day that quiet clay seemed heavier and heavier
    to grow;
And on I went, though the dogs were spent and the grub
    was getting low;

The trail was bad, and I felt half mad, but I swore I would
  not give in;
And I'd often sing to the hateful thing, and it hearkened
  with a grin.

Till I came to the marge of Lake Lebarge, and a derelict
  there lay;
It was jammed in the ice, but I saw in a trice it was called
  the "Alice May."
And I looked at it, and I thought a bit, and I looked at
  my frozen chum;
Then "Here," said I, with a sudden cry, "is my cre-ma-
  tor-e-um."

Some planks I tore from the cabin floor, and I lit the
  boiler fire;
Some coal I found that was lying around, and I heaped the
  fuel higher;
The flames just soared, and the furnace roared — such a
  blaze you seldom see;
And I burrowed a hole in the glowing coal, and I stuffed in
  Sam McGee.

Then I made a hike, for I didn't like to hear him sizzle so;
And the heavens scowled, and the huskies howled, and the
  wind began to blow.
It was icy cold, but the hot sweat rolled down my cheeks,
  and I don't know why;
And the greasy smoke in an inky cloak went streaking down
  the sky.

I do not know how long in the snow I wrestled with grisly
  fear;
But the stars came out and they danced about ere again I
  ventured near;

I was sick with dread, but I bravely said: "I'll just take a peep inside.
I guess he's cooked, and it's time I looked; " . . . then the door I opened wide.

And there sat Sam, looking cold and calm, in the heart of the furnace roar;
And he wore a smile you could see a mile, and he said: "Please close that door!
It's fine in here, but I greatly fear you'll let in the cold and storm —
Since I left Plumtree, down in Tennessee, it's the first time I've been warm."

There are strange things done in the midnight sun
By the men who moil for gold;
The Arctic trails have their secret tales
That would make your blood run cold;
The Northern Lights have seen queer sights,
But the queerest they ever did see
Was that night on the marge of Lake Lebarge
I cremated Sam McGee.

Robert W. Service

THE FAMOUS BALLAD OF THE JUBILEE CUP [2]

(*Condensed Version*)

You may lift me up in your arms, lad, and turn my face to the sun,
For a last look back at the dear old track where the Jubilee Cup was won;
And draw your chair to my side, lad — no, thank ye, I feel no pain —
For I'm going out with the tide, lad; but I'll tell you the tale again.

[2] Don't, I warn you, try to make sense out of this burlesque ballad. It is a mad mixture of all the sporting terms and plays in tennis, yachting, horse-racing, golf, chess, billiards, football, cards, etc. How many do you recognize?

I'm seventy-nine or nearly, and my head it has long turned
    gray,
But it all comes back as clearly as though it was yester-
    day —
The dust, and the bookies shouting around the clerk of the
    scales,
And the clerk of the course, and nobs in force, and 'Is 'Igh-
    ness the Pr**ce of W*les.

'Twas a nine-hole thresh to wind'ard (but none of us cared
    for that),
With a straight run home to the service tee, and a finish
    along the flat,
" Stiff? " ah, well you may say it!   Spot barred, and at five
    stone ten!
But at two and a bisque!   I'd ha' run the risk; for I was
    a greenhorn then.

So we stripped to the B. Race signal, the old red swallow-
    tail —
There was young Ben Bolt and the Portland Colt, and
    Aston Villa, and Yale;
And W. G., and Steinitz, Leander and The Saint,
And the G*rm*n Emp*r*r's Meteor, a-looking as fresh as
    paint;

John Roberts (scratch), and Safety Match, The Lascar,
    and Lorna Doone,
Oom Paul (a bye), and Romany Rye, and me upon Wooden
    Spoon;
And some of us cut for partners, and some of us strung for
    baulk,
And some of us tossed for stations — But there, what use
    to talk?

Three-quarter-back on the Kingsclere crack was station
    enough for me,
With a fresh jackyarder blowing and the Vicarage goal
    a-lee!
And I leaned and patted her center-bit and eased the quid
    in her cheek,
With a " Soh my lass! " and a " Whoa you brute! " — for
    she could do all but speak.

Sir Robert he walked beside me as I worked her down to
    the mark;
" There's money on this, my lad," said he, " and most of
    'em's running dark;
But ease the sheet if you're bunkered, and pack the scrum-
    mages tight,
And use your slide at the distance, and we'll drink to your
    health tonight! "

But I bent and tightened my stretcher. Said I to myself,
    said I —
" John Jones, this here is the Jubilee Cup, and you have
    to do or die."
And the words weren't hardly spoken when the umpire
    shouted " Play! "
And we all kicked off from the Gasworks End with a
    " Yoicks! " and a " Gone Away! "

And at first I thought of nothing as the clay flew by in
    lumps,
But stuck to the old Ruy Lopez, and wondered who'd call
    for trumps,
And luffed her close to the cushion, and watched each one
    as it broke,
And in triple file up the Rowley Mile we went like a trail
    of smoke.

The Lascar made the running but he didn't amount to
much,
For old Oom Paul was quick on the ball, and headed it
back to touch;
And the whole first flight led off with the right as The
Saint took up the pace,
And drove it clean to the putting green and trumped it
there with an ace.

We laid our course for the Warner — I tell you the pace
was hot!
And again off Tattenham Corner a blanket covered the
lot,
Check side! Check side! now steer her wide! and barely
an inch of room,
With the Lascar's tail over our lee rail and brushing Leander's boom.

But none of the lot could stop the rot — nay, don't ask
me to stop!
The villa had called for lemons, Oom Paul had taken his
drop,
And both were kicking the referee. Poor fellow! he'd done
his best;
But, being in doubt, he'd ruled them out — which he always did when pressed.

So, inch by inch, I tightened the winch, and chucked the
sandbags out —
I heard the nursery cannons pop, I heard the bookies
shout:
" The Meteor wins! " " No, Wooden Spoon! " " Check! "
" Vantage! " " Leg Before! "
" Last Lap! " " Pass Nap! " At his saddle-flap I put up
the helm and swore.

You may overlap at the saddle-flap, and yet be loo'd on the
    tape:
And it all depends upon changing ends, how a seven-year-old
    will shape;
It was tack and tack to the Lepe and back — a fair ding-
    dong to the Ridge,
And he led by his forward canvas yet as we shot 'neath
    Hammersmith Bridge.

I could hear the "Conquering 'Ero" a-crashing on God-
    frey's band,
And my hopes fell sudden to zero, just there, with the race
    in hand —
In sight of the Turf's Blue Ribbon, in sight of the um-
    pire's tape,
As I felt the tack of her spinnaker c-rack! as I heard the
    steam escape!

Had I lost at that awful juncture my presence of mind? . . .
    But no!
I leaned and felt for the puncture, and plugged it there
    with my toe. . . .
Hand over hand by the Members' Stand I lifted and eased
    her up,
Shot — clean and fair — to the crossbar there, and landed
    the Jubilee Cup!

"The odd by a head, and leg before," so the Judge he gave
    the word:
And the umpire shouted "Over!" but I neither spoke nor
    stirred.
They crowded round: for there on the ground I lay in a
    dead-cold swoon,
Pitched neck and crop on the turf atop of my beautiful
    Wooden Spoon.

Her dewlap tire was punctured, her bearings all red hot;
She'd a lolling tongue, and her bowsprit sprung, and her
running gear in a knot;
And amid the sobs of her backers, Sir Robert loosened her
girth
And led her away to the knacker's. She had raced her
last on earth!

But I mind me well of the tear that fell from the eye of our
noble Pr*nce,
And the things he said as he tucked me in bed — and I've
lain there ever since;
Tho' it all gets mixed up queerly what happened before my
spill, —
But I draw my thousand yearly: it'll pay for the doctor's
bill.

I'm going out with the tide, lad — you'll dig me a numble
grave,
And whiles you will bring your bride, lad, and your sons,
if sons you have,
And there when the dews are weeping, and the echoes
murmur " Peace! "
And the salt, salt tide comes creeping and covers the pop-
ping-crease;

In the hour when the ducks deposit their eggs with a
boasted force,
They'll look and whisper " How was it? " and you'll take
them over the course,
And your voice will break as you try to speak of the glorious
first of June,
When the Jubilee Cup, with John Jones up, was won upon
Wooden Spoon.

Arthur T. Quiller-Couch

SIMPLE PHILOSOPHY: LITTLE THINGS

But words are things, and a small drop of ink,
Falling like dew upon a thought, produces
That which makes thousands, perhaps millions, think.

— LORD BYRON

SONGS OF JOY

Sing out, my Soul, thy songs of joy;
   Such as a happy bird will sing
Beneath a Rainbow's lovely arch
   In early spring.

Think not of Death in thy young days
   Why shouldst thou that grim tyrant fear,
And fear him not when thou art old,
   And he is near.

Strive not for gold, for greedy fools
   Measure themselves by poor men never;
Their standard still being richer men,
   Makes them poor ever.

Train up thy mind to feel content,
   What matters then how low thy store;
What we enjoy, and not possess,
   Makes rich or poor.

Filled with sweet thought, then happy I
   Take not my state from others' eyes;
What's in my mind — not on my flesh
   Or theirs — I prize.

Sing, happy Soul, thy songs of joy;
　　Such as a Brook sings in the wood,
That all night has been strengthened by
　　Heaven's purer flood.

W. H. Davies

A PRAYER IN SPRING

Oh, give us pleasure in the flowers today;
And give us not to think so far away
As the uncertain harvest; keep us here
All simply in the springing of the year.

Oh, give us pleasure in the orchard white,
Like nothing else by day, like ghosts by night;
And make us happy in the happy bees,
The swarm dilating round the perfect trees.

And make us happy in the darting bird
That suddenly above the bees is heard,
The meteor that thrusts in with needle bill,
And off a blossom in mid air stands still.

For this is love and nothing else is love,
The which it is reserved for God above
To sanctify to what far ends He will,
But which it only needs that we fulfil.

Robert Frost

THANKS

Thank you very much indeed,
River, for your waving reed;
Hollyhocks, for budding knobs;
Foxgloves, for your velvet fobs;

Pansies, for your silky cheeks;
Chaffinches, for singing beaks;
Spring, for wood anemones
Near the mossy toes of trees;
Summer, for the fruited pear,
Yellowing crab,[1] and cherry fare;
Autumn, for the bearded load,
Hazelnuts along the road;
Winter, for the fairy-tale,
Spitting log and bouncing hail.

But, blest Father, high above,
All these joys are from Thy love;
And Your children everywhere,
Born in palace, lane, or square,
Cry with voices all agreed,
" Thank You very much indeed."

Norman Gale

WISE MAN, WISE MAN

Wise man, wise man,
   You who preach,
Kneel to learn what
   Grass-blades teach.
Kneel to dew-drops
   Globing skies,
To show you more of
   Paradise.
Wise man, wise man,
   Do you know,
In your wisdom,
   How green things grow?
How Revelations
   Burst from seeds?
And gospels banner
   Up from weeds?

[1] Here the word "crab" means a crab-apple!

Your Creed is only
  A blinding wall —
Ask a rose-leaf
  To tell you all!
Preacher, preacher,
  Do not pass
Eden's pointing
  Blades of grass!
Wise man, wise man,
  Try to be
Rooted so in
  Divinity!

Louis Ginsberg

RECESSIONAL

(*A Victorian Ode*)

God of our fathers, known of old —
  Lord of our far-flung battle line —
Beneath whose awful hand we hold
  Dominion over palm and pine —
Lord God of Hosts, be with us yet,
Lest we forget — lest we forget!

The tumult and the shouting dies —
  The Captains and the Kings depart —
Still stands Thine ancient sacrifice,
  An humble and a contrite heart.
Lord God of Hosts, be with us yet,
Lest we forget — lest we forget!

Far-called our navies melt away —
  On dune and headland sinks the fire —
Lo, all our pomp of yesterday
  Is one with Nineveh and Tyre!
Judge of the Nations, spare us yet,
Lest we forget — lest we forget!

If, drunk with sight of power we loose
  Wild tongues that have not thee in awe —
Such boastings as the Gentiles use,
  Or lesser breeds without the Law —
Lord God of Hosts, be with us yet,
  Lest we forget — lest we forget!

For heathen heart that puts her trust
  In reeking tube and iron shard — [2]
All valiant dust that builds on dust,
  And guarding calls not Thee to guard,
For frantic boast and foolish word,
  Thy Mercy on Thy People, Lord!
                    Amen.

                    Rudyard Kipling

HILLS

I never loved your plains; —
  Your gentle valleys,
Your drowsy country lanes
  And pleached alleys.

I want my hills! — the trail
  That scorns the hollow.
Up, up the ragged shale
  Where few will follow.

Up, over wooded crest
  And mossy boulder
With strong thigh, heaving chest,
  And swinging shoulder.

So let me hold my way,
  By nothing halted,
Until at close of day,
  I stand, exalted.

[2] shard, in this sense = shells and bullets.

High on my hills of dream —
   Dear hills that know me!
And then, how fair will seem
   The lands below me.

How pure, at vesper-time,
   The far bells chiming!
God, give me hills to climb,
   And strength for climbing!

Arthur Guiterman

THE HAMMERS

Noise of hammers once I heard,
Many hammers, busy hammers,
Beating, shaping, night and day,
Shaping, beating dust and clay
To a palace; saw it reared;
Saw the hammers laid away.

And I listened, and I heard
Hammers beating, night and day,
In the palace newly reared,
Beating it to dust and clay:
Other hammers, muffled hammers,
Silent hammers of decay.

Ralph Hodgson

WORK

Let me but do my work from day to day,
   In field or forest, at the desk or loom,
   In roaring market-place or tranquil room;
Let me but find it in my heart to say,
When vagrant wishes beckon me astray,
   " This is my work; my blessing, not my doom;
   Of all who live, I am the one by whom
This work can best be done in the right way."

Then shall I see it not too great, nor small,
  To suit my spirit and to prove my powers;
  Then shall I cheerful greet the laboring hours,
And cheerful turn, when the long shadows fall
At eventide, to play and love and rest,
Because I know for me my work is best.

Henry van Dyke

TEARS

When I consider Life and its few years —
A wisp of fog betwixt us and the sun;
A call to battle, and the battle done
Ere the last echo dies within our ears;
A rose choked in the grass; an hour of fears;
The gusts that past a darkening shore do beat;
The burst of music down an unlistening street, —
I wonder at the idleness of tears.
Ye old, old dead, and ye of yesternight,
Chieftains, and bards, and keepers of the sheep,
By every cup of sorrow that you had,
Loose me from tears, and make me see aright
How each hath back what once he stayed to weep:
Homer his sight, David his little lad!

Lizette Woodworth Reese

ALONE

'*When I'm alone*' — the words tripped off his tongue
As though to be alone were nothing strange.
'*When I was young,*' he said; '*When I was young.*' . . .

I thought of age, and loneliness, and change.
I thought how strange we grow when we're alone,
And how unlike the selves that meet, and talk,
And blow the candles out, and say good-night.

Alone. . . . The word is life endured and known.
It is the stillness where our spirits walk
And all but inmost faith is overthrown.

Siegfried Sassoon

AFTER SUNSET

I have an understanding with the hills
At evening when the slanted radiance fills
Their hollows, and the great winds let them be,
And they are quiet and look down at me.
Oh, then I see the patience in their eyes
Out of the centuries that made them wise.
They lend me hoarded memory and I learn
Their thoughts of granite and their whims of fern,
And why a dream of forests must endure
Though every tree be slain: and how the pure
Invisible beauty has a word so brief,
A flower can say it or a shaken leaf,
But few may ever snare it in a song,
Though for the quest a life is not too long.
When the blue hills grow tender, when they pull
The twilight close with gesture beautiful,
And shadows are their garments, and the air
Deepens, and the wild veery is at prayer,
Their arms are strong around me; and I know
That somehow I shall follow when you go
To the still land beyond the evening star,
Where everlasting hills and valleys are,
And silence may not hurt us any more,
And terror shall be past, and grief, and war.

Grace Hazard Conkling

ELLIS PARK

Little park that I pass through,
I carry off a piece of you
Every morning hurrying down
To my work-day in the town;
Carry you for country there
To make the city ways more fair.
I take your trees,
And your breeze,
Your greenness,
Your cleanness,
Some of your shade, some of your sky,
Some of your calm as I go by;
Your flowers to trim
The pavements grim;
Your space for room in the jostled street,
And grass for carpet to my feet;
Your fountains take and sweet bird calls
To sing me from my office walls.
All that I can see
I carry off with me.
But you never miss my theft,
So much treasure you have left.
As I find you, fresh at morning,
So I find you, home returning —
Nothing lacking from your grace.
All your riches wait in place
For me to borrow
On the morrow.

Do you hear this praise of you,
Little park that I pass through?

Helen Hoyt

THE LITTLE WAVES OF BREFFNY

The grand road from the mountain goes shining to the sea,
  And there is traffic in it, and many a horse and cart;
But the little roads of Cloonagh are dearer far to me,
  And the little roads of Cloonagh go rambling through my
    heart.

A great storm from the ocean goes shouting o'er the hill,
  And there is glory in it, and terror on the wind;
But the haunted air of twilight is very strange and still,
  And the little winds of twilight are dearer to my mind.

The great waves of the Atlantic sweep storming on their
    way,
  Shining green and silver with the hidden herring shoal;
But the little waves of Breffny have drenched my heart in
    spray,
  And the little waves of Breffny go stumbling through my
    soul.

Eva Gore-Booth

The glories of our blood and state
Are shadows, not substantial things;
There is no armor against fate;
Death lays his icy hand on kings:
Scepter and Crown
Must tumble down,
And in the dust be equal made
With the poor crooked scythe and spade.

— JAMES SHIRLEY

THE DEAD

These hearts were woven of human joys and cares,
  Washed marvellously with sorrow, swift to mirth.
The years had given them kindness. Dawn was theirs,
  And sunset, and the colors of the earth.
These had seen movement, and heard music; known
  Slumber and waking; loved; gone proudly friended;
Felt the quick stir of wonder; sat alone;
  Touched flowers and furs and cheeks. All this is ended.

There are waters blown by changing winds to laughter
And lit by the rich skies, all day. And after,
  Frost, with a gesture, stays the waves that dance
And wandering loveliness. He leaves a white
  Unbroken glory, a gathered radiance,
A width, a shining peace, under the night.

Rupert Brooke

IN FLANDERS FIELDS

In Flanders fields the poppies blow
Between the crosses, row on row,

That mark our place; and in the sky
The larks, still bravely singing, fly
Scarce heard amid the guns below.

We are the Dead. Short days ago
We lived, felt dawn, saw sunset glow,
　Loved and were loved, and now we lie
　　In Flanders fields.

Take up our quarrel with the foe:
To you from failing hands we throw
　The torch; be yours to hold it high.
　If ye break faith with us who die
We shall not sleep, though poppies grow
　　In Flanders fields.

John McCrae

"I HAVE A RENDEZVOUS WITH DEATH"

I have a rendezvous with Death
At some disputed barricade,
When Spring comes back with rustling shade
And apple-blossoms fill the air —
I have a rendezvous with Death
When Spring brings back blue days and fair.
It may be he shall take my hand
And lead me into his dark land
And close my eyes and quench my breath —
It may be I shall pass him still.
I have a rendezvous with Death
On some scarred slope of battered hill,
When Spring comes round again this year
And the first meadow-flowers appear.

God knows 'twere better to be deep
Pillowed in silk and scented down,
Where love throbs out in blissful sleep,
Pulse nigh to pulse, and breath to breath,

Where hushed awakenings are dear. . . .
But I've a rendezvous with Death
At midnight in some flaming town,
When Spring trips north again this year,
And I to my pledged word am true,
I shall not fail that rendezvous.

Alan Seeger

JOURNEY'S END

What will they give me, when journey's done?
Your own room to be quiet in, Son!

Who shares it with me?   There is none
shares that cool dormitory, Son!

Who turns the sheets?   There is but one,
and no one needs to turn it, Son!

Who lights the candle?   Everyone
sleeps without candle all night, Son!

Who calls me after sleeping?   Son!
You are not called when journey's done.

Humbert Wolfe

EASTER

Bring flowers to strew His way,
Yea, sing, make holiday;
Bid young lambs leap,
And earth laugh after sleep.

For now He cometh forth
Winter flies to the north,
Folds wings and cries
Amid the bergs and ice.

Bring no sad palms like those
That led Him to His foes,
Bring wind-flower, daffodil,
From many a vernal hill.

Let there be naught but bloom
To light Him from the tomb
Who late hath slain
Death, and his glory ta'en.

Yea, Death, great Death is dead,
And Life reigns in his stead;
Cometh the Athlete
New from dead Death's defeat.

Bring flowers, make holiday,
In His triumphal way.
Salve ye with kisses
His hurts that make your blisses.

Bring flowers, make holiday,
For His triumphal way:
Yea, fling before Him
Hearts of men that adore Him.

Katharine Tynan

HERE LIES. . . .

When I am gone and all my songs are still
Take up the music ere the harp grows mute,
And pluck the strings so that my soul may thrill
With singing and the sounding of the lute.

I shall be careless of the great acute
Demands that tax our frail and feeble skill;
I shall no longer join the fierce dispute
When I am gone and all my songs are still.

For I shall lie beneath a little hill
And watch the budding of each tender shoot,
Hoping that every May the robins will
Take up the music ere the harp grows mute.

Soon will the impudent phoebe try his flute
Above my narrow casement, and the shrill
Cricket will twang his zither 'neath a root
And pluck the strings so that my soul may thrill.

Come then, let music, bursts of music, kill
The sad-eyed Sorrows and their solemn suit.
Be there rejoicing; let the chambers fill
With singing and the sounding of the lute.

Let voices, blended skillfully, confute
The raven's dismal prophecies, until
Gray Grief shall gnaw her own too-bitter fruit.
Let there be dancing!   Let the goblets spill
                     When I am gone!
                                    Michael Lewis

THE COWARD

Death's a peculiar thing.
If I should meet him grinning at the cross-roads there,
The old sign-post would rather be a joke
With its directions to a man-made thoroughfare.
That sense of following the road would cease
Abruptly, just as if some mighty orchestra had stopped
Midway in the piece —
As if the leader'd turned to stone or dropped.

I'd like to feel that I could out-grin Death —
Could meet him with the manner debonair;
Flushed with old laughter,
Boisterous with the breath of singing winds —

A wind-flower in my hair!
And when I went 'twould be with dancing feet.
I'd dance, and dance, and dance from morn till noon;
I'd out-dance Death upon the hills beyond the sun
And race him down the valleys of the moon —
Scathe him with laughter, rapier-like and sharp,
Until he felt his ghastly-seeming might o'erpowered.
For laughter is a death-cup unto Death,
As laughter is a scourge unto a coward.
And Death's a coward!

R. R. Greenwood

BELLS IN THE RAIN

Sleep falls, with limpid drops of rain,
Upon the steep cliffs of the town.
Sleep falls; men are at peace again
While the small drops fall softly down.

The bright drops ring like bells of glass
Thinned by the wind, and lightly blown;
Sleep cannot fall on peaceful grass
So softly as it falls on stone.

Peace falls unheeded on the dead
Asleep; they have had deep peace to drink;
Upon a live man's bloody head
It falls most tenderly, I think.

Elinor Wylie

MATTER

When I was a live man
A few years ago,
For all I might say,
For all I could do,

I got no attention;
  My life was so small
The world didn't know
  I was living at all.

Such stolid indifference
  I couldn't allow;
I swore that I'd matter —
  Never mind how!

But after a lifetime
  Of hunger and prayer,
I broke my heart trying
  To make the world care.

And now as I lie here,
  Feeding this tree,
I am more to the world
  Than it is to me.

                    Louis Untermeyer

"THE HEART TO FIGHT—AND LOSE"

Let piping swain and craven wight,
Thus weepe and puling crye;
Our business is like men to fight,
And hero-like to die!

— WILLIAM MOTHERWELL

AT THE END OF THE DAY

There is no escape by the river,
There is no flight left by the fen;
We are compassed about by the shiver
Of the night of their marching men.
Give a cheer!
For our hearts shall not give way.
Here's to a dark tomorrow,
And here's to a brave today!

The tale of their hosts is countless,
And the tale of ours a score;
But the palm is naught to the dauntless,
And the cause is more and more.
Give a cheer!
We may die, but not give way.
Here's to a silent morrow,
And here's to a stout today!

God has said: " Ye shall fail and perish;
But the thrill ye have felt tonight
I shall keep in my heart and cherish
When the worlds have passed in might."
Give a cheer!

For the soul shall not give way.
Here's to the greater tomorrow
That is born of a great today!

Now shame on the craven truckler
And the puling things that mope!
We've a rapture for our buckler
That outwears the wings of hope.
Give a cheer!
For our joy shall not give way.
Here's in the teeth of tomorrow
To the glory of today!

Richard Hovey

HIS ALLY

He fought for his soul, and the stubborn fighting
  Tried hard his strength.
" One needs seven souls for this new requiting,"
  He said at length.

" Six times have I come where my first hope jeered me
  And laughed me to scorn;
But now I fear as I never have feared me
  To fall forsworn.

" God! when they fight upright at me
  I give them back
Even such blows as theirs that combat me.
  But now, alack!

" They fight with the wiles of fiends escaping
  And underhand.
Six times, O God, and my wounds are gaping!
  I — reel to stand.

" Six battles' span!   By this gasping breath
  No pantomime.
'Tis all that I can.   I am sick unto death,
  And — a seventh time?

" This is beyond all battles' soreness! "
    Then his wonder cried;
For Laughter, with shield and steely harness,
    Stood up at his side!

William Rose Benét

PREPAREDNESS

For all your days prepare,
    And meet them ever alike:
When you are the anvil, bear —
    When you are the hammer, strike.

Edwin Markham

THE SOLDIER

If I should die, think only this of me:
    That there's some corner of a foreign field
That is forever England.   There shall be
    In that rich earth a richer dust concealed;
A dust whom England bore, shaped, made aware,
    Gave, once, her flowers to love, her ways to roam,
A body of England's, breathing English air,
    Washed by the rivers, blest by suns of home.
And think, this heart, all evil shed away,
    A pulse in the eternal mind, no less
    Gives somewhere back the thoughts by England given;
Her sights and sounds; dreams happy as her day;
    And laughter, learnt of friends; and gentleness,
    In hearts of peace, under an English heaven.

Rupert Brooke

VITAE LAMPADA [1]

There's a breathless hush in the Close to-night —
    Ten to make and the match to win —

[1] *Vitae Lampada* = The Torch of Life.

A bumping pitch and a blinding light,
  An hour to play and the last man in.
And it's not for the sake of a ribboned coat,
  Or the selfish hope of a season's fame,
But his Captain's hand on his shoulder smote
  " Play up! play up! and play the game! "

The sand of the desert is sodden red, —
  Red with the wreck of a square that broke; — [2]
That Gatling's jammed and the Colonel dead,
  And the regiment blind with dust and smoke.
The river of death has brimmed his banks,
  And England's far, and Honor a name,
But the voice of a schoolboy rallies the ranks:
  " Play up! play up! and play the game! "

This is the word that year by year,
  While in her place the School is set,
Every one of her sons must hear,
  And none that hears it dare forget.
This they all with a joyful mind
  Bear through life like a torch in flame,
And falling fling to the host behind —
  " Play up! play up! and play the game! "

Henry Newbolt

FATE DEFIED

As it
Were tissue of silver
I'll wear, O fate, thy grey,
And go mistily radiant, clad
Like the moon.

Adelaide Crapsey

---

[2] See "Fuzzy-Wuzzy" who "bruk a British square."

TO A YOUNG POET WHO KILLED HIMSELF

When you had played with life a space
   And made it drink and lust and sing,
You flung it back into God's face
   And thought you did a noble thing.
" Lo, I have lived and loved," you said,
   " And sung to fools too dull to hear me.
Now for a cool and grassy bed
   With violets to blossom near me."

Well, rest is good for weary feet,
   Although they ran for no great prize;
And violets are very sweet,
   Although their roots are in your eyes.
But hark to what the earthworms say
   Who share with you your muddy haven:
" The fight was on — you ran away.
   You are a coward and a craven.

" The rug is ruined where you bled;
   It was a dirty way to die!
To put a bullet through your head
   And make a silly woman cry!
You could not vex the merry stars
   Nor make them heed you, dead or living.
Not all your puny anger mars
   God's irresistible forgiving.

" Yes, God forgives and men forget,
   And you're forgiven and forgotten.
You might be gaily sinning yet
   And quick and fresh instead of rotten.
And when you think of love and fame
   And all that might have come to pass,
Then don't you feel a little shame?
   And don't you think you were an ass? "

Joyce Kilmer

PRAYER FOR MIRACLE

O God!   No more Thy miracle withhold;
To us in tents give palaces of gold.
And while we stumble among things that are
Give us the solace of a guiding-star!

Anna Wickham

JOAN OF ARC, 1926

I have no solid horse to share with Joan,
I have no wit to contradict a duke
If there were dukes; I dream my dreams alone,
And cannot, in the face of Rome's rebuke,
Consider them divine.   Rather I know
That nations are not worth the men they break,
And tardy Joans are destined to forego
Danger, and the incentive of the stake.

But I shall ride — most surely I shall ride —
Across a field more difficult than France,
Sternly, upon a horse that is my pride,
And make a sword of each foul circumstance
To conquer half the world disdainfully
Before a world, prescribed, can conquer me!

Virginia Moore

PRAYER

God, though this life is but a wraith,
  Although we know not what we use,
Although we grope with little faith,
  Give me the heart to fight — and lose.

Ever insurgent let me be,
  Make me more daring than devout;
From sleek contentment keep me free,
  And fill me with a buoyant doubt.

Open my eyes to visions girt
  With beauty, and with wonder lit —
But let me always see the dirt,
  And all that spawn and die in it.

Open my ears to music; let
  Me thrill with Spring's first flutes and drums —
But never let me dare forget
  The bitter ballads of the slums.

From compromise and things half-done,
  Keep me, with stern and stubborn pride;
And when, at last, the fight is won,
  God, keep me still unsatisfied.

Louis Untermeyer

TOMORROW

Oh yesterday the cutting edge drank thirstily and deep,
The upland outlaws ringed us in and herded us as sheep,
They drove us from the stricken field and bayed us into
    keep;
            But tomorrow
  By the living God, we'll try the game again!

Oh yesterday our little troop was ridden through and
    through,
Our swaying, tattered pennons fled, a broken, beaten few,
And all a summer afternoon they hunted us and slew;
            But tomorrow,
  By the living God, we'll try the game again!

And here upon the turret-top the bale-fire glowers red,
The wake-lights burn and drip about our hacked, disfigured
    dead,
And many a broken heart is here and many a broken head;
            But tomorrow,
  By the living God, we'll try the game again!

John Masefield

ENVOY

Go, little book, and wish to all
Flowers in the garden, meat in the hall,
A bit of wine, a spice of wit,
A house with lawns enclosing it,
A living river by the door,
A nightingale in the sycamore!

— ROBERT LOUIS STEVENSON

YESTERDAY

ALDRICH, THOMAS BAILEY, was born in 1836 at Portsmouth, New Hampshire, and died in 1907. His life was a literary one almost from the start; at nineteen he was already an established critic and his first volume (*The Bells*) was published before he was twenty. He was an intimate friend of the most prominent figures of his day and although his works show their influence, his verses — especially the shorter poems — reveal a clear-cut and refined quality. His *Complete Poems* may be obtained in one volume.

ALLINGHAM, WILLIAM, was born at Ballyshannon, in 1824, and died at Whitby, England, in 1889. Besides being well known as an editor and an authority on ballads, he was a balladist of no mean rank. His first volume, *Poems,* appeared in 1850; his last, *Blackberries,* was published in 1884.

ANSTEY, F., was an English writer little known outside of his own country. His light verse appeared in *Punch* and other humorous publications.

ARNOLD, MATTHEW, was born at Laleham in 1822 and died at Liverpool, England, in 1888. The eldest son of Doctor Thomas Arnold (the famous master of Rugby), Matthew Arnold became one of the greatest thinkers of his day. A critic of life and letters as well as a poet, he wrote essays (particularly those contained in *Literature and Science*) that remain as landmarks of emancipated thought. Much of his poetry is philosophical, " Dover Beach " being one of the finest expressions of its kind.

BEDDOES, THOMAS LOVELL, was born in Clifton, England, in 1803, and died at Basle, Switzerland, in 1849. He was a precocious youth, writing dramas in his adolescence and publishing *The Bride's Tragedy* at the age of nineteen. His posthumous and more powerful play, *Death's Jest Book,* contains some of his most appealing lyrics.

BEECHING, HENRY CHARLES, was born in 1850 and became rector of Yattendon, Berks (England). The best of his verse, which is rather slight, may be found in *Love's Looking Glass.*

BRONTË, EMILY, was born in Yorkshire, England, in 1818, and died there in 1848. Prominent as the author of *Wuthering*

Heights, she adopted the pseudonym of " Ellis Bell " when, with her sister Anne (who took the name of "Acton Bell "), she published a book of verse, *Poems,* in 1846. The novels of the three sisters Brontë (Emily, Anne, and Charlotte) are too famous to require further comment.

BROWN, THOMAS EDWARD, was born on the Isle of Man, England, 1830, and died in 1897. He was headmaster at the school which Henley attended. Although he wrote but little, his work has a distinct charm of utterance. Seven of his quaintly flavored poems are contained in *The Oxford Book of Victorian Verse.*

BROWNING, ELIZABETH BARRETT, was born at Durham, England, 1806, and died in Florence, Italy, 1861. She was a precocious child, learning Hebrew and Italian, and reading Greek poetry and philosophy in her youth. Because of an accident in her thirtieth year, she was confined most of her life to her room, being too fragile to see any but her most devoted friends. When she was almost forty, she met Robert Browning, and although he was six years her junior and though her father forbade the wedding, the two famous poets were married September 12, 1846. After her marriage, she wrote her most memorable work; the exquisite *Sonnets from the Portuguese,* that immortal tribute to her poet-husband, appearing in 1850. She never returned to England, her body lying in the English burying ground at Florence, Italy.

BROWNING, ROBERT, was born at Camberwell (near London), May, 1812, and died at Venice, Italy, December, 1889. His origins were humble; he inherited West-Indian Creole blood from his paternal grandmother. Although his family was poor, he attended the University of London and in his twenty-first year published his fragmentary *Pauline.* The more characteristic *Paracelsus* appeared two years later (1835) and from that time on he wrote ceaselessly. Although his readers were impressed with the originality of his early work, his popularity did not come until middle age, when his admirers ranked him with Milton and Shakespeare. The comparison with the latter, although extreme, is not far-fetched; no one in English literature besides the immortal dramatist has covered so great a range or given the world such studies of character. Stedman calls him " the most profound modern revealer of the human soul," and, although much of his work is awkward in expression and some of it obscure in thought, there can be no question but that the best of it reaches the pinnacles of poetry. Browning died, a vigorous yea-sayer to the last, at the ripe age of seventy-seven and was buried in Westminster Abbey.

BRYANT, WILLIAM CULLEN, was born at Cummington, Mass., November 3, 1794, a direct descendant of John Alden of Plymouth, and died in New York City in 1878. He entered Williams College when he was sixteen and left a year later intending to go to Yale. Circumstances, however, forced him to abandon a college career and take up the study of law. He was admitted to the bar in 1815 and the best of his poetry was written in the few years which followed. "Thanatopsis," though unpublished until 1817, was written in his eighteenth year; his interpretations of nature led many to compare Bryant with the more fertile and far more spontaneous Wordsworth. He became editor of the New York Evening Post in 1828, holding that position for fifty years until his death. Besides his own work, he published excellent blank-verse translations of Homer's *Odyssey* and *Iliad* in 1870–72. Bryant has been called "the father of American poetry" since he was the first poet in this country to receive wide recognition.

CARROLL, LEWIS. Charles Lutwidge Dodgson, a clergyman and scholar, was born in England, in 1833, and died in 1898. After entering the Church, he became a lecturer on mathematics. The "other side of his nature" found expression in his immortal rhymes and tales for children, which he wrote under the pseudonym of "Lewis Carroll." It is certain that the eternally fresh *Alice in Wonderland* (first published in 1865) and *Through the Looking-Glass* (1872) will outlast most of the sedate and more ambitious books of the age.

DICKINSON, EMILY, was born at Amherst, Mass., December 10, 1830, and died there May 16, 1886. Living practically all her life like a hermit, she rarely set foot beyond her own doorstep. She did not need outside contacts or activities; she had a world within herself, a world wider and far richer than that of any but the greatest poets. She cared so little for public approval that, although she wrote hundreds of startling poems, she published only three or four during her lifetime — and these were printed almost against her will. Her poetry is distinguished not only by its intensity of feeling but by its brilliance of "sight and insight." Her vision was as keen in the vivid realities of earth as it was in the world which she beheld only with her spiritual eye. Her slightly "off-color" rhymes seem at first to be only an eccentricity; upon closer acquaintance with Emily Dickinson's intentions, they seem part of her acute and individual imagination. She never sought fame, yet today not only is she the most famous of American women poets, but her work has been called "perhaps the finest by a woman in the English language." No poet since Blake has packed immensities in such compressed stanzas. Her *Complete Poems* were published in one volume in 1924.

DOBSON, AUSTIN, was born at Plymouth, England, in 1840, and died in 1921. It was Dobson who started the revival of French forms in English, and his influence may be seen in the ballades and rondeaus of the period. His own verse is characterized by crisp phrasing and unusual delicacy. His most noted verses are in *Proverbs in Porcelain* (1877) and *At the Sign of the Lyre* (1885), both of these volumes being contained in the *Collected Poems* which were first issued in 1897.

EMERSON, RALPH WALDO, was born in Boston, May 25, 1803, and died at Concord, Mass., April 27, 1882. He studied for the ministry and was ordained in his twenty-sixth year. Although he continued to preach in many different churches he never became regularly connected with any of them. His first volume, a tiny collection called *Nature*, appeared in 1836. It made no particular impression on most of its readers although men like Carlyle were enthusiastic about it. Emerson's position as one of the country's most profound intellects was not established until later. His essays were (and are) stimulating in the deepest sense; his poetry, although sometimes cloudy and overburdened with philosophy, is distinguished by its intensity of thought and its flashing intuitions. His *Complete Poems* may be obtained in a single volume; many of his lines and phrases have become part of our speech.

FIELD, EUGENE, was born in St. Louis, Mo., September 3, 1850, and died in Chicago, Ill., November 4, 1895. He was a journalist all his life and it is said that he was the originator of the daily "colyum." At any rate, his prose and light verse appeared every day for more than fifteen years. He has often been called "the children's laureate," but he was also a genuine scholar and his *Echoes from the Sabine Farm* are witty paraphrases of the odes of Horace. Whether he sang of trumpets and drums, homely philosophy or mythical dinkey birds in amfalula trees, Field was always the natural, high-hearted minstrel. His *Poems* have been collected in a single volume.

FITZGERALD, EDWARD, was born in Suffolk, England, in 1809, and died in Norfolk, 1883. From early youth he was interested in foreign literature, especially the poetry of the East, and published many translations from the Greek, the Spanish, and the Persian, most of which were printed anonymously. His chief fame rests on *The Rubaiyat of Omar Khayyam,* of which there have been a hundred different editions ranging from the very cheapest reprints to the elaborately illustrated gift books. It might be added that the *Rubaiyat* is not so much a translation as a free paraphrase, Fitzgerald deserving fully as much credit for the work as the ancient Persian poet.

GILBERT, W. S., was born in London, 1836, and died at Harrow Weald, England, May, 1911. He is best known as the librettist of *Pinafore, The Mikado, Patience, Iolanthe,* and half a dozen other classic comic operas for which Arthur Sullivan composed the music. Besides being collaborator, Gilbert was the author of a number of dramas. But his *Bab Ballads* would be sufficient to establish his prominence even if all his other work were forgotten, the burlesque grace and rippling rhymes being the most delightful of their type.

HARDY, THOMAS, "the grand old man of modern letters," was born near Dorchester, England, in 1840. Although his first interest was in poetry, he attracted most attention as a novelist, his *Tess of the D'Urbervilles* and *Jude the Obscure* being internationally famous. When he was sixty, he abandoned prose and turned back to **poetry,** which is the form he always loved best. His magnificent *Collected Poems* were issued in 1919. This volume was followed by *Late Lyrics and Earlier* (1922), and in 1925, at the age of eighty-five, Hardy prepared another notable volume of verse. His is a varied genius, one of his greatest gifts being the ability to capture the "feel" of a whole countryside in a single stanza.

HARTE, BRET, was born in Albany, N. Y., August 25, 1839, and died in England, May 6, 1902. Harte is chiefly known as a writer of Western short stories like *The Luck of Roaring Camp,* stories which have been called "the work of a lesser, transplanted Dickens." His verse, notably *East and West*

Poems (1871), vibrates with a mixture of breezy humor and sentiment. A complete *Poetical Works* has been published recently.

HENLEY, WILLIAM ERNEST, was born in Gloucester, England, August 23, 1849, and died at Woking, England, June 11, 1903. Henley was one of the greatest editors of his day and, although he himself was crippled in health, his brave spirit was an inspiration to all who came in contact with him. While recovering from an operation (his foot was amputated and, later, treated by the famous surgeon John Lister) he wrote his splendid series *Hospital Sketches* and met Robert Louis Stevenson, who became his intimate friend. The buoyant note is never absent from his work and *Poems* (first printed in 1898) stir one with the same heartiness that thrilled readers a generation ago.

HOLMES, OLIVER WENDELL, was born in Cambridge, Mass., August 29, 1809, and died in Boston, October 7, 1894. He studied law, but gave it up for medicine, receiving his medical degree in 1836, the same year in which he published his first volume, *Poems*. He taught at Dartmouth and Harvard for more than forty years and, as professor, critic, poet, and wit, occupied one of the most prominent positions in the famous New England group. His *Complete Poems* are obtainable in a single volume which contains his humorous as well as his serious verse. Though not a genius, Holmes was significant of his period; he represented, as has been said, culture rather than creation.

LANG, ANDREW, was born in Scotland in 1844, and died in England in 1912. Lang is chiefly known as a scholarly translator. Among children, his reputation rests securely on the variously colored *Fairy Books* which he edited. With Austin Dobson, he helped popularize the French forms in England and his *Ballades in Blue China* (1880) are excellent examples of " refrain poetry."

LANIER, SIDNEY, was born in Macon, Georgia, February 3, 1842, and died in the mountains of North Carolina, September 7, 1881. Poor health was responsible for his early death and his small output, for it is evident that, had Lanier been robust, his contribution to American poetry would have been among the greatest. A natural musician (at one time he played the flute with the Symphony Orchestra in Baltimore), he was able to make his *Poems* (issued complete in one volume in 1906) rich in musical effects and changing accents.

LEAR, EDWARD, was born near London, in 1812, and died in Italy, in 1888. His ambition was to be a landscape painter and he lived many years in Italy in order to transplant the glamour of the Italian scene to his canvases. In his lighter moments, he wrote nonsense rhymes, illustrating them with even more nonsensical drawings. Today his sober, academic paintings are forgotten while his nonsense lyrics and limericks have become immortal.

LEIGH, H. S., was born in England about 1840 and, though he has written but little, is known as the author of a few extremely clever parodies.

LONGFELLOW, HENRY WADSWORTH, was born in Portland, Maine, February 27, 1807, and died in Cambridge, Mass., March 24, 1882. After graduating from Bowdoin College, he spent three years in Europe studying modern languages. His researches in foreign literature influenced much of his work, and he was one of the first to bring over to America the poetry of Spain, Italy and Germany. But he was also a pioneer in the use of local material; *Hiawatha*, in spite of its familiarity, remains one of the richest pictures of Indian life, while *Evangeline* is a miniature epic of Nova Scotia. So much stress has been laid upon Longfellow's brilliant adaptations of other cultures that readers of today are in danger of forgetting the definitely American quality which gave rise not only to the *Poems on Slavery* (1842) and *The Courtship of Miles Standish* (1858), but to a score of less familiar songs and narratives. As a writer of ballads, Longfellow ranks among the best of the moderns; the swing of his rhythms and the directness of his language are sufficient to account for his constant popularity. A splendid edition of his *Complete Poems* has been published by Houghton Mifflin Company and contains almost 900 pages.

LOWELL, JAMES RUSSELL, was born in Cambridge, Mass., February 22, 1819, and died there, August 12, 1891. He was one of the most fertile as well as one of the best craftsmen of the New England group. He was astonishingly versatile: he wrote Yankee dialect verses as racy as the political *Biglow Papers;* religious poetry, like *The Vision of Sir Launfal,* which was both profound and popular; memorial poems which rank almost as high as his "Harvard Commemoration Ode"; essays which,

though sometimes indiscriminating in judgment, were always individual. His *Complete Poems* are obtainable in a single volume.

MASSEY, GERALD, was born near Tring, England, in 1828
and died at South Norwood, England, in October, 1907. He
was the son of poor laborers and as a boy was forced to earn
his living as a spinner in a silk factory. At the age of twenty-
one he edited a paper entitled *The Spirit of Freedom,* and he
brought out his first volume of poems when he was twenty-
two. He was always a champion of "the under-dog" and his
Poems and Ballads (1854) reveals a struggling but undaunted
spirit.

MEYNELL, ALICE, was born in England in 1850, and died in
1923. After spending her early years in Italy, she married
Wilfrid Meynell, the friend and literary executor of Francis
Thompson. Her *Collected Poems* (1923) are, in the main,
philosophical; but, beneath the intellectual surface, one feels
the warmth of a nature rich in feeling, sensitive in expression.

MILLER, JOAQUIN, was born March 10, 1841, "in a covered
wagon at the time it crossed the line dividing Indiana from
Ohio," and died in California in 1913. His career was a curious
and sensational one. His work failing to arouse any enthusiasm in the country of his birth, Miller left America in despera-
tion and went to England. Even there no publisher would print
his volume and he was forced to undertake the publishing of it
himself. One hundred copies of his *Pacific Poems* were issued
— with startling results. Miller became famous overnight!
The poetry itself suffers from too much straining for effect;
a great deal of Miller's writing is theatrical and exaggerated.
At the best, his verse calls up the wild beauty and spaciousness
of the West, and such a poem as "Columbus" seems sure of
its place in anthologies. Miller's *Complete Poetical Works* were
published recently.

MUNKITTRICK, R. K., was born in Manchester, England, in
1850 and came to America as a child. He lived most of his life
in New Jersey and was on the staff of *Puck,* a humorous weekly,
from 1881 to 1889. Although his work is no longer familiar
to most readers, his light verse had quite a vogue in the
1890's.

NOEL, RODEN, was born in England in 1834, and died in
1894. The son of the Earl of Gainsborough, he spent his childhood in beautiful Rutlandshire, and much of his poetry reflects

the colors of his early surroundings. *My Sea* (1906) contains the best of his posthumous poetry, although the earlier volumes are more favored.

O'SHAUGHNESSY, ARTHUR, was born in London in 1844, and died there in his thirty-seventh year. Although much of his verse is doomed to extinction, he will always be known by two or three poems, of which the most famous is the "Ode," first brought to a wide audience when Palgrave included part of it in his *Golden Treasury*. *The Poems of Arthur O'Shaughnessy*, carefully edited, appeared in 1922.

PATMORE, COVENTRY, was born in Woodford, England, in 1823, and died at Lymington, in 1896. When he was only twenty-three, he became assistant librarian in the British Museum. His work — *The Angel in the House* (1854) being the best known of his volumes — is highly characteristic of his spirit, being a quaint combination of mysticism and simplicity.

POE, EDGAR ALLAN, was born in Boston, Mass., January 19, 1809, and died in Baltimore, Md., October 7, 1849. Although born in New England, Poe is, in every sense, a Southern poet: upon the death of his parents, Poe was taken into the family of Mr. and Mrs. Allan at Richmond, Va., when he was two years old; he entered the University of Virginia in 1826, and lived in Baltimore most of the rest of his life. He was undoubtedly one of the greatest geniuses this country has ever known. When *The Raven and Other Poems* (1845) appeared, it was quoted everywhere. His fame spread rapidly, and he was acclaimed with high plaudits in Europe, where he and Whitman have influenced a great part of modern literature. His grotesque tales, critical as well as personal sketches, scientific essays, and, above all, his few but brilliant poems place him among the true magicians who weave spells with nothing more substantial than shining words.

RILEY, JAMES WHITCOMB, was born October 7, 1849, in Greenfield, Ind., and died in Indianapolis, July 22, 1916. Contrary to the usual stories, Riley was not a poor son of the soil; his father was a lawyer and Riley was not only given a good education but prepared for the law. Nevertheless, Riley's adventurous nature took him from his books and at eighteen he joined a traveling troupe of actors, beat the bass drum during the intermission, painted scenery and wrote new versions of the company's old songs. In 1882, when he was on the staff of the Indianapolis Journal, he wrote his first dialect poems (claiming they were the work of an uneducated farmer, " Benj. F. Johnson, of Boone, the Hoosier poet ") and his work was copied throughout the country. The term " the Hoosier poet " stuck to him, and even people who ordinarily disliked poetry responded (and still respond) to the homely, sentimental rhymes of *Afterwhiles* (1887), *Rhymes of Childhood* (1890) and *Neighborly Poems* (1891).

ROSSETTI, CHRISTINA GEORGINA, was born in London in 1830 and died there in 1894. She was the daughter of the famous political exile and student, Gabriel Rossetti, and sister of the poet and artist, Dante Gabriel Rossetti. During her life she published half a dozen volumes which place her among the greatest of women poets. The delicate purity of her early lyrics is surpassed only by her remarkably musical sonnets; her later work includes some of the richest religious poetry ever written. Swinburne wrote of one of her devotional poems (" Passing Away "), " It is so much the noblest sacred poem in our language that there is none which comes near it enough to stand second." Collected editions of her poetry have appeared on both sides of the Atlantic.

STEVENSON, ROBERT LOUIS, was born in Edinburgh, Scotland, in 1850. He was at first trained to be a lighthouse engineer, but later was called to the bar (in 1875) and practiced law for a few years. His ill-health forced him to abandon the profession and necessitated travel, particularly in warm climates. In 1879 he journeyed to California, where, a year later, he married. Finally he settled at Vailima, in the Samoan Islands, where, after a long struggle against his illness, he died of consumption in 1894. Among adults, Stevenson's chief fame rests on his novels. Young people, however, know him as the immortal author of *Treasure Island* and *A Child's Garden of Verses,* which might be said to have taken its place as a modern Mother Goose.

SWINBURNE, ALGERNON CHARLES, was born at Pimlico, April 5, 1837, and died in England in 1909. As a student at Oxford, he was distinguished for his remarkable command of Greek and Latin, and his poetry reveals his familiarity with the classics. Upon the publication of *Atalanta in Calydon* (1865) and *Poems and Ballads* (1866) it was at once evident that a new genius of rhyme and rhythm had appeared. Although he is too fond of continued alliteration, and too unrestrained in the flow of his syllables, there is a swing in the best of Swinburne's rolling lines which few poets have surpassed.

TENNYSON, ALFRED, LORD, was born in Lincolnshire, England, August 6, 1809, and died at Haslemere, Surrey, October 6, 1892. His youth was spent with his brothers (both of whom were poets) in the county of his birth and near the sea, and to this background, as Stedman notes, " we owe much of the landscape, atmosphere, and truth to nature, of his poetry and its exquisitely idyllic character." The two-volume edition of his *Poems* in 1842 made him universally famous, and upon the death of Wordsworth in 1850 Tennyson was made Poet Laureate. "In Memoriam," which made his position secure, is one of the greatest modern elegies. Although he wrote several dramas, Tennyson's reputation today rests on " The Princess," " Maud," and his shorter pieces, particularly the lyrics which combine music and intellectual power.

WHITMAN, WALT, was born in West Hills, Long Island, May 31, 1819, and died in Camden, New Jersey, March 26, 1892. His father left the Long Island farm, which had been in the family for generations, and went to Brooklyn in 1823, where the young Whitman went to the public schools and learned the printer's trade. Until 1861, he busied himself as printer, editor, and hack-writer. His *Leaves of Grass* had already appeared in 1855, but it was very unlike the amplified and much richer versions that were to appear later. He served as nurse and "wound-dresser" for three years during the Civil War. Following this experience, he was given a position in the Department of the Interior in 1865, but was dismissed by a secretary who had read certain passages in *Leaves of Grass* which displeased him. Meanwhile, the volume had caused its author's name to be spread abroad. Whitman was already becoming a cult in England, where Swinburne and Rossetti were championing the poet of " democratic vistas." His *Drum-Taps* (1866), inspired by the war and the assassination of Lincoln, brought him still wider acclaim. Today his work is hailed not merely as literature but as prophecy throughout the world. His departures in form caused him to be considered one of the great poetic emancipators; in spirit he was one of the most jubilant yea-sayers, one of the greatest lovers of humanity who have ever lived. His work, in its revelation of the " glory of the commonplace," is elemental.

WHITTIER, JOHN GREENLEAF, was born at East Haverhill, Mass., December 17, 1807, and died at Hampton Falls, N. H., September 7, 1892. He had but little schooling and (being a country boy) he was greatly affected by the pastoral lyrics of Robert Burns. Known as "the Quaker poet," he identified himself with the Antislavery movement and never ceased to strike blows for the cause in which he believed. His nature poetry reveals his essential sincerity and a strongly religious sense.

TODAY

(Most of the publishers of the living poets issue pamphlets or circulars giving biographical data and other information concerning their authors.)

ADAMS, LÉONIE, was born in Brooklyn, N. Y., December 9, 1899, and graduated from Barnard College, her first published verse appearing in *The New Republic* while she was still an undergraduate. Since that time she has taught in private schools. Her volume, *Those Not Elect* (1925), is distinguished by a quiet ecstasy, even the landscapes being spiritualized.

AIKEN, CONRAD, was born in Savannah, Ga., August 5, 1889, was class poet at Harvard, traveled extensively after receiving his degree in 1912 and, in 1921, moved his family to England, to the Sussex coast. Besides his poetry, Aiken is the author of a volume of tales, *Bring! Bring!* (1925), which combines the short story and the study, and an excellent volume of advanced critical essays, *Scepticisms* (1919). His poems are remarkable for their music; *Nocturne of Remembered Spring* (1917) and *The House of Dust* (1920) are rich with exquisite effects of word-color and shifting rhythms. *Punch: The Immortal Liar* (1921) is more vigorous and unfolds a more direct narrative. *Priapus and the Pool* (1925) contains not only Aiken's most recent lyrics but some of the most poignant passages he has ever written.

AUSLANDER, JOSEPH, was born in Philadelphia, Pa., October 17, 1897. He was educated at Harvard and the Sorbonne and taught for a while at his Alma Mater in Cambridge. His first volume, *Sunrise Trumpets* (1924), shows the author as an expert phrasemaker as well as a natural musician. *Cyclop's*

Eye (1926) displays the author's gifts with a new restraint.

BELLOC, HILAIRE, was born in France, July 27, 1870, served in the French artillery, moved to England and was naturalized as a British subject, finished his education at Oxford, and in 1906 was elected a member of the House of Commons. As an author, he is extremely versatile: he has written satirical novels, travel books, biographies, religious essays, political articles, serious poems and light verse which has its tongue in its cheek. His *Collected Poems* (1923) include all but the nonsense verses, which many readers have rated even higher than his more dignified lines. Lovers of burlesque will find continual delight in Belloc's *Cautionary Tales* and *The Bad Child's Book of Beasts*.

BENÉT, STEPHEN VINCENT, the younger brother of William Rose Benét, was born in Bethlehem, Pa., in July, 1898. He graduated from Yale in 1919, but even before he had entered college he had written a remarkable little volume, *Five Men and Pompey*, which was published in 1915. With each new volume, Stephen Benét has made great strides; *Heavens and Earth* (1920) shows his whimsical imagination, while *Tiger Joy* (1925) reveals him as one of the best of living ballad-makers.

BENÉT, WILLIAM ROSE, the older brother of Stephen Vincent Benét, was born at Fort Hamilton, N. Y., February 2, 1886, graduating from Yale in 1907. He has been associated with magazines since 1909, becoming one of the founders and editors of *The Saturday Review of Literature* in 1924. The outstanding feature of his work is its vigorous fantasy; even his first volume, *Merchants from Cathay* (1913), is rich with unusual decorations. Of his later volumes, the two most appealing are *The Burglar of the Zodiac* (1918) and *Moons of Grandeur* (1920).

BOGAN, LOUISE, was born in Maine, August 11, 1897, and was educated in New England. She has lived in New York since 1919. Her volume *Body of This Death* (1923) is one of the most brilliant first offerings which any poet of the period has produced. Her verse is sharply edged and her effects are keen but never cold.

BRANCH, ANNA HEMPSTEAD, was born in New London, Conn., and graduated from Smith College in 1897. Her volumes, *The Shoes That Danced* (1905) and *Rose of the Wind*

(1910), attain a high seriousness; the poetry is religious without becoming sentimental. It is consistently philosophical — but Miss Branch is a philosopher who knows how to sing.

BROOKE, RUPERT, was born at Rugby, England, where his father was assistant master, August 3, 1887. When the war came, Brooke enlisted and sailed with the British Mediterranean Expeditionary Force in February, 1915, to take part in the unfortunate Dardanelles campaign. Although the myth has it that Brooke died on the battlefield, the truth is that he never reached his destination. He died of blood-poison and was buried on the Island of Skyros, in the Aegean, April 23, 1915. His early death was one of the greatest losses to modern poetry, for, had Brooke lived, it seems certain he would have been among England's most memorable singers. His lines are passionate without falling into rhetoric, " his world," as Walter de la Mare wrote, " stands out like the towers and pinnacles of a city under the light of a sunny sky." *Collected Poems* appeared with a valuable Memoir late in 1915.

BYNNER, WITTER, was born in Brooklyn, N. Y., August 10, 1881, and graduated from Harvard in 1902. He was assistant editor of various periodicals for several years, but recently has devoted himself entirely to poetry, traveling in the Orient where he prepared his many translations from the Chinese. Although Bynner has identified himself with many causes and has written many semi-political verses championing one propaganda or another, his is primarily a lyric spirit. He is at his best in *Grenstone Poems* (1917) and *A Canticle of Pan* (1920).

CAMPBELL, JOSEPH, was born in Belfast, Ireland, in 1881 and is an artist as well as a poet. *The Rushlight* (1906) is a volume of his poems which is made more attractive by the author's own illustrations. *The Mountainy Singer* (1909) is the best known of his books.

CARMAN, BLISS, was born in Fredericton, New Brunswick, April 15, 1861, but moved to the United States in 1889. He became famous through his association with Richard Hovey, the two poets collaborating and producing the three volumes (*Songs from Vagabondia*) which made such a stir in the Eighteen Nineties. Carman's contribution was frankly pagan and, though its buoyancy was a trifle less than Hovey's, it was never without a bright leap and an athletic humor. Of Carman's later volumes, the most ingratiating is *April Airs* (1916).

CARRYL, GUY WETMORE, was born in New York City, March 4, 1873, and died in 1904. His early death — he had just turned thirty when he died — robbed America of its most brilliant versifier; had he lived, he would undoubtedly have ranked as high as W. S. Gilbert. This country has never known more cleverly turned light verse and rhymes more dazzling than those contained in *Fables for the Frivolous* (1898), *Mother Goose for Grownups* (1900), and the wild variations on fairy tales in *Grimm Tales Made Gay* (1903).

CAWEIN, MADISON, was born in Louisville, Ky., in 1865 and spent most of his life in the state of his birth. Although his occupation kept him confined to the city much of the time, he was a great lover of the countryside about him — he has been christened "the Keats of Kentucky." *The Vale of Tempe* (1905), and *The Poet, the Fool and the Faeries* (1912) contain his most characteristic verses. Cawein died in 1914.

CHESTERTON, G. K., was born in Kensington, England, in 1874, and, next to H. G. Wells, is the most fertile writer of his day. He has to his credit no less than twenty-five volumes, he is the editor of a magazine, a contributor to a score of others, a public speaker, a creator of religious detective stories (the first of their kind!), and an expert draughtsman. *The Flying Inn* (1914) is possibly the best of his extravaganzas; it might be termed a serious comic-opera turned upside down with a score of intoxicating lyrics. What makes these verses so jolly may be discovered by reading the gay *Wine, Women and Song* (1924). The serious Chesterton is to be found in the more earnest *Poems* (1915) and *The Ballad of St. Barbara* (1922).

COATSWORTH, ELIZABETH J., was born in Buffalo, N. Y., in 1893, and, after travel abroad, returned to America, where she divides her time between a residence in California and an old home on the seacoast of Massachusetts. Her first volume was *Fox-Footprints* (1921), a group of studies in the Oriental manner. *Atlas and Beyond* (1924) and the more recent poems have a sharper flavor, a tang of personality which makes Miss Coatsworth one of the most interesting of the younger women.

COLUM, PADRAIC, was born at Longford, Ireland, December 8, 1881, and came to America about 1912. *Wild Earth* (1909) and *Dramatic Poems* (1922) disclose Colum's participation in the Irish revival (he was one of the founders of the Irish

National Theatre) as well as his natural inheritance of racy song.

CONKLING, GRACE HAZARD, was born in New York City in 1878, and graduated from Smith College in 1899. After studying music in Europe she returned to Smith, where she has taught since 1914. Besides being the author of *Afternoons of April* (1915) and *Wilderness Songs* (1920), two volumes disclosing a charm which is rarely cloying, she is the mother of the remarkable child-poet, Hilda.

CONKLING, HILDA, daughter of the poet, Grace Hazard Conkling, was born at Catskill-on-Hudson, October 8, 1910, and came to Northampton, Mass., when she was three years old. When scarcely more than a baby, she began to speak in terms of poetry — she "talked" her fancies to her mother, who copied them down and, later, read them to Hilda for correction. When Hilda was nine years old, her *Poems by a Little Girl* (1920) appeared. *Shoes of the Wind* (1922) followed, two years later. In both of these volumes Hilda displays a beauty of phrase and a sharpness of vision which any poet might envy.

CORNFORD, FRANCES, a descendant of Charles Darwin, was born at Cambridge, England, in 1886. Her two tiny volumes, *Spring Morning* (1915) and *Autumn Midnight* (1923), are scarcely more than pamphlets, but both of them contain the stamp of a distinct personality.

CRANE, NATHALIA, possibly the most remarkable literary phenomenon of the day, was born in New York City, August 11, 1913. She began actually writing at the age of eight, typing out her own verses and sending them to the papers herself. Several of her poems were printed by editors who accepted them wholly on their own merit, and it was only after Nathalia called at the office of the *New York Sun* that the poetry editor realized that the lines which he had praised so highly had been written by a child. From that time on, Nathalia's progress has been sensational. When she was ten, her first volume, *The Janitor's Boy* (1923), was hailed everywhere; it went through seven editions in America and two in England. Late in 1925, *Lava Lane* was published and received even greater applause. Nathalia was invited to join the British Society of Authors and Playwrights, she being the first American poet since Walt Whitman to whom this honor was extended. It must be admitted that there are many who doubt that any child could write such amazing poetry. But there is plenty of evidence to show that, whatever may be the source of her inspiration, Nathalia is the actual author of her two volumes.

CRAPSEY, ADELAIDE, was born in Rochester, N. Y., September 9, 1878, and died at Saranac Lake, N. Y., October 8, 1914. Her early death forced her to leave her work unfinished, her small volume of *Verse* appearing a year after she died. *A Study in English Metrics*, which, even in its incomplete form, is a scholarly examination of rhythm and meter, appeared in 1918.

" D., H. " (HILDA DOOLITTLE), was born September 10, 1886, at Bethlehem, Pa., attended Bryn Mawr College, went abroad in 1911, and has lived in London and in Switzerland since that time. She was one of the founders of Imagism, that school of poets which placed the chief emphasis on " the sharp presentation of an image " and " a concentrated poetry that is hard and clear." Her own work proves her to be not only the best of her group but the only true Imagist. Her *Collected Poems* (1925) are packed with loveliness, even if, at first glance, it seems a frozen beauty.

DALY, T. A., was born in Philadelphia, Pa., May 28, 1871, and left Fordham University at the end of his Sophomore year to enter journalism. Since 1891 he has been a newspaper man, a public speaker, a professional humorist and author of some of the most delectable dialect verse ever written in America. All of his volumes display human sympathy beneath their comic outlines, a sympathy which is tender without being sentimental. Readers who wish to know more of his work are recommended to *Carmina* (1909) and *McAroni Ballads* (1919).

DAVIES, W. H., was born in Monmouthshire, England, April 20, 1870. He was unknown until Bernard Shaw discovered him. Previous to this, Davies had earned his living as a cattleman, a berry-picker and day laborer. Like the American Harry Kemp, he became known as a " tramp poet," but the best of his verse does not concern the workaday world. Davies is first of all an artless lover of nature; his songs are as simple as those of a bird with but a few notes. His is the robin's voice, not the ecstatic nightingale's, but, within his own range, the tones are refreshingly clean and cool. Two volumes of his *Collected Poems* have already appeared; an illustrated *Selected Poems* was published in 1925.

DEANE, ANTHONY C., was born in England in 1870, and, be-

sides being vicar of All Saints, is one of the cleverest of contemporary parodists. His *New Rhymes for Old* (1901), although
little known, is full of surprises.

DE LA MARE, WALTER, was born in Kent, England, in 1873.
He published his early work under the name of " Walter Ramal,"
and did not become famous until the publication of *Peacock Pie*
(1913). There are two distinct notes in de la Mare's poetry.
In one vein, he writes a sort of glorified nursery rhyme, verses
which read like selections from Mother Goose turned into magic
by Shakespeare. In the other mood he expresses the super-
natural world: a world of strange moonlight, half-heard whispers,
and ghostly winds. *The Listeners* (1915) combines both of these
moods and contains some of the most haunting lyrics of the
period. He has written several novels, a few fairy plays, and
compiled a highly personal anthology (*Come Hither*).

DOYLE, CAMILLA, was born in Norwich, England, and is an
artist as well as a poet. *Poems* (1923) is a graceful collection,
expressing large things in a small compass, like a Japanese print.

DUNBAR, PAUL LAURENCE, the most famous of the Negro
poets of America, was born at Dayton, Ohio, in 1872, the son
of slaves. Even while he was writing the verses which were to
become so widely known, he had to earn his living as an elevator
boy. Although he wrote several volumes of short stories and
two novels, he was at his best in the grave and rollicking rhymes
in dialect. *Lyrics of Lowly Life* (1896) and *Lyrics of the
Hearthside* (1899) are sometimes tender, sometimes mocking,
but they are always faithful renderings of Dunbar's own people.
His interpretations have placed Dunbar somewhere between
Eugene Field and James Whitcomb Riley.

FARJEON, ELEANOR, is a young Englishwoman whose *Gypsy
and Ginger* is well known to young readers. Her more ambitious
verse may be found in *Sonnets and Poems* (1918).

FROST, ROBERT, " the voice of New Engand," was born in
San Francisco, Cal., March 26, 1875. Except for " the accident
of birth," Frost is in no sense a Californian; at the age of ten,
he came East to the hills where, for eight generations, his fore-
fathers had lived. He attended Dartmouth and Harvard for a
short time, but graduated from neither. For three years he
taught school, worked in a factory, edited a weekly paper, and,
in 1900, became a farmer at Derry, New Hampshire. For eleven
years he struggled with the soil, writing his poetry in seclusion

ar.d obscurity. A few of his verses had appeared in two magazines, but the peculiar flavor of his poetry seemed to displease
the editors and Frost discontinued submitting his work to the
periodicals. For twenty years he wrote without an audience, and
it was not until he was almost forty that his first volume, *A
Boy's Will* (1913), was published in England. It created a little
comment, but it was not until the American publication of
North of Boston (1914) that Frost came into his own. He was
immediately acclaimed with an enthusiasm that grew with the
two succeeding volumes, *Mountain Interval* (1916) and *New
Hampshire* (1923). (The last named was awarded the Pulitzer
Prize for the best volume of poetry published during the year.)
No poetry ever written has been closer to the earth nor has any
poet communicated a greater love of it. In his longer monologues as well as the lovely " grace notes " he is the true pastoral
poet, one who, though his work is by no means ended, can
already take his place with Virgil and Wordsworth. Universal
in his appeal, Frost is at the same time the most American of
living poets.

FYLEMAN, ROSE, is an Englishwoman chiefly known for her
bright and happy contributions to " Punch " and her own child-
like rhymes. *Fairies and Chimneys* (1918) has gone through
ten editions and a collected edition of her elfin rhymes has
appeared in America.

GALE, NORMAN, was born in Surrey, England, in 1862, was
educated at Oxford, and became a teacher by profession. He
has published eight volumes of graceful, rustic verse, *Collected
Poems* appearing in 1914.

GINSBERG, LOUIS, was born in Newark, N. J., October 1,
1896, was educated at Rutgers, and has been teaching in the
high schools of New Jersey since 1918. His first volume, *The
Attic of the Past* (1920), is lyrical throughout; his more recent
verses attain a much higher level, being both simple and highly
imaginative.

GOING, CHARLES BUXTON, was born in Westchester, N. Y.,
April 5, 1863, and is prominent as a chemical engineer, an
editor of a technical magazine, and the author of several books
on engineering, in addition to being a poet. *Star-Glow and Song*
(1909) shows that Mr. Going can compose delicate lyrics as weil
as hearty narratives, although the outstanding features of the
volume are the rhymed tales and ballads.

GORE-BOOTH, EVA, was born in Sligo, Ireland, in 1871. Though she has written several volumes of verse, of which the most recent is *The Sword of Justice* (1918), she is known principally for the tiny lyric on page 298, without which no anthology of the period would be complete.

GRAVES, ROBERT, son of the Irish poet Alfred Percival Graves, was born in England, July 26, 1895. He was educated at Oxford and, during the war, served three times in France, where he became an intimate friend of that other war-poet, Siegfried Sassoon. Although he shared Sassoon's hatred of war, his own poetry is much lighter in color as well as more buoyant. The mixture of healing humor and rural grace is seen at its best in *Fairies and Fusiliers* (1917) and *Country Sentiment* (1919).

GREENWOOD, ROLLAND R., was born at Worcester, Mass., January 20, 1885, was educated at Clark College, and has been a teacher and lecturer since 1908. His verse has appeared in many magazines, the poem in this volume being first printed in *The New York Times*.

GUITERMAN, ARTHUR, was born in Vienna, Austria, of American parents, November 20, 1871. He came to America as a child and has lived in New York most of his life. A skilled versifier, he originated the " Rhymed Reviews " which appeared in *Life*. Although *The Laughing Muse* (1915) is a wholly humorous collection, *The Mirthful Lyre* (1918) is a still more attractive volume with a greater range of interests.

HARVEY, F. W., was born in Gloucestershire, England, in 1888, became a solicitor in 1912, enlisted in August, 1914, and was taken prisoner two years later. It was in the German prison camp at Gütersloh that he wrote his most noted poems. *Farewell* (1921) is the latest of his volumes.

HODGSON, RALPH, was born in Northumberland, England, 1871, and, for a time, earned his living as journalist, editor, and cartoonist. In non-literary circles he is known as the leading authority on bull terriers. In 1924, he accepted an invitation to visit Japan as lecturer in English literature. As a poet, Hodgson has written only a little — but that little is exquisite. His poems were first issued in broadsides and pamphlets, printed by a small firm of which he was one of the partners. Later the contents of these Chapbooks were collected in the volume *Poems* (1917) which contains some of the rarest and most unforgettable records of beauty of our time.

HOUSMAN, A. E., was born in England, March 26, 1859, and educated at Oxford. He became a professor of Latin in 1892 and has been a teacher ever since. Housman was unknown as a poet until he was thirty-seven, but upon the appearance of *A Shropshire Lad* (1896), he became immediately and internationally famous. In spite of the fact that most of the poems are darkly ironic and the philosophy is altogether pessimistic, these lyrics were continually quoted because of their simplicity and direct music. After a silence of twenty-six years, Housman's second volume, significantly entitled *Last Poems,* appeared in 1922.

HOVEY, RICHARD, was born at Normal, Illinois, May 4, 1864, graduated from Dartmouth in 1885, was a professor of literature at Barnard and died, in his thirty-sixth year, in New York, February 24, 1900. Although several volumes appeared under his own name, Hovey is best known as the collaborator of Bliss Carman, with whom he wrote *Songs from Vagabondia* (1894), *More Songs from Vagabondia* (1896) and *Last Songs from Vagabondia* (1900). His poetry is even more exuberant than Carman's and goes still deeper into experience. His is an almost unique combination of high spirits and high seriousness. *Along the Trail* (1898) is composed entirely of Hovey's own poems.

HOYT, HELEN, was born at Norwalk, Conn., in 1887. She was, for a while, connected with *Poetry: A Magazine of Verse* and was also on the staff of the more radical *Others*. In 1919, she went to California for a visit and remained to marry W. W. Lyman, then instructor at the University of California. Her volume of love poems, *Apples Here in My Basket* (1924), is a complete feminine cycle, the expression of a richly generous nature. Her descriptive poems, particularly " Ellis Park," have been much quoted.

KILMER, JOYCE, was born at New Brunswick, N. J., December 6, 1886, graduated from Rutgers College in 1904, was instructor of Latin, book-salesman, editor, lexicographer, and book-reviewer until the outbreak of the war. In 1917 he enlisted as a private in the National Guard and on July 30, 1918, during the battle of the river Ourcq, was killed in action. Death came before this poet's gift had fully developed, but *Trees and Other Poems* (1914) as well as *Main Street and Other Poems* (1917) express a lovable personality and an almost religious chivalry.

His " Trees " is one of the most popular poems of the last decade.

KIPLING, RUDYARD, was born in Bombay, India, December 30, 1865, was educated in England, returned to India, where he wrote for the Indian press until 1890; then he went to England, where, except for a short stay in America, he has lived ever since. His extremely varied work appeals to readers of every age. For the very young, there are the *Just So Stories;* for those somewhat older, there are the two *Jungle Books;* while all lovers of well-told fiction will continue to be fascinated by *Plain Tales from the Hills* and *Under the Deodars.* As a document of Indian life, *Kim,* who is a sort of Mowgli grown up, is Kipling's masterpiece. Kipling's fame as a novelist is equaled if not surpassed by his popularity as a poet. All of his volumes are liberally sprinkled with infectious verses and his *Collected Poems* (1920), a splendidly inclusive edition, contains some of the most rousing tales in verse we possess. Kipling glorifies the material world; he pierces seemingly commonplace things like machinery, slang, cockney soldiers — and reveals their hidden beauty. For sheer masculine rhythms, his swinging narratives and ballads are without parallel.

LAING, A. K., was born at Great Neck, L. I., August 7, 1903, and was educated at Dartmouth, where he was one of the editors of the college magazine. His own work is neatly executed, especially in the French forms.

LEDWIDGE, FRANCIS, was born in County Meath, Ireland, in 1891. He was, as he once wrote, " educated by life," earning his living as a miner, a farm-hand, a grocer's clerk, and a scavenger. His poetry was discovered by Lord Dunsany, the dramatist, who did much to spread Ledwidge's reputation abroad. Ledwidge served as a corporal in the Great War and was killed on the Flanders front in July, 1917, when he had just turned twenty-six. His delicately descriptive, twilight-colored verse has been collected in *Complete Poems* (1919).

LE GALLIENNE, RICHARD, was born at Liverpool, England, in 1866, entered upon a business career after leaving Liverpool College, but, after five or six years, gave up commercial life to devote himself to literature. He came to America about twenty years ago and has lived here ever since. A very fertile writer, he is the author of more than a score of volumes of essays, prose fancies, novels, adaptations of old myths, and poems. His early *English Poems* (1892) has been considered by many to be his best offering, but *The Lonely Dancer* (1914) is an even more graceful summary of the poet's qualities.

LETTS, WINIFRED M., was born in Ireland and her early work concerned itself entirely with the comedies and tragedies of her background. *Songs from Leinster* (1913) is her most characteristic volume, a book rich in the poetry of simple folk. *Hallow E'en* (1916) is a more recent production by one who delights in calling herself " a back-door sort of bard."

LEWIS, MICHAEL. No biographical data are available concerning this writer. From certain sources of information, however, it has been gathered that " Michael Lewis " is a pseudonym, the pen-name over which an otherwise serious American poet writes occasional light verse.

LINDSAY, VACHEL, was born at Springfield, Ill., November 10, 1879. He was educated at Hiram College and the Art Institute of Chicago. He hoped, at first, to earn his living as an artist and his latest and most inclusive volume, *Collected Poems* (1925), is embellished with many of his fanciful drawings. Tramping the roadside for many years, spreading his " Rhymes to Be Traded for Bread," Lindsay touched the heights and depths of the American countryside, especially in the less cultivated sections of the Middle West. His work is a summary not only of American politics, religion, and middle-class pursuits and pleasures, but an expression of the very *sound* of our energetic civilization. No one else has combined such a blend of rhyme, religion, and ragtime; much of Lindsay's poetry makes us see him as a fiery evangelist, touring the country accompanied by a jazz band. No more genuinely native poet exists; even his quieter and less popular verses are drenched in local color.

LOWELL, AMY, was born in Brookline, Mass., February 9, 1874. She descended from a long line of noted New Englanders, James Russell Lowell being a cousin of her grandfather. Amy Lowell was in no sense a youthful genius; it was in her twenty-eighth year that she determined to be a poet. For eight years she studied and experimented in various forms, refusing to publish any of her attempts, and it was not until 1912 that her first volume, *A Dome of Many-Colored Glass,* appeared. The poet's imaginative powers, however, were not disclosed until the publication of *Sword-Blades and Poppy-Seed* (1914) and *Men, Women and Ghosts* (1916). With these and the following volumes it became evident that an experimenter of unusual brilliance had arrived. Not so much a pioneer, she adapted old and new forms to her own highly individual purpose. She was one of the leading Imagists, possibly the most noted of them all. Where " H. D." is cool and restrained, Amy Lowell was violent and exuberant. Her poems are adventures in excitement; her words seemed to bloom and burst in the same moment, as though issuing from firework flower-pots. As has been said, her work triumphs in recording "motion rather than emotion," in reflecting disturbances of light and surfaces, in the unexpected and illuminating phrase. She died, after a sudden stroke, May 12, 1925.

MARKHAM, EDWIN, was born in Oregon City, Oregon, April 23, 1852, the youngest son of pioneer parents. As a young man, he lived a completely outdoor life, laboring on a cattle ranch and educating himself in the primitive country schools. Unknown as a writer until 1899, Markham was made internationally famous by *The Man with the Hoe* (first published in a San Francisco newspaper). Scarcely second in popularity, " Lincoln, the Man of the People " has been translated into almost every living language, and may be found with many shorter pieces in *Lincoln and Other Poems* (1901). *The Gates of Paradise* (1920) exhibits Markham as a writer of stories in verse.

MASEFIELD, JOHN, was born in Herefordshire, England, June 1, 1878. He went to sea at an early age and worked for several years as a common sailor. At one time, he was employed in a saloon in New York City. At the age of twenty-four he read Chaucer's poetry for the first time and was so thrilled by it that his one ambition was to be a poet. *Salt-Water Ballads* (1902) and *Ballads* (1903) reveal Masefield's close acquaintance with ships and sailormen. They were followed by a set of nautical stories, *A Mainsail Haul* (1905). These volumes interested only a small audience. Masefield's fame was not achieved by them (although his early sea-poems are now widely quoted) but by *The Everlasting Mercy* (1911) and *The Widow in the Bye Street* (1912), two long rhymed narratives showing the strong influence of Chaucer. A comprehensive *Collected Poems*, including the more classical sonnets, was published in 1924.

McCRAE, JOHN, was born in Ontario, Canada, in 1872, finished his studies at Johns Hopkins in Baltimore, and returned to Canada as a doctor. During the World War, he was in charge of the Medical Division of the McGill General Hospital and, after serving two years, he died of pneumonia, January, 1918. His volume, *In Flanders Fields* (1919), appeared shortly after his death, few readers realizing that the title-poem — possibly the most widely quoted poem produced by the war — was written in the strictest of French forms, the rondeau.

McLEOD, IRENE RUTHERFORD, was born in England, August 21, 1891, and though her reputation is by no means great, she has written three volumes of direct and personal poetry. The first, *Songs to Save a Soul* (1915), and third, *Before Dawn* (1918), are the best.

MILLAY, EDNA ST. VINCENT, was born at Rockland, Maine, February 22, 1892. She graduated from Vassar in 1917 and wrote short stories, skits, and burlesques, besides being associated with the Provincetown Players as playwright and actress. Her first published poem, "Renascence," was printed when Miss Millay was not quite twenty; it remains one of the greatest expressions of ecstasy we possess. The lyrics which followed are only a trifle more memorable than the masterly sonnets in *Second April* (1921) and *The Harp-Weaver and Other Poems* (1924), the title-poem of the latter being awarded the Pulitzer Prize in 1922. Everything she touches, from the disillusion and banter in *A Few Figs from Thistles* (1920) to the profound horror of war in *Aria da Capo* (1921) is transformed and heightened. She may well come to be regarded as this generation's leading lyricist.

MONRO, HAROLD, was born in Brussels, Belgium, in 1879, but came to England as a boy and was educated at Cambridge. In 1912, he founded the Poetry Bookshop in London, a gathering place for the younger poets. Soon after, he became a publisher, issuing the quarterly *Poetry and Drama,* the six volumes of the biennial *Georgian Poetry* also coming from his press. As a poet, Monro has four books to his credit, the two most liked being *Strange Meetings* (1917) and *Real Property* (1922). In both of these books, Monro shows the connection between the worlds of reality and fantasy; he gives a half-whimsical, half-mystical sense of the relation between man and the inanimate objects he moves among.

MOORE, VIRGINIA, is a young Southern poet whose work has led her readers to await her future with keen expectation. She was educated at Hollins College, Virginia, and, after receiving her M.A. at Columbia University, supported herself in New York, chiefly by reviewing. Her first volume, *Not Poppy* (1926), is the expression of a spirit which is at once proud and passionate, recorded in a language that is as sensitive as the poet's response to all she observes.

MORLEY, CHRISTOPHER, was born at Haverford, Pa., May 5, 1890, and was Rhodes scholar at New College, Oxford, 1910–1913. Since 1914, he has been on the staff of various newspapers, coming to New York in 1920 to run his column, "The Bowling Green." Morley is a most prolific author and, although *Where the Blue Begins* (1922) is conceded to be his most distinguished work, the verse in *The Rocking Horse* (1919) and *Chimneysmoke* (1922) has a definite if sometimes too conscious charm. He has edited several collections, the most notable being his two series of *Modern Essays*.

NEWBOLT, HENRY, was born in Bilston, England, in 1862, educated at Corpus Christi College, Oxford, and was called to the bar in 1887. He retired from practice twelve years later to become a writer and editor, and with the appearance of *Admirals All* (1897) he attracted a large following. His "Vitae Lampada," reprinted in this volume, is a poem with a message that is not dull and "preachy," an exhortation that is as rousing as its rhythm.

NOYES, ALFRED, was born in Staffordshire, England, September 16, 1880, and was educated at Oxford. He was a poet from his undergraduate days, his first volume, *The Loom of Years* (1902), being written when he was twenty-one. He was appointed Professor of Modern English Literature at Princeton in 1922. His many books have been assembled in three volumes, *Collected Poems,* the first volume (containing his most popular verses) appearing in 1913. Although his later writing is more ambitious, it is less interesting; Noyes' reputation will doubtless rest on ballads like "The Highwayman," "The Barrel-Organ," and a few other rolling measures.

O'NEILL, MOIRA, was born near the county of Wexford in Ireland where she has lived most of her life. *Songs from the Glens of Antrim* (1900) established her reputation as a singer of simple but moving songs. After an interval of more than twenty years she published *More Songs from the Glens of Antrim* (1922) which are almost as musical as the first collection.

QUILLER-COUCH, A. T., was born in Cornwall, England, in 1863. Although he has written many stories and three volumes of verse, he is best known as the editor of the excellent *Oxford Book of English Verse*, which, as a choice compilation, is second only to Palgrave's *Golden Treasury*.

REESE, LIZETTE WOODWORTH, was born near Baltimore, Md., January 9, 1856, and taught English at the Western High School in Baltimore for almost forty years. In 1923 the alumni presented the school with a bronze tablet upon which one of Miss Reese's famous poems ("Tears") was embossed. From the very first — *A Branch of May* appeared in 1887 — it was apparent that here was a singer of high quality. Subsequent volumes emphasized the early enthusiasm. *A Quiet Road* (1896) and *A Wayside Lute* (1909) are full of an artless art, a quiet beauty of form and phrase. The poems written later in life are even more eloquent; *Spicewood* (1920) and *Wild Cherry* (1923) contain the same mixture of sweetness and sorrow, but the tenderness is more compact, the sadness keener than ever. Some one has said that Miss Reese's work, with its old-world elegance, is a poetry of yesterday; in its ageless tensity it is also a poetry of tomorrow.

RICHARDSON, DOROTHY M., was born in England and is known as the author of a sequence of minutely detailed novels. She has published practically no verse, this being the first time that Miss Richardson has allowed any of her poetry to appear in a volume.

ROBERTS, ELIZABETH MADOX, was born near Springfield, Kentucky, and attended the University of Chicago, where she took a degree and won the Fisk Prize in 1921. The prize-winning group with several added poems appeared as *Under the Tree* (1922), a volume written about children though not exclusively for them. The verse is graceful enough where grace is demanded and, where appropriate, childishly awkward in exactly the right manner.

ROBINSON, EDWIN ARLINGTON, was born in the little village of Head Tide, Maine, December 22, 1869, and studied for two years at Harvard. His first privately printed volume, *The Torrent and the Night Before*, was published in 1896 and the few copies that exist bring extraordinarily high prices at book sales. President Roosevelt was one of Robinson's early admirers and, shortly after the publication of *Captain Craig* (1902), the poet was given a position in the New York Custom House. He has sacrificed much to give himself entirely to his work, and no living poet has won a higher position. Robinson has been twice awarded the Pulitzer Prize, in 1921 and 1924. His comprehensive *Collected Poems* (1921) is a volume of which his countrymen may well be proud; it embraces all humanity in its range, from sympathetic portrayal of strange characters to those profound studies of mood and situation for which Robinson is justly famous.

ROBINSON, EDWIN MEADE (no relation to Edwin Arlington Robinson), was born in Lima, Ind., November 1, 1879, and has been connected with newspapers in Ohio since his 'teens. His daily column, which he has conducted since 1906, is bright with "quips and merry saws" as well as skilful light verse. *Piping and Panning* (1920) proves this little known humorist to be an adroit craftsman as well as an artist of burlesque.

SANDBURG, CARL, was born in Galesburg, Ill., January 6, 1878, and went to work at thirteen on a milk-wagon. For almost seven years he earned his living as porter, stage-hand, truck-handler, dish-washer, and harvest-hand. Those who doubt the sincerity of this author's "rough-neck poetry" do not realize how much of it was learned in the "University of Hard Labor." But Sandburg is not without scholastic training. After serving in the Spanish-American War, he attended Lombard College, where he became editor of the college magazine. Since 1910 he has been a newspaper man; for several years he reviewed the "movies" for *The Chicago Daily News*. His *Chicago Poems* (1916) raised a small storm among the critics; Sandburg's work was accused of being formless and merely brutal, coarse and unpoetic. His opponents failed to see that Sandburg, like Whitman, was dignifying material which had been considered "too unpoetical" for poetry, that he was brutal only when describing brutal subjects, and that beneath his toughness he was one of the tenderest of poets. His subsequent volumes proved this. *Cornhuskers* (1918) and *Smoke and Steel* (1920) vibrate with a tremendous energy. Steel mills and slaughterhouses are here, smoke-belching chimneys and many-tongued gangs at work. But quiet is also here: the quiet of open prairies and silent city streets. From the standpoint of language the most striking feature is his use of plain words and the idioms of daily life, which makes his descriptions particularly vivid and recognizably American. Whether he pounds out a "big-fisted slang" or breathes a subtle overtone, he is a pioneer at both extremes. If he exults in expressing the loudest notes in modern poetry, he also whispers some of its softest phrases. His monumental *Abraham Lincoln: The Prairie Years* (1926) is sure to increase Sandburg's literary stature.

SASSOON, SIEGFRIED, was born in Kent, England, September 8, 1886, and was educated at Clare College, Cambridge. He was a captain in the Royal Welsh Fusiliers during the World War and won the Military cross for bringing in wounded under fire. His pre-war poetry is lyric and traditional. But *The Old Huntsman* (1917) sounds an entirely new note; the glamour of war has gone and outraged youth sees the horror stripped of its false "glory." *Counter-Attack* (1918) is even more outspoken and bitter. It is passionate but restrained, the sort of fiery protest that Rupert Brooke might have written had he lived. Sassoon's denunciations will outlive most of the "patriotic violence" produced by all the war-poets of the period.

SCHACHT, MARSHALL W., was born at Brookline, Mass., September 23, 1905, and, after a year at Wesleyan, entered Dartmouth. His verse, written while he was an undergraduate, was immediately commented upon and was one of the bright spots in the anthology *Dartmouth Verse: 1925*.

SEEGER, ALAN, was born in New York City, June 22, 1888, and entered Harvard in 1906, where he became one of the editors of the *Harvard Monthly*. In 1913, he went to Paris and, three weeks after the outbreak of the War, Seeger enlisted in the Foreign Legion of France. He was mortally wounded during the battle of Belloy-en-Santerre on July 4, 1916, and died the next morning. Although there are several excellent passages in his *Poems* (1916), "I Have a Rendezvous with Death," which might have been his own epitaph, is his one famous poem.

SERVICE, ROBERT W., was born in Preston, England, January 16, 1874, was educated in Scotland, emigrated to Canada, tried farming in Vancouver, but deserted agriculture for the more adventurous life, traveling through the wilds of the Pacific coast and the Yukon for eight years. *The Spell of the Yukon* reflects this phase of his career. Later he served as ambulance driver in the World War and his experiences found voice in the more popular *Rhymes of a Red Cross Man* (1917). As poetry, his lines cannot claim high rank, but his stories are told with such gusto and so definite a swing that his admirers have gone so far as to call him " the American Kipling."

STEPHENS, JAMES, was born in Dublin, Ireland, in February, 1882, and worked for a while as typist in a lawyer's office. His *Irish Fairy Tales* (1920) are written in the highly colored prose which his readers have found so admirable. And although his novel *The Crock of Gold* (1912) is even more poetic than most of his poetry, *Insurrections* (1909) and *Reincarnations* (1918) are full of a Puckish humor and an Ariel fantasy.

STRONG, L. A. G., was born in Devon, England, March 8, 1896, was educated at Wadham College, Oxford, and has taught at Summer Fields, a famous preparatory school, since 1921. *Dublin Days* (1921) reveals Strong's Irish ancestry; it is a volume of shrewd humor and keen characterizations.

SYMONS, ARTHUR, was born in Wales in 1865, and was one of the leaders of the group which made the 1890's so prominent in literature. Much of his work is artificial and imitative, but there are many rich and uplifted communications in his *Collected Poems* (1902).

TAYLOR, BERT LESTON, was born in Goshen, Mass., November 13, 1866, was educated at the College of the City of New York, went West and engaged in journalism in 1895. His column " A Line o' Type or Two " became almost as popular as Eugene Field's. *Motley Measures* (1913) contains some of Taylor's best verse, particularly his lusty use of the French forms.

TEASDALE, SARA, was born in St. Louis, Mo., August 8, 1884, and, after her marriage to Ernst Filsinger, moved to New York in 1916. She is one of the best lyric poets of the period, and *Rivers to the Sea* (1915), *Love Songs* (1917) and the more restrained *Flame and Shadow* (1920) explain her popularity. This poetry is both direct and subtle, simple in expression and yet rich in its suggestions. So with the music of Sara Teasdale's lines. The words are precise and straightforward — this singer never relies on a " poetic diction " — and yet the rhythms are both fluent and varied. Hers is, throughout, an emotional poetry, but it is emotion clarified and heightened by intellect. Many of her lyrics have become almost as well known as folk-songs.

THOMAS, EDWARD, was born in England, in 1878, and educated at Lincoln College, Oxford. For many years he earned his living as a critic and author of travel books, essays and "pot-boilers." He first wrote poetry under the influence of Robert Frost, who was in England at the time, and to whom Thomas' *Poems* (1916) was dedicated. This volume, as well as *Last Poems* (1919), shows his kinship with the New England poet; here is the same love of homely details and neglected objects, little things like a child's path, birds' nests uncovered by an autumn wind, sunlight on a wall in November. *Collected Poems*, with an introduction by Walter de la Mare, appeared in 1921.

THOMPSON, FRANCIS, was born in the county of Lancashire, England, December 18, 1859, and died in London, November 13, 1907. Poor from birth, he attempted to earn his living as a clerk, a book-salesman, a messenger — there was a time when he sold matches in the street just before Wilfrid Meynell (an editor whose wife was Alice Meynell) discovered him. Meynell had accepted a poem of Thompson's and had invited him to call. "His appearance was then terrible in its destitution. When he came into the room he half opened the door, and then retreated, and did so twice before he got courage to come inside. He was in rags, his feet without stockings showing through his boots, his coat torn, and no shirt. He seemed in the last stages of physical collapse." Invited to dinner, he talked until about ten o'clock, "when he became uneasy and said he must be going. I asked him what compelled him, and he explained that he was obliged to earn tenpence every day to live. This he did by waiting at the doors of theatres and calling cabs." As a poet, Thompson ranks among the great mystics; there is not a tawdry line or a commonplace thought in all his work. His greatest effort, "The Hound of Heaven," though too long to quote in this volume, is immortal. His *Complete Poems* have recently been gathered in a single volume.

TYNAN, KATHARINE, was born in Dublin in 1861, and educated in Ireland. One of the members though not one of the leaders of the Irish Revival, she has written many novels, miracle plays, and books of verse. Her *New Poems* (1911) and *Flower of Youth* (1914) are winning in their clean sincerities; *A Little Book of XXIV Carols* (1907) is more distinctive and contains the two poems by which she is known to most readers.

UNTERMEYER, JEAN STARR, was born in Zanesville, O., May 13, 1886, took special courses at Columbia University, and married Louis Untermeyer in 1907. Although Mrs. Untermeyer had been writing for several years, her first volume, *Growing Pains*, was not published until 1918. "Here," wrote Amy Lowell, "is no sentimentality, but a great power of emotion. Here we have a poetry of absolutely direct speech, but speech so suffused and heightened that it attains a stark perception of beauty." *Dreams Out of Darkness* (1921) is an even richer revelation of "an essentially feminine or, one might better say, womanly attitude to life."

UNTERMEYER, LOUIS, was born in New York City, October 1, 1885, and attended the De Witt Clinton High School, from which, owing to his inability to understand geometry, he failed to graduate. For twenty years he was engaged in the manufacturing of jewelry as designer and factory manager. He retired from business in 1923, went abroad for two years, and returned to America to devote himself to literature and "informal education." He has written several volumes of poetry, of which *Challenge* (1914) has gone through several editions in America, *Roast Leviathan* (1923) having found most favor in England. Of his four volumes of "critical parodies" the two most popular are *Including Horace* (1919) — a series of paraphrases of the Latin odes — and *Heavens* (1922). *American Poetry Since 1900* (1923) is a large volume of essays and, besides the present collection, three other anthologies have been compiled by the same editor. *The Fat of the Cat* (1925) is a set of short stories freely paraphrased from the original Swiss tales. *Modern American Poetry* and *Modern British Poetry* have been revised several times since their first appearance in 1919.

VAN DYKE, HENRY, was born in Germantown, a suburb of Philadelphia, Pa., in 1852, graduated from Princeton in 1873, from Princeton Theological School in 1877, and, two years later, became pastor of a church in Newport, R. I. After holding two other pastorates, he became Professor of English in Princeton University in 1900, and, in 1913, was appointed Minister to the Netherlands. A complete edition of his stories and poems was published in 1920; several volumes from his pen have appeared since that date. "Sweetness and light" and a certain dogged optimism are the dominant strains in his work.

WATSON, WILLIAM, was born in Yorkshire, England, August 2, 1858, and has written poetry since early youth. *The Hope of the World* (1897) met with instant favor and it seemed likely that Watson would be appointed Poet Laureate. His political verses, however, displeased certain powers at Court and the honor went to the more classical Robert Bridges. His best work is to be found in *Selected Poems* (1902).

WICKHAM, ANNA, was born in Surrey, England, in 1884, studied for the opera in Paris and suddenly gave up music to become a poet. She wrote nine hundred poems in four years — and destroyed most of them in four days. Her first two volumes were combined in one book and published in America as *The Contemplative Quarry* (1921). A smaller pamphlet, *The Little Old House,* appeared a year later. Mrs. Wickham's work is seldom graceful and never " pretty " ; her verse is distinguished by its knotted strength and vigorous phrasing. Even her humor (as shown in " The Tired Man ") is twisted in a wry smile. The best of her work, however, is as clear as it is courageous.

WIDDEMER, MARGARET, was born in Doylestown, Pa., and began writing in her childhood. Although she is the author of several novels, her native expression is poetic. She writes an extremely fluent verse, much of which is keen and refreshing, much of it, also, suffering from an overdose of sentimentality. *The Old Road to Paradise* (1918) divided the Columbia Poetry Prize with Carl Sandburg's *Cornhuskers.* Miss Widdemer's later work is less flowery, her *Ballads and Lyrics* (1925) — from which her two poems in this volume are taken — being her best collection so far.

WILDE, OSCAR, was born in Dublin, Ireland, October 16, 1856, was educated at Trinity College, Dublin, and Magdalen College, Oxford, winning the Newdigate Prize at the latter. He speedily became known as a writer of epigrammatic plays (antedating Shaw's brilliant comedies), paradoxical essays, " perfumed prose," and rather " precious " poetry. He was also notorious socially, becoming an " apostle of artistic house decoration and dress reform." This overemphasis on the aesthetic side of life mars much of Wilde's achievements. But a part of his work will live when his ability to amuse and startle is forgotten. His *Poems* (which have been collected in various editions since 1912) contain many memorable selections and his poems in prose, such as *The Happy Prince and Other Tales,* are even more exquisite and richly tinted than his verse.

WOLFE, HUMBERT, was born in Milan, Italy, January 5, 1885, but went to England as a child. He was educated at Oxford, entered the British Civil Service in 1909, became one of the most valued members of the Ministry of Labour and, in spite of his position, never ceased to criticize the government through his satires and lampoons. Although he had published several volumes, *Kensington Gardens* (1924) was the first one to attract attention beyond a small circle. *The Unknown Goddess* (1925) extended the poet's range and increased his audience. It was hailed both in England and in America as the work of a new and extraordinary melodist; Wolfe's quaint harmonies, curious turns of phrase and, most prominently, his effective use of assonance and " off-color " rhyme, led the reviewers to rank him with de la Mare. But Wolfe's charm is as individual as his humor, and his spicy accent is always his own.

WYLIE, ELINOR, was born in Somerville, N. J., but lived most of her early life in Washington. After several years in England, she returned to America and published her first volume, *Nets to Catch the Wind,* in 1921. This, one of the most brilliant first books of the period, revealed a writer who was, above all, a master of her craft. *Black Armour* (1923) increased her admirers' enthusiasm and emphasized her gifts. Flawless in technique, the second volume sounded greater depths; here was an intensity that was both spirited and patrician. This same fastidiousness of feeling and phrase is evident in Mrs. Wylie's two novels, *Jennifer Lorn* (1923) and *The Venetian Glass Nephew* (1925). She became the wife of William Rose Benét in 1924.

YEATS, WILLIAM BUTLER, was born at Sandymount, Dublin, Ireland, in 1865, and spent his childhood in his native land, where he imbibed the richness of its traditions and folklore. He was one of the originators of the Irish Renaissance and helped found the Irish National Theatre, for which he wrote many of his poetic dramas. Of these plays, *The Land of Heart's Desire* (1904) not only expresses the whole spirit of the Celtic revival but is so universal in its beauty that it has not been spoiled by translation into foreign languages. Although Yeats is an essayist as well as a playwright, it is as a writer of lyrics that he will probably be remembered longest. He has a way of transforming old rhythms and older legends into a fresh and personal music. Using direct speech throughout and discarding all artificial rhetoric, his *Collected Poems* glow with the double light of mystery and candor. His spell is even greater because the magic is so simple.

WHAT IS POETRY?

(Twenty-five Definitions)

To the thousands of unsatisfactory definitions of poetry which we already possess, the editor might add one more: *Poetry is a wild attempt to define the indefinable.* Scientists, with all their graphs and recording needles, have been no more successful than poets, aided only by their intuition, in reducing the essence of poetry to a few phrases. However, the desire to capture the elusive spirit has fascinated almost every writer that ever lived. The following twenty-five statements by twenty-five authorities at least reveal the fact that their definitions are as diverse as the minds which created them.

The poet's eye, in a fine frenzy rolling,
Doth glance from heaven to earth, from earth to heaven;
And as imagination 'bodies forth
The forms of things unknown, the poet's pen
Turns them to shapes, and gives to airy nothings
A local habitation and a name.
        — WILLIAM SHAKESPEARE (1564–1616)

Poetry is the imaginative expression of strong feeling, usually rhythmical . . . the spontaneous overflow of powerful feelings recollected in tranquillity.
        — WILLIAM WORDSWORTH (1770–1850)

A drainless shower
Of light is poesy; 'tis the supreme of power;
'Tis might half slumbering on its own right arm.
        — JOHN KEATS (1795–1821)

Poetry is simply the most beautiful, impressive and widely effective mode of saying things.
        — MATTHEW ARNOLD (1822–1888)

Poetry is the art of uniting pleasure with truth by calling imagination to the help of reason. . . . The essence of poetry is invention; such invention as, by producing something unexpected, surprises and delights.
        — SAMUEL JOHNSON (1709–1784)

349

Poetry is the only verity, — the expression of a sound mind speaking after the ideal, and not after the apparent. . . . The true poem is the poet's mind, the finest poetry was first experience. It does not need that a poem should be long; every word was once a poem. — RALPH WALDO EMERSON (1803–1882)

Poetry is rhythmical, imaginative language expressing the invention, taste, thought, passion and insight of the human soul.
— EDMUND CLARENCE STEDMAN (1833–1908)

Definitions are for the most part alike unsatisfactory and treacherous; but definitions of poetry are proverbially so. Is it possible to lay down invariable principles of poetry? . . . Is it possible for a critic to say of any metrical phrase, stanza, or verse, "This is poetry," or "This is not poetry"? . . . These are questions which have engaged the attention of critics ever since the times of Aristotle.
— THEODORE WATTS-DUNTON (1836–1920)

Poetry is the record of the best and happiest moments of the happiest and best minds. . . . A poem is the very image of life expressed in its eternal truth.
— PERCY BYSSHE SHELLEY (1792–1822)

There is no heroic poem in the world but is at bottom a biography, the life of a man.
— THOMAS CARLYLE (1795–1881)

The proper and immediate object of Science is the acquirement or communication of truth; the proper and immediate object of poetry is the communication of immediate pleasure. . . . I wish our clever young poets would remember my homely definitions of prose and poetry; that is, prose = words in their best order; poetry = the best words in the best order.
— SAMUEL TAYLOR COLERIDGE (1772–1834)

Lyrical poetry is much the same in every age, as the songs of the nightingales in every spring-time.
— HEINRICH HEINE (1799–1856)

By poetry we mean the art of employing words in such a manner as to produce an illusion on the imagination — the art of doing by means of words what the painter does by means of colors. — THOMAS BABINGTON MACAULAY (1800–1859)

Poetry is the music of the soul; and, above all, of great and feeling souls.   — MARIE-FRANÇOIS AROUET DE VOLTAIRE
(1694–1778)

Poetry ought not to take its course through the frigid region of memory; it ought never to convert learning into its interpreter, nor private interest its advocate with the popular mind. It ought to go straight to the heart because it has come from the heart.   — FRIEDRICH SCHILLER (1759–1805)

Poetry is that art which selects and arranges the symbols of thought in such a manner as to excite it the most powerfully and delightfully.

— WILLIAM CULLEN BRYANT (1794–1878)

We shall never explain, though we may do something to distinguish, that transformation by which prose is changed miraculously into poetry.

— ARTHUR SYMONS (1865–   )

The business of words in prose is primarily to *state;* in poetry, not only to state, but also (and sometimes primarily) to *suggest*.   — JOHN LIVINGSTON LOWES (1867–   )

What is poetry? Is it a mosaic
      Of colored stones which curiously are wrought
      Into a pattern? Rather glass that's taught
By patient labor any hue to take
And glowing with a sumptuous splendor, make
      Beauty a thing of awe.

— AMY LOWELL (1874–1925)

Poetry is a language that tells us, through a more or less emotional reaction, something that cannot be said. All poetry, great or small, does this. And it seems to me that poetry has two outstanding characteristics. One is that it is, after all, undefinable. The other is that it is eventually unmistakable.

— EDWIN ARLINGTON ROBINSON (1869–   )

Poetry is a series of explanations of life, fading off into horizons too swift for explanations. . . . Poetry is the opening and closing of a door, leaving those who look through to guess what is seen during a moment.

— CARL SANDBURG (1878–

Poetry (from poet, Greek *poietes, a maker,* from the verb *poieo, I make*). Without attempting to define poetry, it may be broadly stated as that form of expression which language takes when it consists of a definite number of measures in some fixed relation to each other, and accompanied by a discernible and more or less definite rhythm.

— *Encyclopedia Americana* (1904)

Poetry: The art of apprehending and interpreting ideas by the faculty of imagination; the art of idealizing in thought and in expression. — *Webster's International Dictionary*

It is absurd to think that the only way to tell if a poem is lasting is to wait and see if it lasts. The right reader of a good poem can tell the moment it strikes him that he has taken an immortal wound — that he will never get over it. That is to say, permanence in poetry as in love is perceived instantly. It hasn't to await the test of time. The proof of a poem is not that we have never forgotten it, but that we knew at sight that we never could forget it. — ROBERT FROST (1875–   )

If I read a book and it makes my whole body so cold no fire can ever warm me, I know that is poetry. If I feel physically as if the top of my head were taken off, I know that is poetry. These are the only ways I know it. Is there any other way?

— EMILY DICKINSON (1830–1886)

FAMOUS OLDER POEMS

In connection with the selections in this volume it may be desirable to read and compare certain poems on similar themes by the older poets. All of the following poems not only have attained the rank of famous classics but are the best examples of their kind. All of them, incidentally, are easily procurable, since they can be found in either *The Oxford Book of English Verse* or Palgrave's *Golden Treasury,* many of them being contained in both of these admirable collections. The following lists are arranged chronologically:

OLD SONGS AND CAROLS

Carol (I sing of a maiden)........	Anonymous (15th Century)
There Is a Lady Sweet and Kind...	Anonymous (17th Century)
Crabbèd Age and Youth	William Shakespeare
O Mistress Mine.................	William Shakespeare
Hark! Hark! the Lark............	William Shakespeare
"Drink to me only with thine eyes"	Ben Jonson
"Pack, clouds, away, and welcome, day"	Thomas Heywood
The Lover's Resolution	George Wither
"Gather ye rosebuds while ye may"	Robert Herrick
To Music	Robert Herrick
Go, Lovely Rose	Edmund Waller
Sally in Our Alley	Henry Carey
Song (from Aella)	Thomas Chatterton
Jean	Robert Burns
Auld Lang Syne	Robert Burns
"Piping down the valleys wild " ...	William Blake
For Music	Lord Byron
The Indian Serenade	Percy Bysshe Shelley
Music, when soft voices die	Percy Bysshe Shelley
Song of the Indian Maid (from "Endymion ")	John Keats
Fair Ines	Thomas Hood
"She is not fair to outward view"..	Hartley Coleridge

OLD LEGENDS AND BALLADS

TWENTY GREAT LOVE–POEMS
OF THE PAST

THIRTEEN GREAT SONNETS OF THE PAST

TWELVE GREAT ODES AND ELEGIES OF THE PAST

PORTRAITS AND PEOPLE

DRUMS, BANNERS, BATTLE–CRIES

GOLDEN TEXTS

These Suggestions for Study are, as the phrase implies, merely *suggestions*. They do not pretend to cover the entire field nor all the material presented by this volume, being sketches rather than detailed outlines. There has been no attempt to "interpret" every line of every poem, a custom which robs poetry of much of its appeal and which, the editor is happy to note, is rapidly being discarded. If poetry can actually, in the old sense of the word, be *taught* — a problem which is highly debatable — an interest in the art can best be fostered by contact and individual enthusiasm, rather than by lists of irritating questions which make the reading of poetry less like an adventure and more like a problem in mathematics.

Since the emphasis of this collection is placed on the poems rather than on the poets, the Suggestions for Study have been divided by subjects and types of verse. Certain readers may be encouraged to devote time to a more thorough study of individual poets. The last five Suggestions are for such students, giving hints as to the preparation of such studies as well as information leading to supplementary reading. (The section entitled *Who's Who Among the Poets* will be an aid in this direction, since it contains not only condensed biographies but a list of the poets' most important works.)

It should be added that these suggestions are not intended to be given as assignments for all grades. It must be left to the initiative of the teacher and the response of the student to determine along what lines the studies should be pursued. One group may wish to specialize in one kind of poetry, another may instinctively turn to an entirely different angle of approach. One class of teacher (or reader) may prefer detailed reading in one particular field; another may obtain happier results by a general or widely scattered interest.

It should also be added that these suggestions are not merely the editor's own, but the condensation of those of many advisers. Most of them have been tried out in different classes and have formed the basis of further studies. The aim of this collection, it must be repeated, is stimulation fully as much as instruction.

I. THE ENJOYMENT OF POETRY

Read "The Poets," by Arthur O'Shaughnessy (p. 2). This poem might serve as an introduction to poetry itself.

What is the central idea of the poem? What phrases does the poet use to bring out this idea?

When the poet says that "deathless ditties" may "build up the world's great cities" he means that songs about some famous town preserve its fame long after the city has gone to dust. We remember Troy, a tiny village, because of what Homer wrote about it. Babylon is "built up" in our minds by dead singers. What other cities or towns have been celebrated by poets? What famous legends or poems are connected with Sherwood Forest? Bethlehem? Sleepy Hollow? Plymouth? Hamelin?

It is evident that the author believes that poetry is very important to the world. Why does he think so? Do you share his opinion? In what way do you disagree?

What kind of poem do you like best: the poem that (a) tells a story? (b) teaches a lesson? (c) paints a picture? (d) describes a character? (e) rouses an emotion? or (f) merely sings a song? Choose three examples from this volume illustrating your choice.

When you were very little, what were the first things you learned by heart? Were they stories or jingles? Were they Nursery Rhymes? Why do you think that, for many generations, infants have found such delight in Mother Goose?

II. THE POET AS OBSERVER

Read poems from the section "Common Miracles" (p. 3) in connection with those in "Daily Life" (p. 139).

Which do you prefer, the group in *Yesterday* or the one in *Today?* What, in general, is your impression of the two groups? Do they contradict or amplify each other? What one poem do you find (a) the most vivid? (b) the most human? (c) the most generally likable? Why?

Although poetry is chiefly a matter of *feeling,* the poet who paints a picture for us must also be a keen observer. Some one has said that the true poet is "a reporter of the universe." It is not only sharp vision which is required of the poet but a knowledge of just which details to emphasize; the artist becomes great by what he leaves out as well as by what he puts in.

Read, as examples of the poets' observation, the following poems:

> "A Memory" (*Yesterday*), by William Allingham (p. 3)
>
> From "Snowbound" (*Yesterday*), by John Greenleaf Whittier (p. 6)
>
> "Miracles" (*Yesterday*), by Walt Whitman (p. 10)
>
> "Week-End" (*Today*), by Harold Monro (p. 140)
>
> "The Wood-Pile" (*Today*), by Robert Frost (p. 146)
>
> "The Covered Bridge" (*Today*), by Madison Cawein (p. 147)
>
> "The Prettiest Things" (*Today*), by Camilla Doyle (p. 148)
>
> "Cargoes" (*Today*), by John Masefield (p. 149)

In each of these poems the poet has selected certain details to make his picture clearer. For instance, in "Week-End," Harold Monro makes the scene very actual by such phrases as "the tea-pot with *contented* spout *thinks* of the boiling water," "the stair will *grumble* at our feet," "*contented* evening" and "the *snoozing* fire." Can you find similar details or sharper phrases in the eight poems listed in this section?

In "The Eagle" (p. 24) Tennyson gives us the very look of disturbed water by speaking of "the *wrinkled* sea." In "Pigeons Just Awake" (p. 185) Hilda Conkling, although only a child, shows an *exact* observation when she speaks of "the *curved* flight of pigeons" with feet "the color of new June strawberries."

What are some of the details in other poems illustrating this same gift? Do these details show a sharp eye, a quick imagination, or both?

Select other poems to show the poet's power of "sight and insight."

III. THE POET AS MUSICIAN

The poet is known not only for his power to see, but for his ability to *sing*. Music is the very base of poetry, and melody is achieved in various ways — by rhyme, rhythm, cadence, etc. — the separate words being like notes or chords in a bar of music. The best poems must please the ear even more than the eye — which is one reason why no poem yields its complete magic until it is read aloud.

Read " The Song of the Chattahoochee " (*Yesterday*, p. 57), by Sidney Lanier. Notice how Lanier gives us the rush and chatter of the little river by his hurrying rhymes. What passage do you think achieves this effect best? Notice, also, how he gives his lines a watery sound by the use of the liquid l's and w's, as in the phrase, " wilful waterweeds." Can you find other phrases carrying out this or a similar effect?

Read " The Bees' Song " (*Today*, p. 208), by Walter de la Mare. This is a half-humorous, fanciful lyric, exaggerated in spelling for a definite purpose. What is that purpose? What sound is the poet trying to capture by the continued use of the letter *z?* Can you name any other poems in which the principal feature is the *sound* rather than the sense?

Read " The Broncho That Would Not Be Broken " (*Today*, p. 189), by Vachel Lindsay. Notice that the form of this poem suggests the light-footed pace of the broncho, not the heavy plodding of an ordinary farm horse. (Vachel Lindsay says that he himself saw this incident out West when some ranchmen forced a prancing colt to do the labor of ordinary mules.) Show, by reference to the poem, the contrast between the spirited little creature and the duller animals. Why does the poet speak of the broncho's " boyish heart "? What other figures of speech are especially striking? Note, above all, the musical effects by which the poet emphasizes his theme. Observe the way " dancing " is rhymed and half-rhymed throughout; the same is true of the word " paces." Does this seem to you to bring out the effect of dancing? Which appeals to you more in these verses, the music or the story itself?

Most lyrics, however, do not depend on any letter or vowel for their musical effect but on the *combination* of syllables. These sounds are assembled in order to reflect the *mood* of the particular poem. A love song will, naturally, have softer syllables and a quieter music than a brisk song of the road or a burly sea-chanty.

Read " To Helen " (*Yesterday*, p. 59), by Edgar Allan Poe
  " A Musical Instrument " (*Yesterday*, p. 60), by Elizabeth Barrett Browning
  " A Birthday " (*Yesterday*, p. 62), by Christina Rossetti

"Break, Break, Break" (*Yesterday*, p. 63), by Alfred Lord Tennyson

"On the South Downs" (*Today*, p. 171), by Sara Teasdale

"Wind Song" (*Today*, p. 171), by Carl Sandburg

"Vagabond Song" (*Today*, p. 172), by Bliss Carman

"Sea-Fever" (*Today*, p. 174), by John Masefield

"Sea-Song" (*Today*, p. 173), by Irene Rutherford McLeod

Notice that the swing of the lines differs in each case. What mood is called up by each poem? What lines present this mood most clearly in each poem? What is your favorite poem among the above nine? Why?

Do you remember the words of your favorite song, or only the melody? Would these words still be beautiful without the tune?

IV. THE POET AS STORY–TELLER

Although describing and singing may be said to be the chief qualities of poetry, many poets have an additional faculty: the ability to tell a story. All the old ballads are, first of all, tales in verse. In fact most of the stories we remember longest are those which have been told to us by the poets, for the use of rhyme and a regular rhythm gives a clearer edge to the sentences and makes the tale itself more vivid.

Read "King Robert of Sicily" (*Yesterday*, p. 34), by Henry Wadsworth Longfellow

"Annabel Lee" (*Yesterday*, p. 66), by Edgar Allan Poe

"The Deacon's Masterpiece" (*Yesterday*, p. 67), by Oliver Wendell Holmes

"Barbara Frietchie" (*Yesterday*, p. 71), by John Greenleaf Whittier

"The Laboratory" (*Yesterday*, p. 78), by Robert Browning

"Off the Ground" (*Today*, p. 211), by Walter de la Mare

"Mandalay" (*Today*, p. 227), by Rudyard Kipling

"Fuzzy-Wuzzy" (*Today*, p. 229), by Rudyard Kipling

9, 10, 11 in practice activities

"Ballad of the Battle of Gibeon" (*Today*, p. 236), by
G. K. Chesterton
"The Highwayman" (*Today*, p. 243), by Alfred
Noyes
"The Bombardment" (*Today*, p. 256), by Amy Lowell
"The Mountain Whippoorwill" (*Today*, p. 259), by
Stephen Vincent Benét

What, if anything, has been gained by telling these stories
in verse instead of in prose? Do the different forms and methods
seem natural to the unfolding of the plots or ideas? Which
strikes you as (a) the most exciting? (b) the most picturesque?
(c) the most appealing? (d) the truest to life? (e) the best
told? What reasons can you give for your choice? Which
would you care to learn by heart?

Read "The Ballad of the Harp-Weaver" (*Today*, p. 231),
by Edna St. Vincent Millay. What do you like most in this
poem — (a) the simplicity of the verses? (b) the fairy-tale atmosphere of the whole poem? or (c) the theme of mother-love
which it celebrates?

Read "Skipper Ireson's Ride" (*Yesterday*, p. 73), by John
Greenleaf Whittier, and "The True Story of Skipper Ireson"
(*Today*, p. 239), by Charles Buxton Going. Here are two versions of an old legend. Which do you prefer? As a piece of
narrative verse, which seems the better story? As a story,
which seems the more likely to have happened?

Can you name any other legends which have been treated
from two different points of view?

What effects do you hear or feel in "The Highwayman" (p.
243) and "The Mountain Whippoorwill" (p. 259) which could
not be obtained in prose?

V. THE POET AS PORTRAIT–PAINTER

Some people find their chief pleasure not in the sound of
poetry nor in its narratives, but in its famous portraits. One
of the first things that the poet learns to do is to condense his
thoughts; and, since poetry is so much more concentrated than
prose, it can characterize in a much smaller space and in a far
more vivid manner.

Read "A Dutch Picture" (*Yesterday*, p. 32), by Henry
Wadsworth Longfellow

"Her Letter" (*Yesterday,* p. 40), by Bret Harte
"The Courtin'" (*Yesterday,* p. 43), by James Russell Lowell
"Lady Clara Vere de Vere" (*Yesterday,* p. 53), by Alfred Lord Tennyson
"Lincoln, the Man of the People" (*Today,* p. 191), by Edwin Markham
"The Sleeper" (*Today,* p. 193), by Walter de la Mare
"The Old Woman" (*Today,* p. 196), by Joseph Campbell
"The Old Woman of the Roads" (*Today,* p. 196), by Padraic Colum
"Songs for My Mother" (*Today,* p. 194), by Anna Hempstead Branch

What sort of persons are suggested to you by each of these poems? Do any of the poems give you a background or a scene as well as a description of the character? Does the scene bring out more fully the person described — or vice versa?

Find certain phrases or passages that bring out the spiritual qualities of the characters described. For example, in "Lincoln, the Man of the People" which symbols are used to make us see Lincoln's strength, his homely beginning, his high place among his countrymen? What metaphor seems to you the most beautiful? Which seems to be the most descriptive? Which fits best your conception of Lincoln's character?

Read "Ulysses" (*Yesterday,* p. 76), by Alfred Lord Tennyson. Ulysses, as most of you know, was the famous general and mariner who, after the fall of Troy, spent so many years on the sea, journeying home. What is there in this poem which suggests the old seaman's restlessness? Why does he prefer the hazardous adventures of the sea to the comfort and security of his home? What lines contain a note of heroism?

VI. THE POET AS NATURALIST

Nature, which ordinarily means so little to the hurrying modern man, is brought sharply to our notice by the poets, and we who read, even though we run, are made to thrill with surprises hidden in the most familiar roadside objects. The best descriptions of nature are, therefore, no mere photographic reproductions. " I never observed such colors in a sunset," said a lady when shown one of Whistler's paintings. "No," replied the painter. " Don't you wish you had! " So with the poems in the groups entitled " This Spacious Earth " (*Yesterday*, p. 13), and " The Good Ground " (*Today*, p. 155). Here we have the combination of the actual scene and the poetic imagination acting upon each other. We not only have the landscape in terms of the poet, but (because every poem gives us a glimpse into its composer's mind) the poet in terms of the landscape! In other words, the more sensitively a writer describes a field or a flower, the more fully does he reveal himself.

Read " God's World " (*Today*, p. 155), by Edna St. Vincent Millay. This is, first of all, the painting of a day in autumn when the woods are brilliant with reds and golds — but it is much more than a mere description. What else is it? Which do you feel more, the actuality of the scene or the intensity of the poet's emotion? What particular phrases make you feel the keenness of Miss Millay's love of earth? What phrase shows that beauty is so great that it almost hurts? What do you see when she speaks of woods that " ache and sag and all but cry with color! " Do the three verbs add to the strength of the poet's emotion? Which is the most vivid of the three? Why does the poet plead " Let fall no burning leaf; let no bird call " ?

Read " The Mountain " (*Yesterday*, p. 13), by Emily Dickinson

" The Grass " (*Yesterday*, p. 14), by Emily Dickinson

" Weathers " (*Yesterday*, p. 15), by Thomas Hardy

" Home Thoughts from Abroad " (*Yesterday*, p. 16), by Robert Browning

" Mariners' Song " (*Yesterday*, p. 20), by Thomas Lovell Beddoes

" Amends to Nature " (*Today*, p. 157), by Arthur Symons

" A Ballad of Spring's Unrest " (*Today*, p. 159), by Bert Leston Taylor

" The Good Ground " (*Today*, p. 155), by Virginia Moore

" Spring Song " (*Today*, p. 160), by Bliss Carman

" May Is Building Her House " (*Today*, p. 163), by Richard Le Gallienne

"Buttercups" (*Today*, p. 168), by Louis Ginsberg
"On the South Downs" (*Today*, p. 171), by Sara Teasdale
"The Sea Gypsy" (*Today*, p. 173), by Richard Hovey

What is the particular *picture* painted by each of these poems? What is the principal *mood?* What seems to be the more clearly painted? Why? What lines in particular reflect the poet's experiences or emotions? Select two or three poems by different poets on the same subject and show in what way they differ. Is the difference due to the actual scene or to the poet's point of view?

Read "A Vagabond Song" (*Today*, p. 172), by Bliss Carman. What is the "something" in autumn that is "native to the blood" of the poet? Do you feel it too? Does the poet mean that only the "vagabond" nature can be thrilled by what he describes, or does he mean that there are a few drops of gypsy blood in all of us? Compare this poem with "God's World" (*Today*, p. 155), by Edna St. Vincent Millay. Which of the two poems speaks more directly to you? Which of the two would you care to memorize?

Read the sections "Birds, Beasts, and Flowers" (*Yesterday*, p. 22), and "Hoof, Claw, and Wing" (*Today*, p. 175). Which section do you find (a) the more vivid? (b) the more interesting? (c) the more memorable? In which do you most easily recognize the objects named? In which poems do the animals seem the most natural? In which do they seem most "human"? Do you relish the combination of seriousness and humor in "Ducks" (*Today*, p. 186)? Would this poem have been better if the author had been humorous or solemn throughout?

Read "To a Waterfowl," by William Cullen Bryant (*Yesterday*, p. 22). This is one of the most famous poems about a bird ever written. Are there any other poems about birds, either in this volume or in any other, which you prefer?

Some modern writer has said that "The Bull" (*Today*, p. 175), by Ralph Hodgson, will some day be considered "one of the most powerful poems of an animal ever written." What reasons can you give for this opinion? What part of the poem impresses you the most strongly: the passages describing the bull's babyhood, his vigorous and mature strength, or his feeble last hours? By the repetition of what lines does the poet continually remind us of the bull's oncoming death? Compare this poem with other verses which glorify or describe other animals.

Which is your favorite "flower poem" in this collection? Contrast it with some other that you may already know. What is the reason for your preference?

VII. THE POET AS TEACHER AND INSPIRER

A great number of people believe that poets must not only sing and describe, but teach. This is a matter which has been much disputed, for there are many people who say, with Emerson, that "beauty is its own excuse for being," and that the best "lesson" which art can teach is its own loveliness. Nevertheless, anything which really touches or moves us adds to our experience — and, in that sense, teaches. There are, for all of us, "sermons in stones, books in the running brooks."

Read "Rabbi Ben Ezra" (*Yesterday*, p. 105), by Robert Browning. What is the lesson contained in it? Does the poet think that we are helped or harmed by struggle? Does he refer only to physical or also to spiritual conflict? Does he believe that the body and the soul are two separate things, or that they act with each other? Is the general tone of the poem discouraging or uplifting? Select what you consider the most inspiring passage.

Read "The Potter's Song" (*Yesterday*, p. 111), by Henry
       Wadsworth Longfellow
"Invictus" (*Yesterday*, p. 126), by William Ernest
       Henley
"Einar Tamberskelver" (*Yesterday*, p. 129), by
       Henry Wadsworth Longfellow
"Quiet Work" (*Yesterday*, p. 15), by Matthew
       Arnold
"The Deserter from the Cause" (*Yesterday*, p. 132),
       by Gerald Massey
"So Nigh Is Grandeur" (*Yesterday*, p. 133), by
       Ralph Waldo Emerson
"Columbus" (*Yesterday*, p. 134), by Joaquin Miller
"Songs of Joy" (*Today*, p. 289), by W. H. Davies

"Hills" (*Today*, p. 293), by Arthur Guiterman
"After Sunset" (*Today*, p. 296), by Grace Hazard Conkling
"At the End of the Day" (*Today*, p. 306), by Richard Hovey
"His Ally" (*Today*, p. 307), by William Rose Benét
"Prayer" (*Today*, p. 311), by Louis Untermeyer
"Tomorrow" (*Today*, p. 312), by John Masefield

What is the leading message of each of these poems? Select the three or four which appeal to you most. In "Einar Tamberskelver" (p. 129) we have one of the finest descriptions of a sea battle ever written. Even though it is of a time long perished and the poem itself is part of a much longer story, the *feeling* stirs us almost as much as though we were in the Viking ship. Every line vibrates with the spirit of courage. What other poems would you say contain "the life-blood of bravery"? What relation can you find in "Hills" (p. 293), "At the End of the Day" (p. 306), and "Prayer" (p. 311)? Can you find other poems here or elsewhere which also bear a relation to each other? In what way are they connected?

Read "Trees" (*Today*, p. 167), by Joyce Kilmer. In answer to a questionnaire concerning recent poetry, this poem received the most votes. Can you see why "Trees" has become such a favorite? Do you think this poem is popular for *what* it says or the *way* it says it? Notice that the tree itself is "personified" in various ways. What figure of speech do you like best? What is the simple thought which the poet is trying to impress upon us?

VIII. THE POET AS HUMORIST

The poet is not always the solemn graybeard that many of the portraits declare him to be. There is often, even when his face is straight, the ghost of a smile on his lips and, behind his spectacles, we can detect an eye that twinkles. Frequently, indeed, the poet breaks into open outbursts of mirth, and there is nothing so contagious as rhyme that chuckles, laughs, and digs one between the ribs. Once in this mood, we surrender completely to the poet's whims; the madder his measures, the more we like them.

Read " The Duel " (*Yesterday*, p. 81), by Eugene Field
   " The Captain and the Mermaids " (*Yesterday*, p. 82), by W. S. Gilbert
   " A Nightmare " (*Yesterday*, p. 88), by W. S. Gilbert
   " Jest 'Fore Christmas " (*Yesterday*, p. 91), by Eugene Field
   " The Man in the Moon " (*Yesterday*, p. 92), by James Whitcomb Riley
   " The Walrus and the Carpenter " (*Yesterday*, p. 94), by Lewis Carroll
   " The Pobble That Has No Toes " (*Yesterday*, p. 98), by Edward Lear
   " Dutchman's Breeches " (*Today*, p. 253), by Arthur Guiterman
   " The Ballad of Jack and Jill " (*Today*, p. 265), by Anthony C. Deane
   " The Harmonious Heedlessness of Little Boy Blue " (*Today*, p. 268), by Guy Wetmore Carryl
   " The Gastronomic Guile of Simple Simon " (*Today*, p. 270), by Guy Wetmore Carryl
   " Matilda " (*Today*, p. 272), by Hilaire Belloc
   " Encouragement " (*Today*, p. 276), by Paul Laurence Dunbar
   " The Cremation of Sam McGee " (*Today*, p. 279), by Robert W. Service

In some of these poems the humor is of a quiet kind, in others it is boisterous. Select a few of both classes. Which do you prefer? " The Ballad of Jack and Jill " (p. 265) is not only a witty enlargement of the old nursery rhyme, but a burlesque of Rudyard Kipling's style. Does this poem make you like Kipling any the less? Would any of these stories be more appealing if they were told in a wholly serious vein?

Read " The Famous Ballad of the Jubilee Cup " (*Today*, p. 283), by Arthur T. Quiller-Couch. This, although it seems to tell a story, is sheer nonsense, plus a very rollicking rhythm. Do you like it? Do you know any other famous nonsense poem? Which of those included in this volume do you like best? *Alice in Wonderland* is possibly the greatest of all nonsense books, a close second being the little known *Davy and the Goblin* (by

Charles E. Carryl, father of Guy Wetmore Carryl). Do you know any verses from either of these books?

Samuel Johnson said: "Any man can write sense. Only the gifted few can write nonsense." Try to write a nonsense poem — and see if you agree with Johnson.

IX. THE POET AS PATRIOT

Patriotism is a quality which means many different things. The patriot may be the first to rush to arms — on the other hand he may be the first to oppose a war which he considers unjust. The true patriot is one who is passionately in love with his country at all times, one who does not need fifes, drums, and the display of flags to rouse him. "Peace has her victories no less than war" and the poet-patriot is the first to celebrate these bloodless triumphs.

> *Read* "England, My England" (*Yesterday*, p. 127), by William Ernest Henley
>
> "Marching Along" (*Yesterday*, p. 128), by Robert Browning
>
> "Concord Hymn" (*Yesterday*, p. 131), by Ralph Waldo Emerson
>
> "Barbara Frietchie" (*Yesterday*, p. 71), by John Greenleaf Whittier
>
> "The Dead" (*Today*, p. 299), by Rupert Brooke
>
> "The Soldier" (*Today*, p. 308), by Rupert Brooke
>
> "In Flanders Fields" (*Today*, p. 299), by John McCrae
>
> "I Have a Rendezvous with Death" (*Today*, p. 300), by Alan Seeger

Which one of these poems seems to strike the deepest note? Which expresses the most intense love of country? Select one of the poems and show what particular quality the poet admires most in his own country. What draws the poet closest to his native land: (a) its past history? (b) its struggles? (c) its traditions? (d) its present glory? Do you know any other poems with patriotic sentiments?

Read "Home Thoughts from Abroad" (*Yesterday*, p. 16), by Robert Browning. Although this is a tribute to nature, could it also be classed as a patriotic poem? If you think so, state why.

Under the section *Famous Older Poems* you will find a group called " Drums, Banners, Battle-Cries " (p. 357). Compare two or three of those poems with the patriotic ones in this book. What differences do you find? Which appeal to you most? Why?

X. THE POET AND ETERNITY

Death to many has seemed a grim and painful subject. But the poet does not always find it so. To some of the poets, death is merely a continuance of life in a new form; to others, it is "the last summons," a time of "peaceful backward glances"; to others it is "a long and vivid holiday."

Read "Prospice" (*Yesterday*, p. 114), by Robert Browning
From "Thanatopsis" (*Yesterday* p. 115), by William Cullen Bryant
"The Old" (*Yesterday*, p. 116), by Roden Noel
"O Captain! My Captain!" (*Yesterday*, p. 117), by Walt Whitman
"Death Chant" (from "When Lilacs Last") (*Yesterday*, p. 118), by Walt Whitman
"Afterwards" (*Yesterday*, p. 124), by Thomas Hardy
"Requiem" (*Yesterday*, p. 125), by Robert Louis Stevenson
"The Dead" (*Today*, p. 299), by Rupert Brooke
"Here Lies . . . " (*Today*, p. 302), by Michael Lewis
"The Coward" (*Today*, p. 303), by R. R. Greenwood
"Matter" (*Today*, p. 305), by Louis Untermeyer

What different attitudes toward death are present in these poems? Which appeals to you most? Why?

Notice that not one of these poems shows any fear of dying. Instead of being depressing, most of them are actually inspiring and courageous. Explain, by reference to the poems themselves, why this is so. Select a poem which expresses the mood of reminiscence, of "backward glances." Select two which, though they have death as their subject, are actually celebrating life.

What type of poem about death is "Afterwards," by Thomas Hardy (p. 124)? Do you understand what the poet means by the first line? What phrases show his quiet but intense love of little things? Although the poem is pitched in a low key, do you find it less courageous than the more assertive "Prospice," by Robert Browning (p. 114)?

XI. THE POET AS CRAFTSMAN

So far, practically nothing has been said about the different forms of poetry; the emphasis has been placed on the *matter* rather than on the *manner*. But the poet is also a craftsman and it may be well to devote a little time to a consideration of his craft.

RHYTHM AND RHYME

Before listing any of the principal forms, the student should be acquainted with a few elementary principles of verse. Underlying all poetry (and, for that matter, all writing) is the broad current of rhythm. Rhythm is merely the beat — which may be regular or irregular — of a passage. It is a stress or emphasis by which words are given a certain musical effect.

When *rhythm* becomes altogether regular, it is known as *meter*. *Meter* is a word taken from the Greek meaning measure. In poetry, it means a *regular* succession of beats arranged according to some particular pattern. (Free verse, of which you will find a few examples in this volume, is rhythmical but not metrical.)

Read " The Psalms " or part of " The Book of Job," all of which are strongly rhythmical. Does this seem to you to be poetry? In order to stir you, does poetry need a regular meter? or rhyme?

Every poet uses certain devices or technical tricks in order to accomplish his effects. Among the most important are *rhyme, alliteration,* and *onomatopoeia*.

Rhyme is the matching of words which are partly alike and partly unlike in sound. Tom Hood states the principle of rhyme exactly when he writes: "A rhyme must commence on an *accented* syllable. From the accented vowel of the syllable to the end, the rhymed words must be *identical* in sound — but the letter or letters *preceding* the accented vowel must be *unlike* in sound." Thus " write " and " right " are not rhymes at all, for, though the spelling may be different, there is nothing *un*like in sound. "Light," " site," " fight," and " height " are all perfect rhymes for " write " — and unaccented syllables may be added to these words without affecting the perfection of the rhyme, as: " fighting," " writing," etc.

Although rhymes as a rule occur at the ends of the lines, many poets have used what is known as *interior* rhyme. This gives the poem a doubly musical ring and is a device of which Kipling, among others, is very fond. A poem which is built on a mixture of end-rhyme and interior rhyme is the editor's own " Boy and Tadpoles " (*Today,* p. 223). Can you find some of the inside rhymes in a given passage of this poem? Does it seem to you that, as one critic wrote, " these interwoven sounds give the effect of a tapestry in which the colors are words " ? Does this duplication of rhyme add to or detract from the fantastic pictures?

Read " The Bombardment " (*Today,* p. 256), by Amy Lowell. This is an even more complicated arrangement of mixed rhymes, alliteration, and assonance. When we first see this poem on the printed page it appears to be prose, for it is arranged in paragraphs rather than in the usual line-divisions. The poet herself called this form " polyphonic prose " (prose with many voices), for it is a curious blend of rhythmical prose and all the devices of poetry. Can you discover some of these devices? Does not this very mixture of effects give you something of the excitement which the inhabitants of a city must feel during an attack? The poem is a series of pictures, each picture giving us the point of view of a different person. First we have a general description; then a room in some magnificent house; then a poet's attic; then a child's bedroom; then a chemist's laboratory. Which description seems to you the most vivid? Which passage is the most regular in rhyme and rhythm? Do you think that for the purpose of this poem the regular passages or those that are more irregular are more suited to the theme?

Alliteration is the repetition of the *same* letter in words succeeding each other or close together. It is sort of rhyming of consonants rather than vowels. Little Nathalia Crane is very fond of this device and uses it almost as often as Swinburne. Note, for example, the f's, p's and r's in her verse:

> " Fear not for a moment's defection,
>   Though pansies and poppies may pose;
> For after a bit of reflection
>   The rover returns to the rose."

Possibly the most famous example of alliteration is the one in which the letter *m* expresses the humming sound of bees and the murmur of leaves in Tennyson's:

> " The moan of doves in immemorial elms,
>   And murmur of innumerable bees."

Onomatopoeia is the formation of a word by the imitation of some particular sound. Some of these words which give the *effect* or the *motion* of a thing they describe are: " whiz," " smash," " bang," " whisper," " hiss," " boom," " crack."

THE FIXED FORMS
THE SONNET

Of the fixed forms, the most important is undoubtedly the *sonnet,* of which there are several varieties. *Sonnets,* however, can be recognized by the fact that all of them have exactly fourteen lines and that most of them are divided into two parts. When they are so divided, the first eight lines are known as the *octave,* and the second part of six lines, the *sestet.* In English versification, the two most popular types of sonnet are the *Petrarcan* (named after the Italian poet, Petrarch) and the *Shakespearean* sonnet, so called not because Shakespeare invented it but because he popularized it. The Shakespearean sonnet is easily recognized since it always ends in a couplet — two lines rhyming together.

" Week-End " (*Today,* p. 140), by Harold Monro, is a series of Shakespearean sonnets. A beautiful example of the Petrarcan sonnet is " Abandoned " (*Today,* p. 165), by Madison Cawein. Compare the two forms for similarities and differences.

Read " Mowing " (*Today,* p. 159), by Robert Frost
    " The Covered Bridge " (*Today,* p. 147), by Madison Cawein
    " The Sheaves " (*Today,* p. 165), by Edwin Arlington Robinson

"Tears" (*Today,* p. 295), by Lizette Woodworth
   Reese
"Work" (*Today,* p. 294), by Henry van Dyke
"The Soldier" (*Today,* p. 308), by Rupert Brooke
"Joan of Arc, 1926" (*Today,* p. 311), by Virginia
   Moore

These are all sonnets from the second part of this book. Can you discover some of the differences in them? Can you select the sonnets in the first section of the book? Compare these with some of the "Fourteen Great Sonnets of the Past" listed in *Famous Older Poems* (p. 355). Which is your favorite? Has your choice been determined by the thought or the form of the poem, or by both?

William Sharp, a noted critic who was also a poet, said that "for the concise expression of a single poetic thought, the sonnet is by all odds the finest medium." Do you agree that the very shortness of the sonnet helps the poet to condense his thought? If you were to write on a solemn theme, would you choose the sonnet form, the lyric, or the ballade? Why?

THE BALLAD

The *ballad* (not to be confused with the *ballade*) has no strict form. Originally "a song intended to accompany a dance," it was afterwards applied to "a light, simple song of any kind." The ballad as we know it has been defined by Dr. Murray as "a simple, spirited poem in short stanzas, in which some popular story is graphically told." Ballads have been popular ever since men learned "to lisp in numbers" and they have as firm a hold on our affections today as they had in the days when Robin Hood's exploits were sung in every English lane. Most of the poems in the sections "Ballads and Legends" (*Yesterday,* p. 65) and in "Tales Old and New" (*Today,* p. 227) fulfil the requirements of Dr. Murray's definition.

Can you find other poems in other sections of this volume which seem to you to be true ballads? Compare the ballads in this book with some of those in "The Oxford Book of Ballads," which is the best collection of its kind. Do you prefer the modern or the ancient stories? Select your favorite and write (or explain) why you have chosen it.

THE BALLADE

The *ballade* is not only the oldest but the most popular of the French forms. (The French forms are so called because they originated in the country of the troubadours as early as the Fourteenth Century.) It was introduced into England as early as the Fifteenth Century but was little favored until Austin Dobson began using it toward the end of the Nineteenth Century. Other famous poets of the period (Andrew Lang, William Ernest Henley, and A. C. Swinburne) followed Dobson, and by 1890 the ballade was almost as well known as the sonnet.

The structure of the ballade is strict but not complicated. It consists of three stanzas of eight lines and an additional stanza of four lines called *The Envoy*. The rhymes of all the stanzas must follow the order of the first verse — which might be expressed thus: a-b-a-b-b-c-b-c. The outstanding feature of the ballade is its *refrain*. The refrain is the line which ends every stanza and, being repeated in its entirety, gives a unity to the poem itself. An excellent example of this form is "A Ballade of Spring's Unrest" (*Today*, p. 159), by Bert Leston Taylor. Compare this with other ballades in Helen Louise Cohen's *Lyric Forms from France* or in some other collection. Does the repeating of the same rhyme make the poem (a) more monotonous? (b) more musical? Have you ever read anything of François Villon, the gutter-poet who was called the "Prince of Ballade-Makers"? Robert Louis Stevenson's short story, "A Lodging for the Night," gives an excellent picture of his times, although the tale itself is pure fiction.

THE RONDEAU, THE TRIOLET, ETC.

There are several other French forms which are highly interesting and more or less complicated in structure. Lacking the space to analyze each of them, we may list the more popular as follows:

The *rondeau*, one of the most charming of these forms, consists of thirteen lines, written throughout on two rhymes — the *ends* of the second and third verses being the same as the *beginning* of the first verse. "In Vain To-day" (*Yesterday*, p. 100), by Austin Dobson, is an excellent example of this form.

A more modern example, in which the refrain is punned on, is "A Song to One" (*Today*, p. 202), by T. A. Daly.

The *triolet* is possibly the neatest of these forms. It is a single stanza of eight lines with only two rhymes — two of the lines being repeated *in their entirety* in a certain order. The chief characteristic of the triolet is a neat playfulness, as may be seen in "To a Fat Lady Seen from the Train" (*Today*, p. 203), by Frances Cornford. But, though most of the triolets are amusing rather than profound, "Triolet" (*Today*, p. 221), by A. K. Laing, turns this tiny form to a serious purpose.

The *villanelle* has been defined by Henley as follows:

> "A dainty thing's the villanelle
> Sly, musical, a jewel in rhyme;
> It serves its purpose passing well."

It, also, is built entirely upon two rhymes; but, rather than have the structure defined, the student will be able to understand it better by analyzing "When I Saw You Last, Rose" (*Yesterday*, p. 51), by Austin Dobson, and "The House on the Hill" (*Today*, p. 214), by Edwin Arlington Robinson, the two finest villanelles of their periods.

XII. AN OUTLINE OF HENRY WADSWORTH LONG-FELLOW

(For biographical and critical details, refer to the section entitled "Who's Who Among the Poets," p. 321.)

Among the results of a questionnaire, it was discovered that the names of five poets "led all the rest." These five — Longfellow, Whitman, Browning, Kipling, and Frost — were practically tied for first place in the affections of teachers and students. It is interesting to note the division in time and country: three of the favorite poets belong to *Yesterday*, two of them to *Today*, two of these leaders are English poets, three of them are Americans.

Since Longfellow was surely the most beloved poet of his period and since he still has his devoted readers, young and old, many a student will like to examine his work in greater detail.

Read "A Dutch Picture" (p. 32)
 "King Robert of Sicily" (p. 34)
 "Einar Tamberskelver" (p. 129)
 "The Potter's Song" (p. 111)

These poems (all of which may be found in the section *Yesterday*) have been less quoted than other stanzas of Longfellow's which have become "household words." Do they give you a different picture of the poet from the one you may already have formed of him?

There are today many critics who find fault with Longfellow because he "mixed preaching and poetry" and was "continually tagging morals on to the ends of his poems, as in 'The Village Blacksmith.'" Do you believe this is true of all of Longfellow's work? Do his poems in this book bear out the above criticism, or do they contradict it?

"A Dutch Picture" and "King Robert of Sicily" are, primarily, portraits of two different types of person, but they are also "story poems." In which do you think Longfellow excels, in the description of a character or in the telling of a tale?

Read seven or eight of the poems listed below:
 "My Lost Youth"
 "The Day Is Done"
 * "The Children's Hour"
 * "The Slave's Dream"
 "Hymn to the Night"
 "Sandalphon"
 "The Skeleton in Armor"
 "Nature" (a sonnet)
 "A Psalm of Life"
 "The Wreck of the Hesperus"
 "The Building of the Ship"
 "Paul Revere's Ride"
 "The Birds of Killingworth"
 "The Jewish Cemetery at Newport"
 "The Arrow and the Song"
 "The Clock on the Stairs"

All of these poems may be found in one volume — *Complete Poems of Henry Wadsworth Longfellow,* published by Houghton Mifflin Company. Those with an asterisk (*) may be found in *This Singing World.*

After choosing seven or eight of the above, would you say, as one critic has said, that "Longfellow is essentially a moralist, harping always on the same theme," or would you agree with another critic who maintains that "no American writer has been so fertile, so varied in subject, so rich in ideas"?

Have you read "Hiawatha," "The Courtship of Miles Standish," or "Evangeline"? Do you prefer these longer poems to Longfellow's shorter ones? Do you see any relation between the young Hiawatha and the young Mowgli of Kipling's *Jungle Books?*

Write an article on (a) Longfellow as Historian, (b) Longfellow as a Writer of American Epics, (c) Longfellow as Lyric Poet, (d) Longfellow as Moral Guide, (e) Longfellow as Nature-Lover — or, if you prefer, a general essay combining as many of the qualities as you admire in this poet.

XIII. AN OUTLINE OF WALT WHITMAN

(For biographical and critical details, refer to the section entitled "Who's Who Among the Poets," p. 325.)

The rise of Walt Whitman to popular esteem is due to the extraordinary interest in modern poetry. Although during his lifetime he had his admirers who championed him valiantly, those who loved Whitman's lines were in the minority and the mere mention of his name in literary circles was the signal for a long and bitter battle. Whitman's great work, "Leaves of Grass," was first published before the Civil War, but as late as 1900 the importance of his contribution to literature was still disputed. Today he is acclaimed as "one of the major prophets" in every country of the civilized world. His poems and "democratic chants" have been translated into practically every language and an entire literature has resulted from his universal influence.

Read the poems listed below (from the section *Yesterday*) and see if you can understand the reason for Whitman's greatness.

"Miracles" (p. 10)
"When I Heard the Learn'd Astronomer" (p. 11)
"Song of the Open Road" (p. 18)
"From 'Leaves of Grass'" (p. 28)

"O Captain! My Captain!" (p. 117)
"When Lilacs Last in the Dooryard Bloom'd" (p. 118)

The last two poems cited are tributes to Abraham Lincoln and were written shortly after the assassination of the President. These two are part of a series in which the "good gray poet" wrote about the "martyr-chief" without sentimentalizing or prettifying him. Whitman did not treat Lincoln from the literary but from the human standpoint. "After Whitman is done with him," so writes John Burroughs, "Lincoln still remains Lincoln. No way reduced. No way aggrandized. Only better understood."

The last poem on the above list, "When Lilacs Last in the Dooryard Bloom'd," is one of the noblest memorial poems ever written. It has been praised by thousands, none of whom has written about it more beautifully than John Burroughs, from whom is quoted the following:

"At first it would seem to defy analysis, so rapt is it, and so indirect. No reference whatever is made to the mere fact of Lincoln's death; the poet does not even dwell upon its unprovoked atrocity, and only occasionally is the tone that of lamentation; but, with the intuition of art which is most complex when it seems most simple, he seizes upon three beautiful facts of nature, which he weaves into a wreath for the dead President's tomb. The central thought is of death, but around this he curiously twines, first, the early-blooming lilacs which the poet may have plucked the day the dark shadow came; next the song of the hermit thrush, heard at twilight in the dusky cedars; and with these the evening star, which, night after night in the early part of that eventful spring, hung low in the west with unusual and tender brightness.

"The attitude, therefore, is not that of being bowed down and weeping hopeless tears, but of singing a commemorative hymn, in which the voices of nature join, and fit that exalted condition of the soul which serious events and the presence of death induce."

Does this interpretation by Burroughs help you to appreciate the beauties of this classic? Do the long, irregular lines disturb you, or do you like " the uneven music, like the orchestral rhythms of the sea " ? Which passage in particular means the most to you?

Read five or six of the poems listed below:
" Pioneers, O Pioneers! "
" Give Me the Splendid Silent Sea "
* " The First Dandelion "
* " I Am He That Walks "
* " The Runner "
* " What Is the Grass "
" Out of the Cradle Endlessly Rocking "
" I Hear America Singing "
" Crossing Brooklyn Ferry "
" Come Up from the Fields "
" A Sight in Camp "

(Those with an asterisk (*) may be found in *This Singing World*.)

What is the chief characteristic of this poetry? Do you agree with the author that " whosoever touches this book, touches a man " ? Which is most prominent in this poetry: the power of description or the power of emotion? Would you say that this work is " characteristically American " ? What reasons would you give (a) for thinking so? or (b) for disagreeing?

XIV. AN OUTLINE OF ROBERT BROWNING

(For biographical and critical details, refer to the section entitled " Who's Who Among the Poets," p. 316.)

It is doubtful whether there has ever existed a more many-sided, continually stimulating poet than Robert Browning. His was a mind in which poetry and intellect were equally balanced, a balance which gave even the least of his lyrics that peculiarly intense quality which is so typical of Browning. " No modern English poet," says Richard Garnett, " comes so near as Robert Browning to painting a panorama of life. . . . Had Browning lived in the age of Shakespeare, he would have been the second greatest English dramatist." Every line that Browning wrote — even the most philosophic one — is animated by this dramatic spirit. He was — some of his critics have charged — an incorrigible optimist; his affirmative spirit, with its " God's in his heaven, all's right with the world," has annoyed many skeptics. But Browning's philosophy is never meekly submissive; when he accepts, it is only after testing his soul against struggle; his " yea" is no light response, but the courageous reply to self-questioning.

Read " Rabbi Ben Ezra " (*Yesterday*, p. 105).

Here Browning expresses a religious philosophy which recognizes the perfection of some divine plan, a philosophy which joyfully accepts old age, death, and rebuffs as a means for perfecting the growth of the soul. According to Charlotte Porter, " the very failure of man in the flesh, showing his infinite possibilities of growth, removes him from the brute, and gives assurance both of God and of man's tendency Godwards."

Rabbi Ben Ezra was a medieval Jewish seer, born in Toledo, who became famous as a theologian, physician, astronomer, and poet. Besides the philosophy of this poem, do you get a picture of Rabbi Ben Ezra himself? What would you say were his chief characteristics? Do you think that Browning has identified himself with the ancient Jewish thinker? What passage or passages impress you the most because of (a) their power? (b) their beauty? (c) their message?

Read " Prospice " (p. 114).

Do you find any relation between this poem and " Rabbi Ben Ezra " ? If you do, show the similarity by the selection of phrases or passages. In this poem, the speaker anticipates death as the climax and fulfilment of life; the end of the poem suggests the reunion with his " other soul." Remembering that Elizabeth Barrett Browning died almost thirty years before her husband, would you say that the poem was autobiographical? Does the philosophical or the personal element move you more?

Read " Home Thoughts from Abroad " (p. 16)
   " De Gustibus —— " (p. 7)
   " The Laboratory " (p. 78)
   " Marching Along " (p. 128)

In these poems (all from *Yesterday*) we have Browning in entirely different moods. The Cavalier tune reflects the spirit of the rallying of the nobles to the cause of King Charles against the Parliament. It is in a galloping measure. " Home Thoughts from Abroad " is a lyric expressing the longing for home of a person to whom the " gaudy melon flower " of Italy is not half so lovely as the little buttercup of England. "De Gustibus" is a more whimsical lyric on the same theme. "The Laboratory" is a highly dramatic episode, depicting a jealous court lady preparing to poison her rival and showing us, at the same time, the social conditions of the feudal period which she represents.

Which of these four poems do you care for most? Do you like Browning best as (a) philosopher? (b) story-teller? (c) portrait-painter? (d) lyricist? or (e) moral guide? Show, by extracts from the poems, the reasons for your choice.

Read seven or eight of the poems listed below:
  "Love Among the Ruins"
  * "Incident of the French Camp"
  * "Service" ("All service ranks the same with God")
  * "The Year's at the Spring" (from *Pippa Passes*)
  * "Apparitions"
  "The Pied Piper of Hamelin"
  "Saul"
  "The Glove"
  "Hervé Riel"
  "Youth and Art"
  "The Boy and the Angel"
  "How They Brought the Good News from Ghent to Aix"
  "My Star"
  "The Lost Leader"
  "Andrea del Sarto"
  "Evelyn Hope"
  "My Last Duchess"
  "James Lee's Wife" (Selections)
  "Confessions"

(Practically all of these can be found in any one volume of Browning's selected poems. Those marked with an asterisk (*) may be found in *This Singing World*.)

Do the poems which you have read display Browning's "many-mindedness"? Do they make you see why he has been regarded as one of the greatest dramatic poets since Shakespeare? Do his characters seem merely the mouthpieces of the poet or do you feel that they are alive? If you were given the opportunity of becoming acquainted with any of Browning's men and women, whom would you like most to meet?

XV. AN OUTLINE OF RUDYARD KIPLING

(For biographical and critical details, refer to the section entitled "Who's Who Among the Poets," p. 336.)

Among the living poets it is doubtful whether any has achieved wider recognition than Rudyard Kipling. Although an Englishman, born in India, he is as popular in America as in his native land. Heartiness, a marching rhythm, a belief in England's destiny, and an infectious gusto characterize the greater part of his work and make us see why he has been called "the British Empire's unofficial laureate."

Read "Fuzzy-Wuzzy" (p. 229)
      "Mandalay" (p. 227)
      "To James Whitcomb Riley" (p. 203)
      "Recessional" (p. 292)

All of these poems appear in the section *Today*. Which one appeals to you most? Do you like it best because of (a) its description? (b) its vigorous language? (c) its ability to make you feel what the poet is feeling? or (d) the ease with which it reads?

"Fuzzy-Wuzzy" is merely the tale of one of the minor engagements of the British soldiery in the Soudan, but it is much more than the depiction of a battle. It is a tribute both to the bravery of the untrained native and to the proverbial "good sportsmanship" of the English. Are both qualities apparent to you? Does the humorous tone of the verse affect the sincerity of the tribute?

"Recessional" was written at the end of Queen Victoria's Diamond Jubilee in 1897 which celebrated the sixty years of her reign. Many poems in honor of the glory of her rule were written at the time; "Recessional" is the only one which survives. Does the poem strike you as a mere celebration of the British Empire or is it also a warning? Does Kipling believe that power and armies will make England live forever? What does he suggest by his reference to the ancient cities of Nineveh and Tyre? Even though the "Amen" were not added to the poem, what would make you feel that it is a prayer? What effect is given by the repetition of the phrase "Lest we forget"?

"Mandalay" is possibly the most famous of Kipling's soldier poems although it is in a quieter key than most. Do you like it more or less than the more vigorous verses? What phrases have become bywords in our speech? Which image do you find the most striking? This poem has been set to music by several composers. If you have heard it sung, do you think that the melody adds anything, or do you think that the lines are sufficient music in themselves?

Read six or seven of the poems listed below:

* "The Ballad of East and West"
* "Danny Deever"
* "If —"
† "Gunga Din"
† "The Return"
† "The Conundrum of the Workshops"
† "An Astrologer's Song"
  "The Explorer"
  "The Law of the Jungle"
  "Rhymes from *Just So Stories*"
  "The Overland Mail"
  "The Last Chantey"
  "The Feet of the Young Men"
  "The Gipsy Trail"
  "General Summary"
  "The Long Trail"
  "The Sons of Martha"
  "Tommy Atkins"

All of these poems are contained in the splendid one-volume *Inclusive Edition* published by Doubleday, Page and Company. Those marked with an asterisk (*) are in *This Singing World;* those marked with a dagger (†) are in *Modern British Poetry.*

Which of these would you like (a) to reread? (b) to recite? (c) to write about in a composition? Take two or three similar poems and write an article emphasizing one phase of Kipling's poetry. Take two or three entirely different types of poems from the above list and write an essay showing the variety of Kipling's gifts. Other compositions might be written on (a) Indian life in Kipling's poetry; (b) Kipling and "Tommy Atkins" — Tommy Atkins being the ordinary British soldier; (c) Kipling as Patriot; (d) Kipling as Popularizer of Poetry.

XVI. AN OUTLINE OF ROBERT FROST

(For biographical and critical details, refer to the section "Who's Who Among the Poets," p. 332.)

Read "The Code" (p. 142)
  "The Wood-Pile" (p. 146)
  "Mowing" (p. 159)
  "Wind and Window-Flower" (p. 255)
  "A Prayer in Spring" (p. 290)

All of these poems are in the section entitled *Today*. From a reading of them, what do you think has caused critics to call Robert Frost "the laureate of the soil, the most sympathetic recorder of farm and field"? In "Mowing" notice how the poet gives you the feeling of being alone in a silent world in the first two lines. Could any description be better than that of the scythe "whispering"?

Do you find a similar sense of solitude in "The Wood-Pile"? In spite of its serious theme, would you say that the poem is without lightness? What passage would you select as an example of Frost's "elfin fantasy" and banter? What does the poet mean by "the slow smokeless burning of decay"?

Although Frost has been rated higher than any other living American poet, he has sometimes been accused of having no humor. Do you agree with this? Does "The Code" bear this out, or does it contradict it?

Read seven or eight of the poems listed below:
  "Into My Own" from *A Boy's Will*
  "Storm Fear" from *A Boy's Will*
  "To the Thawing Wind" from *A Boy's Will*
 *† "The Tuft of Flowers" from *A Boy's Will*
 *† "The Pasture" from *North of Boston*
  * "Mending Wall" from *North of Boston*
  * "The Death of the Hired Man" from *North of Boston*
  "After Apple-Picking" from *North of Boston*
  "The Mountain" from *North of Boston*
  * "Birches" from *Mountain Interval*
  "An Old Man's Winter Night" from *Mountain Interval*

> * " Fire and Ice " from *New Hampshire*
> " Nothing Gold Can Stay " from *New Hampshire*
> *† " The Runaway " from *New Hampshire*
> *† " Stopping by Woods on a Snowy Evening " from *New Hampshire*
> * " Goodbye and Keep Cold " from *New Hampshire*
> * " Two Look at Two " from *New Hampshire*
> † " A Hillside Thaw " from *New Hampshire*

Those poems which are marked with an asterisk (*) are also to be found in the revised edition of *Modern American Poetry;* those with a dagger (†) are also contained in *This Singing World*.

Do these poems give you a clearer picture of (a) the New England countryside? (b) the New England character? (c) the poet himself? or (d) all these things combined? Do you find that the actual language of these poems is different from that of most of the others? In what way? Is it a " literary " language, or can you hear the " tones of speech " as they would come from a person talking to you? What else, if anything, interests you in these poems?

Robert Frost has given this bit of advice to young poets: " A poem must be at least as good as the prose it might have been. A poem is a box with a *set* or assortment of sentences that just fit together to fill it. You are rhyming sentences and phrases, not just words." Does this help to explain why his words are straightforward and why they " smell of the hills and meadows rather than of dusty libraries "?

XVII. SUPPLEMENTARY SUGGESTIONS

It is taken for granted that when (or if) the student reaches this point, he has already covered the ground outlined in the previous suggestions. These supplementary hints and questions merely amplify the preceding ones — the teacher may not only vary them but add any others which the collection may suggest.

1. Has your interest in poetry, as a whole, been stimulated or lessened by the questions?

2. Would you yourself like to prepare a set of questions on any feature of this volume? Following the outlines of these suggestions for study, could you — from the contents of this

volume — make a study outline on *The Poet as Lover? The Poet as Optimist? The Poet as Comrade? The Poet as Historian? The Poet as Child? The Poet and the Fairies?*

3. Write an essay on any of the above or similar subjects, with quotations from the poems themselves.

4. Write a composition on the use of color in poetry. Show how Amy Lowell and certain other writers make their work sparkle with "words that shimmer and glow."

5. To which of the five senses does poetry appeal most? Choose one or two examples which appeal most to the sense of (a) sight, (b) hearing, (c) taste, (d) smell, (e) touch.

6. Are you sufficiently interested in the forms of poetry to try to write (a) a ballad? (b) a lyric? or (c) a sonnet?

Choose some object with which you are familiar, or some person whom you know, and try to describe this in verse. Take some popular story, of either the past or the present, and make a simple ballad of it. Using as your subject "The Sea" or "Mountains" or "The Road" or one of the months, try to write a sonnet, following the form of one of the sonnets in this collection. (Study the length of lines and note that they all are not only *even* in beat, but of exactly the same length.)

7. Aided by the poets' own works as well as the suggestions in the foregoing pages, write an article on Henry Wadsworth Longfellow, Walt Whitman, Rudyard Kipling, Robert Browning, or Robert Frost. If you wish to go further and do your own "research" work, prepare a similar outline or essay on Ralph Waldo Emerson, William Ernest Henley, Carl Sandburg, John Masefield, Walter de la Mare, or Edna St. Vincent Millay.

8. Do you agree with the modern poets that there is no particular "poetic diction"? Or do you believe that such a poem as "To a Waterfowl" (which uses such "poetic" words as *whither, plashy, 'midst, seek'st, marge, o'er*) is more truly poetry than the poems of Robert Frost or Carl Sandburg which contain only words which are used in everyday speech?

9. Suppose you were the final judge of the winner in a Poetry Contest and the following six poems were submitted to you:

> "King Robert of Sicily" — Longfellow (p. 34)
> "Annabel Lee" — Poe (p. 66)
> "Columbus" — Miller (p. 134)
> "Ballad of the Harp-Weaver" — Millay (p. 231)

"The Bull" — Hodgson (p. 175)
"Mandalay" — Kipling (p. 227)

To which would you award the prize? Would personal taste be the only factor in your decision? Give other reasons for your choice.

10. Suppose it is the year 5219; American civilization has entirely disappeared from the earth, but a copy of this volume is dug up and deciphered by scholars. Which of the poems do you think you would understand and enjoy? Would you have any emotional response to such poems as "Marching Along" (p. 128)? "The Ballad of the Oysterman" (p. 80)? "Invictus" (p. 126)? "At the End of the Day" (p. 306)? "The Code" (p. 142)? What is the quality about any of these which might make them "last"? Name any other poem (or poems) which you think might have such a lasting power, and state why you think so.

11. Why I would elect ———— ———— Poet Laureate of our school.

12. After Lizette Woodworth Reese had retired from the high school in Baltimore, the pupils whom she had taught for many years presented the school with a bronze tablet commemorating her work. On this tablet was inscribed her sonnet, "Tears" (p. 295). If a similar tablet were to be placed on the wall of your school, which poem would you like to see engraved upon it?

13. Suppose you could have any poet whose work is included in this book (whether he is now living or dead) read to you from his own writings. Whom would you choose and why?

14. Suppose a Chinese poet, an excellent English scholar, is making an anthology and writes to you, asking you to send him six modern poems to be translated into his native language. Which poems would you send him?

A SUPPLEMENTARY READING LIST

The following is a list of volumes classified according to their *kind* for those readers who wish to study the poetry of the periods in greater detail. It is taken for granted that the pupil knows the existence of the older standard authorities (such as Palgrave's *Golden Treasury of Songs and Lyrics*), and this list, therefore, represents the comparatively recent or the less familiar collections. An asterisk (*) in front of a title means that the book thus marked is either of a technical nature or for advanced students.

GENERAL

For a general consideration of poetry, the following titles will repay study:

AN INTRODUCTION TO POETRY, *Hubbell and Beatty*. The Macmillan Company, 1922.

* ESSENTIALS OF POETRY, *William Allan Neilson*. Houghton Mifflin Company, 1912.

ENJOYMENT OF POETRY, *Max Eastman*. Charles Scribner's Sons, 1915.

* THE KINDS OF POETRY, *John Erskine*. Duffield and Company, 1923.

* A STUDY OF POETRY, *Bliss Perry*. Houghton Mifflin Company.

A DEFENCE OF POETRY, *Percy Bysshe Shelley*. Bobbs-Merrill Company.

* CONVENTION AND REVOLT IN POETRY, *John Livingston Lowes*. Houghton Mifflin Company, 1919.

* SCEPTICISMS: NOTES ON CONTEMPORARY POETRY, *Conrad Aiken*. Alfred A. Knopf, 1919.

* ON ENGLISH POETRY ("Being an irregular approach to the psychology of the art from evidence mainly subjective "), *Robert Graves*. Alfred A. Knopf, 1922.

STUDIES OF CONTEMPORARY POETRY (confined to a study of the contemporary English poets), *Mary C. Sturgeon*. Dodd, Mead and Company, 1919.

* SOME CONTEMPORARY POETS (this is also confined to recent English poets), *Harold Monro*. Leonard Parsons (London), 1920.

* A NEW STUDY OF ENGLISH POETRY (twelve essays on such subjects as "Poetry and Rhythm," "Poetry and Education," "British Ballads"), *Henry Newbolt*. E. P. Dutton and Company, 1919.
* NEW VOICES, *Marguerite Wilkinson*. The Macmillan Company, 1921.
* AMERICAN POETRY SINCE 1900, *Louis Untermeyer*. Henry Holt and Company, 1923.

COLLECTIONS

It would be impossible to list the many anthologies which cover the ground with varying thoroughness. However, as *reference* volumes and for those who wish to study the individual poets in greater detail, the following larger collections may be recommended.

THE HOME BOOK OF VERSE. Edited by *Burton E. Stevenson*. Henry Holt and Company, 1918. (4000 pages)
* THE OXFORD BOOK OF ENGLISH VERSE. Edited by *A. T. Quiller-Couch*. Oxford University Press, 1919. (1080 pages)
* THE OXFORD BOOK OF VICTORIAN VERSE. Edited by *A. T. Quiller-Couch*. Oxford University Press, 1919. (1000 pages)
AN AMERICAN ANTHOLOGY (from 1787 to 1900). Edited by *Edmund Clarence Stedman*. Houghton Mifflin Company, 1900. (860 pages)
A VICTORIAN ANTHOLOGY (from 1837 to 1895). Edited by *Edmund Clarence Stedman*. Houghton Mifflin Company, 1895. (740 pages)
ROMANTIC AND VICTORIAN POETRY. Edited by *C. E. Andrews* and *M. O. Percival*. A. A. Adams & Company (Columbus, Ohio), 1924. (980 pages)
* THE NEW POETRY: AN ANTHOLOGY OF TWENTIETH CENTURY VERSE IN ENGLISH. Edited by *Harriet Monro* and *Alice Corbin Henderson*. The Macmillan Company, 1923. (611 pages)
AN ANTHOLOGY OF MODERN VERSE (devoted exclusively to recent English poets). Chosen by *A. Methuen*. Methuen and Company (London), 1921. (240 pages)
MODERN BRITISH POETRY (from 1840 to 1925). Revised and

Enlarged Edition. Edited by *Louis Untermeyer*. Harcourt, Brace and Company, 1925. (400 pages)

MODERN AMERICAN POETRY (from 1830 to 1925). Revised and Enlarged Edition. Edited by *Louis Untermeyer*. Harcourt, Brace and Company, 1925. (620 pages)

COLLECTIONS FOR YOUNGER READERS

THE HOME BOOK OF VERSE FOR YOUNG FOLKS, *Burton Egbert Stevenson*. Henry Holt and Company, 1915.

GOLDEN NUMBERS. Chosen and classified by *Kate Douglas Wiggin* and *Nora Archibald Smith*. McClure, Phillips and Company, 1903.

THE LISTENING CHILD, *Lucy W. Thacher*. The Macmillan Company, Revised Edition, 1924.

RAINBOW GOLD, *Sara Teasdale*. The Macmillan Company, 1922.

POEMS FOR YOUTH, *William Rose Benét*. E. P. Dutton and Company, 1925.

COME HITHER, *Walter de la Mare*. Alfred A. Knopf, 1923.

OPEN GATES, *Susan Thompson Spaulding* and *Francis Trow Spaulding*. Houghton Mifflin Company, 1924.

THIS SINGING WORLD, *Louis Untermeyer*. Harcourt, Brace and Company, 1923.

BALLADS

The best collections of older or popular ballads are, without doubt, the following:

PERCY'S RELIQUES or RELIQUES OF ANCIENT ENGLISH POETRY, *Thomas Percy, Lord Bishop of Dromore*. Thomas Y. Crowell and Company.

THE BALLAD BOOK. Edited by *William Allingham*. D. Lothrop and Co.

THE OXFORD BOOK OF BALLADS. Edited by *A. T. Quiller-Couch*. Oxford University Press.

BALLADS AND LYRICS OF LOVE. Edited by *Frank Sidgwick*. F. A. Stokes Company.

LEGENDARY BALLADS. Edited by *Frank Sidgwick*. F. A. Stokes Company.

ENGLISH AND SCOTTISH POPULAR BALLADS. Edited from the collection of Francis J. Child by *Helen Child Sargent* and

George Lyman Kittredge. Houghton Mifflin Company, 1904.

(A particularly splendid résumé is Andrew Lang's article on the ballad in *The Encyclopaedia Britannica*.)

Excellent examples of the *modern American ballad* may be found in:

COWBOY SONGS AND OTHER FRONTIER BALLADS. Collected and edited by *John A. Lomax*. The Macmillan Company.

* POETIC ORIGINS AND THE BALLAD, *Professor Louise Pound*. The Macmillan Company, 1921.

AMERICAN BALLADS AND SONGS. Collected by *Professor Louise Pound*. Charles Scribner's Sons, 1922.

THE BOOK OF AMERICAN NEGRO POETRY. Edited by *James Weldon Johnson*. Harcourt, Brace and Company.

KENTUCKY MOUNTAIN SONGS and LONESOME TUNES. (Two volumes, with Music.) *Loraine Wyman* and *Howard Brockway*. Oliver Ditson Company.

THE FRENCH FORMS

The two best collections, as well as the two most detailed analyses of the French forms are:

BALLADES AND RONDEAUS, SESTINAS, VILLANELLES, etc. Selected by *Gleeson White*. The Walter Scott Publishing Company.

LYRIC FORMS FROM FRANCE: THEIR HISTORY AND THEIR USE. Edited by *Helen Louise Cohen*. Harcourt, Brace and Company.

VERS DE SOCIÉTÉ

(*Light Verse*)

The collections of Vers de Société are almost as numerous as the usual type of anthology. Carolyn Wells has been a pioneer in this field; three of her most enticing collections are listed below:

A VERS DE SOCIÉTÉ ANTHOLOGY. Collected by *Carolyn Wells*. Charles Scribner's Sons.

A WHIMSY ANTHOLOGY. Collected by *Carolyn Wells*. Charles Scribner's Sons.

A PARODY ANTHOLOGY. Collected by *Carolyn Wells*. Charles Scribner's Sons.

Other standard volumes are:

AMERICAN FAMILIAR VERSE. Edited by *Brander Matthews.* Longmans, Green and Co.

VERS DE SOCIÉTÉ. Edited by *Charles H. Jones.* Henry Holt and Company.

LYRA ELEGANTIARUM. Edited by *Frederick Locker-Lampson.* Ward, Lock and Co.

THE LITTLE BOOK OF SOCIETY VERSE. Compiled by *Claude Moore Fuess* and *Harold Crawford Stearns.* Houghton Mifflin Company.

A LITTLE BOOK OF LIGHT VERSE. Edited by *Anthony C. Deane.* Dodd, Mead and Company.

A TREASURY OF HUMOROUS POETRY, *Frederick Lawrence Knowles.* Dana Estes and Company.

FREE VERSE

The best discussion of free verse occurs in two volumes, both of them rather technical, which present two almost opposed points of view. These two volumes are:

* TENDENCIES IN MODERN AMERICAN POETRY, *Amy Lowell.* The Macmillan Company.

* THE RHYTHM OF PROSE, *William Morrison Patterson.* Columbia University Press.

Amy Lowell's introduction to her *Can Grande's Castle* contains not only the basic idea of free verse, but also a complete explanation of "polyphonic prose."

THE EPIC

The best consideration of the epic principle is to be found in:

* ENGLISH EPIC AND HEROIC POETRY, *Professor W. MacNeile Dixon,* M.A. London: J. M. Dent and Sons, 1911.

THE SONNET

The most thorough consideration as well as the best historical survey of the subject of the sonnet itself is:

THE ENGLISH SONNET, *T. W. H. Crossland.* Dodd, Mead and Company, 1917.

There is no recent collection of modern sonnets which is particularly notable. There are, however, three general compilations which are excellent. The first covers the field from Henry Howard, Earl of Surrey (1517–1547), to the New England poets; the second is devoted entirely to poets of the Nineteenth Century:

THE BOOK OF THE SONNET. Edited by *Leigh Hunt* and *S. Adams Lee*. (This is in two volumes.)

SONNETS OF THIS CENTURY. (With a Critical Introduction on the Sonnet.) *William Sharp.*

THE GOLDEN BOOK OF ENGLISH SONNETS. Selected by *William Robertson*. London: George G. Harrap and Company, 1913.

THE LYRIC

The best discussion as well as the most comprehensive analysis of the English lyric is to be found in:

* LYRIC POETRY. (From the earliest Norman melodies to the literary lyrics of the late Victorians.) *Ernest Rhys.* E. P. Dutton and Company, 1913.

There are several collections of purely lyrical verses, the best being:

ENGLISH LYRICAL POETRY (1500–1700). Edited by *Frederic Ives Carpenter*. Charles Scribner's Sons.

SELECTIONS FROM MODERN POETS. Made by *J. C. Squire*. London: Martin Secker, 1921.

SHORTER LYRICS OF THE TWENTIETH CENTURY, 1900–1922. Selected by *W. H. Davies*. London: The Poetry Bookshop.

A POCKET DICTIONARY OF VERSE

THE FORMS OF POETRY, *Louis Untermeyer*. Harcourt, Brace and Company, 1926.

This book is divided into three parts: *A Handbook of Poetic Terms*, in which all the terms are simply defined with hundreds of quotations; *Forms of Poetry*, in which the forms themselves are analyzed and illustrated by famous examples; and *An Outline of English Poetry*, which traces the development of the art from the Tenth Century to the present day.

ACKNOWLEDGMENTS

My debt to the poets for their assistance as well as their permission to reprint their poems in this volume is only a trifle greater than my gratitude to the many teachers without whose coöperation this book would have been impossible. The collection was planned chiefly for use in the first and second years of high schools and, from the beginning, I realized that such a book should represent something more than the personal enthusiasms and prejudices of any one editor. Even before the first sketch of the volume was completed, a number of questionnaires (as has already been stated in the Preface) were sent to a selected list of teachers and Heads of English Departments with a note asking for the teachers' preferences, and, as far as possible, the pupils' own reactions. The results were more than merely gratifying — at least to the editor — and the contents of this volume has been greatly determined by the suggestions so generously given. Without the ample lists (reflecting, parenthetically, a broad familiarity with the poetry of the period), the many letters and countless other helps, this collection would not have appeared. It is, with a genuine sense of obligation, that I wish to record the invaluable aid of the following teachers — this acknowledgment being a declaration rather than a discharge of my debt:

Miss *Olga Achtenhagen*, High School, Appleton, Wisconsin.

Miss *Edith Adams*, Senior High School, New Britain, Connecticut.

Robert F. Allen, East Boston High School, East Boston, Massachusetts.

Miss *Rosemary Arnold*, Eastern High School, Washington, D. C.

Miss *Helen B. Baker*, Horace Mann School, Teachers' College, New York City.

William Avery Barras, Peddie Institute, Hightstown, New Jersey.

Miss *Maria Beatty*, Englewood High School, Chicago, Illinois.

Miss *Miriam B. Booth*, East High School, Erie, Pennsylvania.

Richard Warner Borst, Fullerton Union High School and Junior College, Fullerton, California.

Miss *Fannie J. Boswell,* La Junta Senior High School, La Junta, Colorado.

Stanley Burnshaw, Pittsburgh, Pennsylvania.

Miss *Anna P. Butler,* High and Latin Schools, Cambridge, Massachusetts.

Ray Cecil Carter, Albany High School, Albany, New York.

Miss *Agnes A. Cawley,* and members of the English Department of the High School, Bayonne, New Jersey.

Miss *Mary S. Cline,* High School, Easton, Pennsylvania.

Harry E. Coblentz, South Division High School, Milwaukee, Wisconsin.

Miss *Ella M. Cockrell,* Moline High School, Moline, Illinois.

Miss *Etta Cohen,* Masten Park High School, Buffalo, New York.

Miss *Helen Louise Cohen,* Washington Irving High School, New York City.

Miss *Marjorie Cook,* High School, De Kalb, Illinois.

Miss *Pauline Cope,* Haverford Township High School, Upper Darby Branch, Philadelphia, Pennsylvania.

M. J. Costello, Technical High School, Scranton, Pennsylvania.

Miss *Florence A. Crocker,* La Salle-Peru Township High and Junior College, La Salle, Illinois.

Miss *M. Theresa Dallam,* Western High School, Baltimore, Maryland.

Miss *Sally Freeman Dawes,* Quincy High School, Quincy, Massachusetts.

Miss *Jeanette Deane,* Central High School, Kalamazoo, Michigan.

Miss *Eleanora F. Deem,* Mechanic Arts High School, St. Paul, Minnesota.

Miss *Susan B. Dinsmore,* Bonita High School, La Verne, California.

Miss *Margaret Dixon,* Lindblom High School, Chicago, Illinois.

Harold T. Eaton, Brockton High School, Brockton, Massachusetts.

Miss *Mary P. Eaton,* The Wadleigh High School, New York City.

Miss *Laura V. Edwards,* Glenville High School, Cleveland, Ohio.

William B. Elwell, Crosby High School, Waterbury, Connecticut.

Mrs. *I. H. FitzGerald,* Hartford Public High School, Hartford, Connecticut.

B. E. Fleagle, Baltimore City College, Baltimore, Maryland.

Miss *Anne Louise Forsythe,* Lexington High School, Lexington, Massachusetts.

Claude M. Fuess, Phillips Academy, Andover, Massachusetts.

Miss *Ellen E. Garrigues* and members of the English Department of the De Witt Clinton High School, New York City.

Miss *Mabel Garwood,* East High School, Aurora, Illinois.

Miss *Mabel Goddard,* Technical High School, Indianapolis, Indiana.

Mrs. *M. B. Goodall,* University High School, Eugene, Oregon.

Ward H. Green, Central High School, Tulsa, Oklahoma.

R. R. Greenwood, North High School, Worcester, Mass.

Miss *M. Isabelle Hall,* Hope Street High School, Providence, Rhode Island.

Miss *Olive Ely Hart,* South Philadelphia High School for Girls, Philadelphia, Pennsylvania.

Miss *Clara N. Hawkes,* J. Sterling Morton High School, Cicero, Illinois.

Miss *Winifred C. Hays,* Washington High School, Portland, Oregon.

Miss *Jean Hoard,* University High School, Madison, Wisconsin.

Mrs. *Margaret K. Hoover,* Brantwood Hall, Bronxville, New York.

Miss *Mary C. Houston,* High School, Newark, Delaware.

Miss *Mary H. Hutchinson,* Libbey High School, Toledo, Ohio.

Miss *Grace Inman,* Bloomington High School, Bloomington, Illinois.

Miss *E. Florence Kimmins* and members of the English Department of the Technical High School, Buffalo, New York.

John A. Lester, The Hill School, Pottstown, Pennsylvania.

Miss *Celina H. Lewis,* The High School, Brookline, Massachusetts.

Miss *Anna M. Mashek,* High School, La Crosse, Wisconsin.

Miss *G. Eunice Meers*, Roosevelt High School, Des Moines, Iowa.

Miss *Emma L. Newitt* and members of the English Department, Philadelphia High School for Girls, Philadelphia, Pennsylvania.

Miss *Mary E. Noone*, High School, Kingston, New York.

A. F. Olney, Phoenix Union High School, Phoenix, Arizona.

Merrill P. Paine, New Haven High School, New Haven, Connecticut.

Miss *Inez Parshall*, Central High School, Akron, Ohio.

Frank J. Platt, Oak Park High School, Oak Park, Illinois.

Miss *N. Octavia Pleé*, Northeastern High School, Detroit, Michigan.

Miss *Ethel Pope*, High School, Santa Maria, California.

Miss *Susie McD. W. Rabourn*, Fresno High School, Fresno, California.

Miss *Eulalie A. Richardson*, Kodak High School, Rochester, New York.

Miss *Fannie L. Rosenberg*, Beloit High School, Beloit, Wisconsin.

Charles L. Sanders, High School, Greenwich, Connecticut.

Mrs. *Mary Hill Sankey*, Garfield High School, Terre Haute, Indiana.

H. C. Schweikert, Central High School, St. Louis, Missouri.

Miss *Clara B. Shaw*, High School of Practical Arts, Boston, Massachusetts.

Harvey L. Sherwood, Central High School, Kalamazoo, Michigan.

Miss *Sarah E. Simons*, Head of the Department of English, High Schools, Washington, D. C.

Miss *Clara M. Sloat*, High School, Watertown, New York.

Miss *Anne M. Smith*, High School, Bloomfield, New Jersey.

Milton M. Smith, Horace Mann School for Boys, New York City.

Orrin Henry Smith, Roxbury High School, Roxbury, Massachusetts.

Miss *Edna O. Spinney*, English High School, Lynn, Massachusetts.

Dr. *Stewart A. Steger*, Centenary College of Louisiana, Shreveport, Louisiana.

Paul J. Thayer, Shead Memorial High School, Eastport, Maine.

Miss *Anna J. Thomas,* Central High School, Columbus, Ohio.

Miss *Laura Thompson,* Beloit High School, Beloit, Wisconsin.

Miss *Helen G. Todd,* High School, Elyria, Ohio.

A. Francis Trams, Joliet Township High School and Junior College, Joliet, Illinois.

O. Fred Umbaugh, Thornton Township High School, Harvey, Illinois.

Charles Fowler Van Cleve, Central High School, Kalamazoo, Michigan.

Miss *Bertha Evans Ward,* Hughes High School, Cincinnati, Ohio.

Charles B. Weld, The Taft School, Watertown, Connecticut.

Miss *Frances E. Yerkes,* High School, Gloversville, New York.

A further and special acknowledgment must be made to Winifred Howell Davies, not only for her secretarial services, but for her many helpful suggestions during the progress of the work.

There remains my appreciation of the courtesy of the many publishers for their permissions to reprint the selections for which they hold the copyright. This indebtedness is alphabetically acknowledged to the following:

D. APPLETON AND COMPANY — for the selections from *Poetical Works of William Cullen Bryant.*

BARSE AND HOPKINS — for a selection from *The Spell of the Yukon* by Robert W. Service.

BASIL BLACKWELL (Oxford, England) — for the selection from *Poems* by Camilla Doyle.

BOBBS-MERRILL COMPANY — for the selections from *Rhymes of Childhood and Neighborly Poems* by James Whitcomb Riley.

BONI AND LIVERIGHT — for selections from *Collected Poems of H. D.* and *Dublin Days* by L. A. G. Strong.

BRANDT AND BRANDT (as agents for Edna St. Vincent Millay) — for permission to reprint "God's World" and "When the Year Grows Old," from *Renascence and Other Poems,* published by Harper & Brothers, Copyright 1917, by Edna St.

Vincent Millay, and "The Ballad of the Harp-Weaver" from *The Harp Weaver and Other Poems,* published by Harper & Brothers. Copyright 1920, 1921, 1922, 1923, by Edna St. Vincent Millay.

BRENTANO'S — for the selection from *Collected Poems* by Francis Ledwidge.

DODD, MEAD & COMPANY — for selections from *The Complete Poems of Rupert Brooke, Lyrics of Lowly Life* by Paul Laurence Dunbar, *Lyrics of Love and Laughter* by Paul Laurence Dunbar, and *The Lonely Dancer* by Richard Le Gallienne.

GEORGE H. DORAN COMPANY — for the selections from *Tiger Joy* by Stephen Vincent Benét (Copyright 1925), *Trees and Other Poems* by Joyce Kilmer (Copyright 1914), *Chimneysmoke* by Christopher Morley (Copyright 1917, 1919, 1920, 1921). The poems from all of these volumes are reprinted by permission of, and by special arrangement with, George H. Doran Company, publishers.

DOUBLEDAY, PAGE & COMPANY — for selections from *Lincoln and Other Poems* by Edwin Markham and *The Gates of Paradise and Other Poems* by Edwin Markham.

E. P. DUTTON & COMPANY — for selections from *Counter-Attack* by Siegfried Sassoon, and *The Wild Knight* by G. K. Chesterton.

HARPER & BROTHERS — for selections from *Mother Goose for Grown-Ups* by Guy Wetmore Carryl, *Star-Glow and Song* by Charles Buxton Going, *The Mirthful Lyre* by Arthur Guiterman, *Ballads of Old New York* by Arthur Guiterman, *Hawthorn and Lavender* by William Ernest Henley, *The Harp Weaver and Other Poems* by Edna St. Vincent Millay and *Renascence and Other Poems* by Edna St. Vincent Millay.

HARCOURT, BRACE AND COMPANY — for selections from *A Miscellany of American Poetry — 1925, Canzoni* by T. A. Daly, *Carmina* by T. A. Daly, *Selected Poems* by W. H. Davies, *Not Poppy* by Virginia Moore, *Piping and Panning* by Edwin Meade Robinson, *Smoke and Steel* by Carl Sandburg, *Challenge* by Louis Untermeyer, *Roast Leviathan* by Louis Untermeyer, *The Contemplative Quarry* by Anna Wickham, *Ballads and Lyrics* by Margaret Widdemer, *The Unknown Goddess* by Humbert Wolfe, *Nets to Catch the Wind* by

Elinor Wylie, and *Lyric Forms from France* by Helen Louise Cohen.

HARR WAGNER PUBLISHING COMPANY — for the selection from *The Complete Poetical Works of Joaquin Miller.*

HENRY HOLT AND COMPANY — for selections from *Wilderness Songs* by Grace Hazard Conkling, *The Listeners* by Walter de la Mare, *Peacock Pie* by Walter de la Mare, *North of Boston* by Robert Frost and *A Boy's Will* by Robert Frost.

HOUGHTON MIFFLIN COMPANY — The selections from *The Complete Poems of Thomas Bailey Aldrich, Complete Poems of Ralph Waldo Emerson, Her Letter* by Bret Harte, *The Complete Poems of Oliver Wendell Holmes, The Complete Poems of Henry Wadsworth Longfellow, The Complete Poems of James Russell Lowell, The Complete Poems of John Greenleaf Whittier, The Shoes That Danced* by Anna Hempstead Branch, *Pictures of the Floating World* by Amy Lowell and *Men, Women and Ghosts* by Amy Lowell are used by permission of, and by special arrangement with Houghton Mifflin Company.

ALFRED A. KNOPF, INC. — for the selection from *Grenstone Poems* by Witter Bynner.

LITTLE, BROWN & COMPANY — for the selections from *The Complete Poems of Emily Dickinson.*

THE MACMILLAN COMPANY — for the selections from *The Collected Poems of Vachel Lindsay, Cowboy Songs and Other Frontier Ballads,* collected by John A. Lomax, *Salt Water Ballads* by John Masefield, *The Story of a Round House* by John Masefield, *Dionysus in Doubt* by Edwin Arlington Robinson, *Songs from the Clay* by James Stephens, and *Flame and Shadow* by Sara Teasdale.

ROBERT M. McBRIDE & COMPANY — for selections from *Those Not Elect* by Léonie Adams, and *Body of This Death* by Louise Bogan.

JOHN P. MORTON & COMPANY — for selections from *The Garden of Dreams* by Madison Cawein.

THOMAS B. MOSHER — for selections from *A Quiet Road* by Lizette Woodworth Reese and *A Wayside Lute* by Lizette Woodworth Reese.

THE POETRY BOOKSHOP (London, England) — for selections from *Spring Morning* by Frances Cornford, *Autumn Midnight* by Frances Cornford, *Poems* by Ralph Hodgson,

Strange Meetings by Harold Monro and *Children of Love* by Harold Monro.

G. P. PUTNAM'S SONS — for the title poem from *In Flanders Fields and Other Poems* by John McCrae.

NORMAN REMINGTON COMPANY — for the selection from *Wild Cherry* (Copyright 1923) by Lizette Woodworth Reese.

CHARLES SCRIBNER'S SONS — for selections from *Poems of Childhood* by Eugene Field, *The Poems of Sidney Lanier*, *Collected Poems* by Alice Meynell, *The Children of the Night* by Edwin Arlington Rcbinson, *Poems* by Alan Seeger, *Poems of Henry van Dyke,* and *Poems* by William Ernest Henley.

SIEGFRIED SASSOON — for a poem from the privately printed *Lingual Exercises for Advanced Vocabularians.*

THOMAS SELTZER, INC. — for selections from *The Janitor's Boy and Other Poems* by Nathalia Crane and *Lava Lane* by Nathalia Crane.

SMALL, MAYNARD & COMPANY — for selections from *Songs from Vagabondia* and *More Songs from Vagabondia* by Bliss Carman and Richard Hovey.

FREDERICK A. STOKES COMPANY — The poems by Hilda Conkling are reprinted by permission from *Shoes of the Wind*, Copyright 1922, and the poem "The Highwayman" is reprinted by permission from *Collected Poems*, Volume I, Copyright 1906, by Alfred Noyes.

THE VIKING PRESS (and B. W. HUEBSCH) — for selections from *Swords for Life,* by Irene Rutherford McLeod, *Under the Tree* by Elizabeth Madox Roberts, *Growing Pains* by Jean Starr Untermeyer and *Dreams Out of Darkness* by Jean Starr Untermeyer.

THE YALE UNIVERSITY PRESS — for the selection from *Merchants from Cathay* by William Rose Benét.

For permission to reprint several poems which have appeared in recent publications but which have not yet been collected in any volume by their authors, thanks are due to the following magazines:

THE CHAPBOOK (London, England) — for a poem by Camilla Doyle.

THE LITERARY REVIEW OF THE NEW YORK EVENING POST — for a poem by Elinor Wylie.

THE MIDLAND — for a poem by Helen Hoyt.

THE NEW REPUBLIC — for a poem by William Rose Benét.

POETRY: A MAGAZINE OF VERSE — for poems by Helen Hoyt, Sara Teasdale, and Dorothy M. Richardson.

PUNCH (London, England) — for a poem by Rose Fyleman.

THE SATURDAY REVIEW OF LITERATURE — for poems by Nathalia Crane and Elizabeth J. Coatsworth.

VOICES — for a poem by Louis Ginsberg.

INDEX OF AUTHORS

INDEX OF TITLES

Index of Titles 415